Mary Noailles Murfree

The Prophet of the Great Smoky Mountains

Mary Noailles Murfree

The Prophet of the Great Smoky Mountains

ISBN/EAN: 9783337035969

Printed in Europe, USA, Canada, Australia, Japan

Cover: Foto ©Lupo / pixelio.de

More available books at **www.hansebooks.com**

THE PROPHET

OF THE

GREAT SMOKY MOUNTAINS

BY

CHARLES EGBERT CRADDOCK

BOSTON AND NEW YORK
HOUGHTON, MIFFLIN AND COMPANY
The Riverside Press, Cambridge
1885

THE PROPHET

OF THE

GREAT SMOKY MOUNTAINS.

I.

ALWAYS enwrapped in the illusory mists, always touching the evasive clouds, the peaks of the Great Smoky Mountains are like some barren ideal, that has bartered for the vague isolations of a higher atmosphere the material values of the warm world below. Upon those mighty and majestic domes no tree strikes root, no hearth is alight; humanity is an alien thing, and utility set at naught. Below, dense forests cover the massive, precipitous slopes of the range, and in the midst of the wilderness a clearing shows, here and there, and the roof of a humble log cabin; in the valley, far, far lower still, a red spark at dusk may suggest a home, nestling in the cove. Grain grows apace in these scanty clearings, for the soil in certain favored spots is mellow; and the weeds grow, too, and in a wet season the ploughs are fain to be active. They are of the bull-tongue variety, and are sometimes drawn by oxen. As often as otherwise they are followed by women.

. In the gracious June mornings, when winds are astir and wings are awhirl in the wide spaces of the sunlit air, the work seemed no hardship to Dorinda Cayce, — least of all one day when another plough ran parallel to the furrows of her own, and a loud, drawling, intermittent conversation became practicable. She paused often, and looked idly about her: sometimes at the distant mountains, blue and misty, against the indefinite horizon; sometimes down at the cool, dense shadows of the wooded valley, so far below the precipice, to which the steep clearing shelved; sometimes at the little log cabin on the slope above, sheltered by a beetling crag and shadowed by the pines; sometimes still higher at the great "bald" of the mountain, and its mingled phantasmagoria of shifting clouds and flickering sheen and glimmering peak.

"He 'lowed ter me," she said, suddenly, " ez he hev been gin ter view strange sights a many a time in them fogs, an' sech."

The eyes lifted to the shivering vapors might never have reflected aught but a tropical sunshine, so warm, so bright, so languorously calm were they. She turned them presently upon a young man, who was ploughing with a horse close by, and who also came to a meditative halt in the turn-row. He too was of intermittent conversational tendencies, and between them it might be marveled that so many furrows were already run. He wore a wide-brimmed brown wool hat, set far back upon his head; a mass of straight yellow hair hung down to the collar of his brown jeans coat. His brown eyes were slow and contemplative. The corn was knee-high, and hid the great boots drawn over his trousers. As he moved there sounded the unexpected jingle of spurs. He looked, with the stolid, lack-lustre expression of the mountaineer, at the girl, who continued, as she leaned lightly on the plough-handles: —

"I 'lowed ter him ez mebbe he hed drempt them visions. I knows I hev thunk some toler'ble cur'ous thoughts myself, ef I war tired an' sleepin' hard. But he said he reckoned I hed drempt no sech dreams ez his'n. I can't holp sorrowin' fur him some. He 'lowed ez Satan hev hunted him like a pa'tridge on the mounting."

The young man's eyes dropped with sudden significance upon his plough-handles. A pair of pistols in their leather cases swung incongruously there. They gave a caustic suggestion of human adversaries as fierce as the moral pursuit of the Principle of Evil, and the girl's face fell. In absence of mind she recommenced her work.

"Waal," she gently drawled, as the old ox languidly started down the row, " 'pears like ter me ez it ain't goin' ter be no differ, nohow; it won't hender ye none."

Her face was grave, but there was a smile in her eyes, which had the lustre and depth of a sapphire, and a lambent glow like the heart of a blue flame. They were fringed by long, black lashes, and her hair was black, also. Her pink calico sun-bonnet, flaring toward the front, showed it lying in moist tendrils on her brow, and cast an unwonted roseate tint upon the clear, healthful pallor of her complexion. She wore a dark blue homespun dress, and, despite her coarse garb and uncouth occupation and the gaunt old ox, there was something impressive in her simple beauty, her youth, and her elastic vigor. As she drove the ploughshare into the mould she might have seemed the type of a young civilization, — so fine a thing in itself, so roughly accoutred.

When she came down the slope again, facing him, the pink curtain of her bonnet waving about her shoulders, her blue skirts fluttering among the blades of corn, a winged shadow sweeping along as if attendant upon her, while a dove flew high above to its nest in the pines, he raised his hand with an imperative gesture, and she paused obediently. He had flushed deeply; the smouldering fire in his eyes was kindling. He leaned across the few rows of corn that stood between them.

"I hev a word ter ax right now. Who air under conviction hyar?" he demanded.

She seemed a trifle startled. Her grasp shifted uncertainly on the plough-handles, and the old ox, accustomed to rest only at the turn-row, mistook her intention, and started off. She stopped him with some difficulty, and then, "Convicted of sin?" she asked, in a voice that showed her appreciation of the solemnity of the subject.

"I hev said it," the young man declared, with a half-suppressed irritation which confused her.

She remained silent.

"Mebbe it air yer granny," he suggested, with a sneer.

She recoiled, with palpable surprise. "Granny made her peace fifty year ago," she declared, with pride in this anciently acquired grace, — "fifty year an' better."

"The boys air convicted, then?" he asked, still leaning over the corn and still sneering.

"The boys hev got thar religion, too," she faltered, looking at him with wide eyes, brilliant with astonishment, and yet a trifle dismayed. Suddenly, she threw herself into her wonted confiding attitude, leaning upon her plough-handles, and with an appealing glance began an extenuation of her spiritual poverty: " 'Pears like ez I hev never hed a call ter tell you-uns afore ez I hev hed no time yit ter git my religion. Granny bein' old, an' the boys at the still, I hev hed ter spin, an' weave, an' cook, an' sew, an' plough some, — the boys bein' mos'ly at the still. An' then, thar be Mirandy Jane, my brother Ab's darter, ez I hev hed ter l'arn how ter cook vittles. When I went down yander ter my aunt Jerushy's house in Tuckaleechee Cove, ter holp her some with weavin', I war plumb cur'ous ter know how Mirandy Jane would make out whilst I war gone. They 'lowed ez she hed cooked the vittles toler'ble, but ef she had washed a skillet or a platter in them three days *I* could n't find it."

Her tone was stern; all the outraged housekeeper was astir within her.

He said nothing, and she presently continued discursively, still leaning on the plough-handles: "I never stayed away but them three days. I war n't sati'fied in my mind, nohow, whilst I bided down thar in Tuckaleechee Cove. I hankered cornsider'ble arter the baby. He air three year old now, an' I hev keered fur him ever sence his mother died, — my brother Ab's wife, ye know, — two year ago an' better. They hed fedded him toler'ble whilst I war away, an' I fund him fat ez common. But they hed crost him somehows, an' he war ailin' in his temper when I got home, an' hed ter hev cornsider'ble coddlin'."

She paused before the rising anger in his eyes.

"Why air Mirandy Jane called ter l'arn how ter cook vittles?" he demanded, irrelevantly, it might have seemed.

She looked at him in deprecating surprise. Yet she turned at bay.

"I hev never hearn ez ye war convicted yerself, Rick Tyler!" she said, tartly. "Ye war never so much ez seen a-scoutin' round the mourner's bench. Ef I hev got no religion, ye hev got none, nuther."

"Ye air minded ter git married, D'rindy Cayce," he said, severely, solving his own problem, "an' that's why Mirandy Jane hev got ter be l'arned ter take yer place at home."

He produced this as if it were an accusation.

She drew back, indignant and affronted, and with a rigid air of offended propriety. "I hev no call ter spen' words 'bout sech ez that, with a free-spoken man like you-uns," she staidly asseverated; and then she was about to move on.

Accepting her view of the gross unseemliness of his mention of the subject, the young fellow's anger gave way to contrition. "Waal, D'rindy," he said, in an eager, apologetic tone, "I hev seen that critter, that thar preacher, a-hangin' round you-uns's house a powerful deal lately, whilst I hev been obleeged ter hide out in the woods. An' bein' ez nobody thar owns up ter needin' religion but ye, I reckoned he war a-tryin' ter git ye ter take him an' grace tergether. That man hev got his mouth stuffed chock full o' words, — more 'n enny other man I ever see," he added, with an expression of deep disgust.

Dorinda might be thought to abuse her opportunities. "He ain't studyin' 'bout'n me, no more 'n I be 'bout'n him," she said, with scant relish for the spectacle of Rick Tyler's jealousy. "Pa'son Kelsey jes' stops thar ter the house ter rest his bones awhile, arter he comes down off'n the bald, whar he goes ter pray."

"In the name o' reason," exclaimed the young fellow petulantly, "why can't he pray somewhar else? A man ez hev got ter h'ist hisself on the bald of a mounting ten mile high — except what 's lackin' — ter git a purchase on prayer hain't got no religion wuth talkin' 'bout. Sinner ez I am, I kin pray in the valley — way down yander in Tuckaleechee Cove — ez peart ez on enny bald in the Big Smoky. That critter air a powerful aggervatin' contrivance."

Her eyes still shone upon him. "'Pears like ter me ez it air no differ, nohow," she said, with her consolatory cadence. As she again started down the row, she added, glancing over her shoulder and relenting even to explanation, "'T war granny's word ez Mirandy Jane hed ter be l'arned ter cook an' sech. She air risin' thirteen now, an' air toler'ble bouncin' an' spry, an' oughter be some use, ef ever. An' *she* mought marry when she gits fairly grown, an'," pausing in the turn-row for argument, and looking with earnest eyes at him, as he still stood in the midst of the waving corn, idly holding his plough-handles, where the pistols swung, " ef she did marry, 'pears like ter me ez she would be mightily faulted ef she could n't cook tasty."

There was no reasonable doubt of this proposition, but it failed to convince, and in miserable cogitation he completed another furrow, and met her at the turn-row.

"I s'pose ez Pa'son Kelsey an' yer granny air powerful sociable an' frien'ly," he hazarded, as they stood together.

"I dunno ez them two air partic'lar frien'ly. Pa'son Kelsey air in no wise a sociable critter," said Dorinda, with a discriminating air. "He ain't like Brother Jake Tobin, — though it 'pears like ter me ez his gift in prayer air manifested more survigrus, ef ennything." She submitted this diffidently. Having no religion, she felt incompetent to judge of such matters. "'Pears like ter me ez Pa'son Kelsey air more like 'Lijah an' 'Lisha, an' them men, what he talks about cornsider'ble, an' goes out ter meet on the bald."

"He don't meet them men on the bald; they air dead," said Rick Tyler, abruptly.

She looked at him in shocked surprise.

"That's jes' his addling way o' talkin'," continued the young fellow. "He don't mean fur true more 'n haffen what he say. He 'lows ez he meets the sperits o' them men on the bald."

Once more she lifted her bright eyes to the shivering vapors, — vague, mysterious, veiling in solemn silence the barren, awful heights.

An extreme gravity had fallen upon her face. "Did they live in thar life-time up hyar in the Big Smoky, or in the valley kentry?" she asked, in a lowered voice.

"I ain't sure 'bout'n that," he replied, indifferently.

"'Crost the line in the old North State?" she hazarded, exhausting her knowledge of the habitable globe.

"I hearn him read 'bout'n it wunst, but I furgits now."

Still her reverent, beautiful eyes, full of the dreamy sunshine, were lifted to the peak. "It must hev been in the Big Smoky Mountings they lived," she said, with eager credulity, "fur he tole me ez the word an' the prophets holped him when Satan kem a-huntin' of him like a pa'tridge on the mounting."

The young fellow turned away, with a gesture of angry impatience.

"Ef he hed ever hed the State o' Tennessee a-huntin' of him he would n't be so feared o' Satan. Ef thar war a warrant fur *him* in the sher'ff's pocket, an' the gran' jury's true bill fur murder lyin' agin *him* yander at Shaftesville, an' the gov'nor's reward, two hunderd dollars blood money, on *him*, he would n't be a-humpin' his bones round hyar so peart, a-shakin' in his shoes fur the fear o' Satan." He laughed, — a caustic, jeering laugh. "Satan's mighty active, cornsiderin' his age, but I 'd be willin' ter pit the State o' Tennessee agin him when it kem ter huntin' of folks like a pa'tridge."

The sunshine in the girl's eyes was clouded. They had filled with tears. Still leaning on the plough-handles, she looked at him, with suddenly crimson cheeks and quivering lips. "I dunno how the State o' Tennessee kin git its own cornsent ter be so mean an' wicked ez it air," she said, his helpless little partisan.

Despite their futility, her words comforted him. "An' I hev done nuthin', nohow!" he cried out, in shrill self-justification. "I could no more hender 'Bednego Tynes from shootin' Joel Byers down in his own door 'n nuthin' in this worl'. I never even knowed they hed a grudge. 'Bednego Tynes, he tole me ez he owed Joel a debt, an' war goin' ter see him 'bout'n it, an' wanted somebody along ter hear his word an' see jestice done 'twixt 'em. Thar air fower Byers boys, an' I reckon he war feared they would all jump on him at wunst, an' he wanted me ter holp him ef they did. An' I went along like a fool sheep, thinkin' 'bout nuthin'. An' when we got way down yander in Eskaqua Cove, whar Joel Byers's house air, he gin a hello at the fence, an' Joel kem ter the door. An' 'Bednego whipped up his rifle suddint an' shot him through the head, ez nip an' percise! An' thar stood Joel's wife, seein' it all. An' 'Bednego run off, nimble, I tell ye, an' I war so flustrated I run, too. Somebody cotched 'Bednego in the old North State the nex' week, an' the gov'nor hed ter send a requisition arter him. But sence I fund out ez they 'lowed I war aidin' an' abettin' 'Bednego, an' war goin' ter arrest me 'kase I war thar at the killin', they hev hed powerful little chance o' tryin' me in the court. An' whilst the gov'nor hed his hand in, he offered a reward fur sech a lawless man ez I be."

He broke off, visibly struggling for composure; then he recommenced in increasing indignation: " An' these hyar frien's o' mine in the Big Smoky, I 'll be bound they hanker powerful arter them two hunderd dollars blood money. I know ez I 'd hev been tuk afore this, ef it war n't fur them consarns thar." He nodded frowningly at the pistols. " Them 's the only frien's I hev got."

The girl's voice trembled. " 'Pears like ye mought count me in," she said, reproachfully.

" Naw," he retorted, sternly, " ye go round hyar sorrowin' fur a man ez hev got nuthin' ter be afeard of but the devil."

She made no reply, and her meekness mollified him.

" D'rindy," he said, in an altered tone, and with the pathos of a keen despair, " I hed fixed it in my mind a good while ago, when I could hev hed a house, an' lived like folks, stiddier like a wolf in the woods, ter ax ye ter marry me; but I war hendered by gittin' skeered 'bout'n yer bein' all in favor o' Amos Jeemes, ez kem up ter see ye from Eskaqua Cove, an' I did n't want ter git turned off. Mebbe ef I hed axed ye then I would n't hev tuk ter goin' along o' Abednego Tynes an' sech, an' the killin' o'

Joel would n't hev happened like it done. Would ye — would ye hev married me then?"

Her eyes flashed. "Ye air fairly sodden with foolishness, Rick!" she exclaimed, angrily. "Air you-uns thinkin' ez I 'll 'low ez I would hev married a man four month ago ez never axed me ter marry, nohow?" Then, with an appreciation of the delicacy of the position and a conservation of mutual pride, she added, "An' I won't say nuther ez I *would n't* marry a man ez hev never axed me ter marry, nohow."

Somehow, the contrariety of the proprieties, as she translated them, bewildered and baffled him. Even had he been looking at her he might hardly have interpreted, with his blunt perceptions, the dewy wistfulness of the eyes which she bent upon him. The word might promise nothing now. Still she would have valued it. He did not speak it. His eyes were fixed on Chilhowee Mountain, rising up, massive and splendid, against the west. The shadows of the clouds flecked the pure and perfect blue of the sunny slopes with a dusky mottling of purple. The denser shade in the valley had shifted, and one might know by this how the day wore on. The dew had dried from the long, keen blades of the Indian corn; the grasshoppers droned among them. A lizard basked on a flat, white stone hard by. The old ox dozed in the turn-row.

Suddenly Rick Tyler lifted his hand, with an intent gesture and a dilated eye. There came from far below, on the mountain road, the sound of a horse's hoof striking on a stone, again, and yet again. A faint metallic jingle — the air was so still now — suggested spurs. The girl's hand trembled violently as she stepped swiftly to his horse and took off the plough-gear. He had caught up a saddle that was lying in the turn-row, and as hastily buckled the girth about the animal.

"Ef that air ennybody a-hankerin' ter see me, don't you-uns be a-denyin' ez I hev been hyar, D'rindy," he said, as he put his foot in the stirrup. "I reckon they hev fund out by now ez I be in the kentry round about. But keep 'em hyar ez long ez ye kin, ter gin me a start."

He mounted his horse, and rode noiselessly away along the newly turned mould of the furrow.

She stood leaning upon her plough-handles, and silently watching him. His equestrian figure, darkly outlined against the far blue mountains and the intermediate valley, seemed of heroic size against the landscape, which was reduced by the distance to the minimum of proportion. The deep shadows of the woods, encompassing the clearing, fell upon him presently, and he, too, was but a shadow in the dusky monochrome of the limited vista. The dense laurel closed about him, and his mountain fastnesses, that had befriended him of yore, received him once again.

Then up and down the furrows Dorinda mechanically followed the plough, her pulses throbbing, every nerve tense, every faculty alert. She winced when she heard the frequent striking of hoofs upon the rocky slopes of the road below. She was instantly aware when they were silent and the party had stopped to breathe the horses. She began accurately to gauge their slow progress.

"'T ain't airish in no wise ter-day," she said, glancing about at the still, noontide landscape; "an' ef them air valley cattle they mus' git blowed mightily travelin' up sech steep mountings ez the Big Smoky." She checked her self-gratulation. "Though I ain't wantin' ter gloat on the beastis' misery, nuther," she stipulated.

She paused presently at the lower end of the clearing, and looked down over the precipice, that presented a sheer sandstone cliff on one side, and on the other a wild confusion of splintered and creviced rocks, where the wild rose bloomed in the niches and the grape-vine swung. The beech-trees on the slope below conserved beneath their dense, umbrageous branches a tender, green twilight. Loitering along in a gleaming silver thread by the roadside was a mountain rill, hardly gurgling even when with slight and primitive shift it was led into a hollow and mossy log, that it might aggregate sufficient volume in the dry season to water the horse of the chance wayfarer.

The first stranger that rode into this shadowy nook took off a large straw hat and bared his brow to the refreshing coolness. His grizzled hair stood up in front after the manner denominated "a roach." His temples were deeply sunken, and his strongly marked face was long and singularly lean. He held it forward, as if he were snuffing the air. He had a massive and powerful frame, with not an ounce of superfluous flesh, and he looked like a hound in the midst of the hunting season.

It served to quiet Dorinda's quivering nerves when he leisurely rode his big gray horse up to the trough, and dropped the rein that the animal might drink. If he were in pursuit he evidently had no idea how close he had pressed the fugitive. He was joined there by the other members of the party, six or eight in number, and presently a stentorian voice broke upon the air. "Hello! Hello!" he shouted, hailing the log cabin.

Mirandy Jane, a slim, long-legged, filly-like girl of thirteen, with a tangled black mane, the forelock hanging over her wild, prominent eyes, had at that moment appeared on the porch. She paused, and stared at the strangers with vivacious surprise. Then, taking sudden fright, she fled precipitately, with as much attendant confusion of pattering footfalls, flying mane, and excited snorts and gasps as if she were a troop of wild horses.

"Granny! Granny!" she exclaimed to the old crone in the chimney corner, "thar's a man on a big gray critter down at the trough, an' I ain't s'prised none ef he air a raider!"

The hail of the intruders was regarded as a challenge by some fifteen or twenty hounds that suddenly materialized among the bee-hives and the althea bushes, and from behind the ash-hopper and the hen-house and the rain-barrel. From under the cabin two huge curs came, their activity impeded by the blocks and chains they drew. These were silent, while the others yelped vociferously, and climbed over the fence, and dashed down the road.

The horses pricked up their ears, and the leader of the party awaited the onslaught with a pistol in his hand.

The old woman, glancing out of the window, observed this demonstration.

"He'll kill one o' our dogs with that thar shootin'-iron o' his'n!" she exclaimed in trepidation. "Run, Mirandy Jane, an' tell him *our* dogs don't bite."

The filly-like Mirandy Jane made great speed among the hounds, as she called them off, and remembered only after she had returned to the house to be afraid of the "shootin'-iron" herself.

The old woman, who had come out on the porch, stood gazing at the party, shading her eyes with her hand, and a long-range colloquy ensued.

"Good-mornin', madam," said the man at the trough.

"Good-mornin', sir," quavered the old crone on the mountain slope.

"I'm the sher'ff o' the county, madam, an' I'd like ter know ef" —

"Mirandy Jane," the old woman interrupted, in a wrathful undertone, "'pears like I hev hed the trouble o' raisin' a idjit in you-uns! Them ain't raiders, 'n nuthin' like it. Run an' tell the sher'ff we air dishin' up dinner right now, an' ax him an' his gang ter' light an' hitch, an' eat it along o' we-uns."

The prospect was tempting. It was high

noon, and the posse had been in the saddle since dawn. Dorinda, with a beating heart, marked how short a consultation resulted in dismounting and hitching the horses; and then, with their spurs jingling and their pistols belted about them, the men trooped up to the house.

As they seated themselves around the table, more than one looked back over his shoulder at the open window, in which was framed, as motionless as a painted picture, the vast perspective of the endless blue ranges and the great vaulted sky, not more blue, all with the broad, still, brilliant noontide upon it.

"Ye ain't scrimped fur a view, Mis' Cayce, an' that's the Lord's truth!" exclaimed the officer.

"Waal," said the old woman, as if her attention were called to the fact for the first time, "we kin see a power o' kentry from this spot o' ourn, sure enough; but I dunno ez it gins us enny more chance o' ever viewin' Canaan."

"It's a sight o' ground ter hev ter hunt a man over, ez ef he war a needle in a haystack," and once more the officer turned and surveyed the prospect.

The room was overheated by the fire which had cooked the dinner, and the old woman actively plied her fan of turkey feathers, pausing occasionally to readjust her cap, which had a flapping frill and was surmounted by a pair of gleaming spectacles. A bandana kerchief was crossed over her breast, and she wore a blue-and-white-checked homespun dress of the same pattern and style that she had worn here fifty years ago. Her hands were tremulous and gnarled and her face was deeply wrinkled, but her interest in life was as fresh as Mirandy Jane's.

The great frame of the warping-bars on one side of the room was swathed with a rainbow of variegated yarn, and a spinning-wheel stood near the door. A few shelves, scrupulously neat, held piggins, a cracked blue bowl, brown earthenware, and the cooking utensils. There were rude gun-racks on the walls. These indicated the fact of several men in the family. It was the universal dinner-hour, yet none of them appeared. The sheriff reflected that perhaps they had their own sufficient reason to be shy of strangers, and the horses hitched outside advertised the presence and number of unaccustomed visitors within. When the usual appetizer was offered, it took the form of whiskey in such quantity that the conviction was forced upon him that it was come by very handily. However, he applied himself with great relish to the bacon and snap-beans, corn dodgers and fried chicken, not knowing that Mirandy Jane, who was esteemed altogether second rate, had cooked them, and he spread honey upon the apple-pie, ate it with his knife, and washed it down with buttermilk, kept cold as ice in the spring, — the mixture being calculated to surprise a more civilized stomach.

Not even his conscience was roused, — the first intimation of a disordered digestion. He listened to old Mrs. Cayce with no betrayal of divination when she vaguely but anxiously explained the absence of her son and his boys in the equivocal phrase, "Not round about ter-day, bein' gone off," and he asked how many miles distant was the Settlement, as if he understood they had gone thither. He was saying to himself, the brush whiskey warming his heart, that the revenue department paid him nothing to raid moonshiners, and there was no obligation of his office to sift any such suspicion which might occur to him while accepting an unguarded hospitality.

He looked with somewhat appreciative eyes at Dorinda, as she went back and forth from the table to the pot which hung in the deep chimney-place above the smouldering coals. She had laid aside her bonnet. Her face was grave; her eyes were bright and excited; her hair was drawn back, except for the tendrils about her brow, and coiled, with the aid of a much-prized "tuckin' comb," at the back of her head in a knot discriminated as Grecian in civilization. He remarked to her grandmother that he was a family man himself, and had a daughter as old, he should say, as Dorinda.

"D'rindy air turned seventeen now," said Mrs. Cayce, disparagingly. "It 'pears like ter me ez the young folks nowadays air awk'ard an' back'ard. I war married when I war sixteen, — sixteen scant."

The girl felt that she was indeed of advanced years, and the sheriff said that his daughter was not yet sixteen, and he thought it probable she weighed more than Dorinda.

He lighted his pipe presently, and tilted his chair back against the wall.

"Yes 'm," he said, meditatively, gazing out of the window at the great panorama, "it's a pretty big spot o' kentry ter hev ter hunt a man over. Now ef 't war one o' the town folks we could make out ter overhaul him somehows; but a mounting boy, — why, he's ez free ter the hills ez a fox. I s'pose ye hain't seen him hyar-abouts?"

"I hain't hearn who it air yit," the old woman replied, putting her hand behind her ear.

"It's Rick Tyler; he hails from this deestric'. I won't be 'stonished ef we ketch him this time. The gov'nor has offered two hunderd dollars reward fur him, an' I reckon somebody will find it wuth while ter head him fur us."

He was talking idly. He had no expectation of developments here. He had only stopped at the house in the first instance for the question which he had asked at every habitation along the road. It suddenly occurred to him as polite to include Dorinda in the conversation.

"Ye hain't seen nor hearn of him, I s'pose, hev ye?" inquired the sheriff, directly addressing her.

As he turned toward her he marked her expression. His own face changed suddenly. He rose at once.

"Don't trifle with the law, I warn ye," he said, sternly. "Ye hev seen that man."

Dorinda was standing beside her spinning-wheel, one hand holding the thread, the other raised to guide the motion. She looked at him, pale and breathless.

"I hev seen him. I ain't onwillin' ter own it. Ye never axed me afore."

The other members of the party had crowded in from the porch, where they had been sitting since dinner, smoking their pipes. The officer, realizing his lapse of vigilance and the loss of his opportunity, was sharply conscious, too, of their appreciation of his fatuity.

"Whar did ye see him?" he asked.

"I seen him hyar — this mornin'." There was a stir of excitement in the group. "He kem by on his beastis whilst I war a-ploughin', an' we talked a passel. An' then he tuk Pete's plough, ez war idle in the turnrow, an' holped along some; he run a few furrows."

"Which way did he go?" asked the sheriff, breathlessly.

"I dunno," faltered the girl.

"Look-a-hyar!" he thundered, in rising wrath. "Ye'll find yerself under lock an' key in the jail at Shaftesville, ef ye undertake ter fool with me. Which way did he go?"

A flush sprang into the girl's excited face. Her eyes flashed.

"Ef ye kin jail me fur tellin' all I know, I can't holp it," she said, with spirit. "I kin tell no more."

He saw the justice of her position. It did not make the situation easier for him. Here he had sat eating and drinking and idly talking while the fugitive, who had escaped by a hair's breadth, was counting miles and miles between himself and his lax pursuer. This would be heard of in Shaftesville, — and he a candidate for reëlection! He beheld already an exchange of significant glances among his posse. Had he asked that simple question earlier he might now be on his way back to Shaftesville, his prisoner braceleted with the idle handcuffs that jingled in his pocket as he moved.

He caught at every illusive vagary that might promise to retrieve his error. He declared that she could not say which way Rick Tyler had taken because he was not gone.

"He's in this house right now!" he exclaimed. He ordered a search, and the guests, a little while ago so friendly, began exploring every nook and cranny.

"No, no!" cried the old woman, shrilly, as they tried the door of the shed-room, which was bolted and barred. "Ye can't tech that thar door. It can't be opened, — not ef the Gov'nor o' Tennessee war hyar himself, a-moanin' an' a-honin' ter git in."

The sheriff's eyes dilated. "Open the door, — I summon ye!" he proclaimed, with his imperative official manner.

"No! — I done tole ye," she said indignantly. "The word o' the men folks hev been gin ter keep that thar door shet, an' shet it's goin' ter be kep'."

The officer laid his hand upon it.

"Ye mustn't bust it open!" shrilled the old woman. "Laws-a-massy! ef thar be many sech ez you-uns in Shaftesville, I ain't s'prised none that the Bible gits ter mournin' over the low kentry, an' calls it a vale o' tears an' the valley o' the shadder o' death!"

The sheriff had placed his powerful shoulder against the frail batten door.

"Hyar goes!" he said.

There was a crash; the door lay in splinters on the floor; the men rushed precipitately over it.

They came back laughing sheepishly. The officer's face was angry and scarlet.

"Don't take the bar'l, — don't take the bar'l!" the old woman besought of him, as she fairly hung upon his arm. "I dunno *how* the boys would cavort ef they kem back an' fund the bar'l gone."

He gave her no heed. "Why n't ye tell me that man war n't thar?" he asked of the girl.

"Ye did n't ax me that word," said Dorinda.

"No, 'Cajah Green, ye did n't," said one of the men, who, since the abortive result of their leader's suspicion, were ashamed of their mission, and prone to self-exoneration. "I'll stand up ter it ez she answered full an' true every word ez ye axed her."

"Lor'-a'mighty! Ef I jes' knowed aforehand how it will tech the boys when they view the door down onto the floor!" exclaimed the old woman. "They mought jounce round hyar ez ef they war bereft o' reason, an' all thar hope o' salvation hed hung on the hinges. An' then agin they mought 'low ez they hed ruther hev no door than be at the trouble o' shettin' it an' barrin' it up ez they come an' go. They air mighty onsartin in thar temper, an' I hev never hankered ter see 'em crost. But fur the glory's sake, don't tech the bar'l. It's been sot thar ter age some, ef the Lord will spare it."

In the girl's lucent eyes the officer detected a gleam of triumph. How far away in the tangled labyrinths of the mountain wilderness, among the deer-paths and the cataracts and the cliffs, had these long hours led Rick Tyler!

He spoke on his angry impulse: "An' I ain't goin' ter furgit in a hurry how I hev fund out ez ye air a-consortin' with criminals, an' aidin' an' abettin' men ez air fleein' from jestice an' wanted fur murder. Ye look out; ye'll find yerself in Shaftesville jail 'fore long, I'm a-thinkin'."

"He stopped an' talked ez other folks stop an' talk," Dorinda retorted. "I could n't hender, an' I hed no mind ter hender. He took no bite nor sup ez others hev done. 'Pears like ter me ez we hev gin aid an' comfort ter the off'cer o' the law, ez well ez we could."

And this was the story that went down to Shaftesville.

The man, his wrath rebounding upon himself, hung his head, and went down to the trough, and mounted his horse without another word.

The others hardly knew what to say to Dorinda. But they were more deliberate in their departure, and hung around apologizing in their rude way to the old woman, who convulsively besought each to spare the barrel, which had been set in the shed-room to "age some, ef it could be lef' alone."

Dorinda stood under the jack-bean vines, blossoming purple and white, and watched the men as they silently rode away. All the pride within her was stirred. Every sensitive fibre flinched from the officer's coarse threat. She followed him out of sight with vengeful eyes.

"I wish I war a man!" she cried, passionately.

"A-law, D'rindy!" exclaimed her grandmother, aghast at the idea. "That ain't manners!"

The shadows were beginning to creep slowly up the slopes of the Great Smoky Mountains, as if they came from the depths of the earth. A roseate suffusion idealized range and peak to the east. The delicate skyey background of opaline tints and lustre made distinct and definite their majestic symmetry of outline. Ah!

and the air was so clear! What infinite lengths of elastic distances stretched between that quivering trumpet-flower by the fence and the azure heights which its scarlet horn might almost seem to cover! The sun, its yellow blaze burned out, and now a sphere of smouldering fire, was dropping down behind Chilhowee, royally purple, richly dark. Wings were in the air and every instinct was homeward. An eagle, with a shadow skurrying through the valley like some forlorn Icarus that might not soar, swept high over the landscape. Above all rose the great "bald," still splendidly illumined with the red glamour of the sunset, and holding its uncovered head so loftily against the sky that it might seem it had bared its brow before the majesty of heaven.

When the "men folks," great, gaunt, bearded, jeans-clad fellows, stood in the shed-room and gazed at the splintered door upon the floor, it was difficult to judge what was the prevailing sentiment, so dawdling, so uncommunicative, so inexpressive of gesture, were they.

"We knowed ez thar war strangers prowlin' roun'," said the master of the house, when he had heard his mother's excited account of the events of the day. "We war a-startin' home ter dinner, an' seen thar beastises hitched thar a-nigh the trough. An' I 'lowed ez mebbe they mought be the revenue devils, so I jes' made the boys lay low. An' Sol war set ter watch, an' he gin the word when they hed rid away."

He was a man of fifty-five, perhaps, tough and stalwart. His face was as lined and seamed as that of his mother, who had counted nearly fourscore years, but his frame was almost as supple as at thirty. This trait of physical vigor was manifested in each of his muscular sons, and despite their slow and lank uncouthness, their movements suggested latent elasticity. In Dorinda, his only daughter, it graced her youth and perfected her beauty. He was known far and wide as "Ground-hog Cayce," but he would tell you, with a flash of the eye, that before the war he bore the Christian name of John.

Nothing more was said on the subject until after supper, when they were all sitting, dusky shadows, on the little porch, where the fireflies sparkled and the vines fluttered, and one might look out and see the new moon, in the similitude of a silver boat, sailing down the western skies, off the headlands of Chilhowee. A cricket was shrilling in the weeds. The vague, sighing voice of the woods rose and fell with a melancholy monody. A creamy elder blossom glimmered in a corner of the rail fence, hard by, its delicate, delicious odor pervading the air.

"I never knowed," said one of the young men, "ez this hyar sher'ff — this 'Cajah Green — war sech a headin' critter."

"He never teched the bar'l," said the old woman, not wishing that he should appear blacker than he had painted himself.

"I s'pose you-uns gin him an' his gang a bite an' sup," remarked Ground-hog Cayce.

"They eat a sizable dinner hyar," put in Mirandy Jane, who, having cooked it, had no mind that it should be belittled.

"An' they stayed a right smart while, an' talked powerful frien'ly an' sociable-like," said old Mrs. Cayce, "till the sher'ff got addled with the notion that we hed Rick Tyler hid hyar. An' unless we-uns hed tied him in the cheer or shot him, nuthin' in natur' could hev held him. I 'lowed 't war the dram he tuk, though D'rindy thinks differ. They never teched the bar'l, though."

"An' then," said Dorinda, with a sudden gush of tears, all the afflicted delicacy of a young and tender woman, all the overweening pride of the mountaineer, throbbing wildly in her veins, her heart afire, her helpless hands trembling, "he said the word ez he would lock me up in the jail at Shaftesville, sence I hed owned ter seein' a man ez he war n't peart enough ter ketch. He spoke that word ter me, — *the jail!*"

She hung sobbing in the doorway.

There was a murmur of indignation among the group, and John Cayce rose to his feet with a furious oath.

"He shell rue it!" he cried, — "he shell rue it! Me an' mine take no word off'n nobody. My gran'dad an' his three brothers, one hunderd an' fourteen year ago, kem hyar from the old North State an' settled in the Big Smoky. They an' thar sons rooted up the wilderness. They crapped. They fit the beastis; they fit the Injun; they fit the British; an' this last little war o' ourn they fit each other. Thar hev never been a coward 'mongst 'em. Thar hev never been a key turned on one of 'em, or a door shet. They hev respected the law fur what it war wuth, an' they hev stood up fur thar rights agin it. They answer fur thar word, an' others hev ter answer." He paused for a moment.

The moon, still in the similitude of a silver boat, swung at anchor in a deep indentation in the summit of Chilhowee that looked like some lonely pine-girt bay; what strange, mysterious fancies did it land from its cargo of sentiments and superstitions and uncanny influences!

"D'rindy," her father commanded, "make a mark on this hyar rifle-bar'l fur 'Cajah Green's word ter be remembered by."

There was a flash in the faint moonbeams, as he held out to her a long, sharp knife. The rifle was in his hand. Other marks were on it commemorating past events. This was to be a foregone conclusion.

"No, no!" cried the girl, shrinking back aghast. "I don't want him shot. I would n't hev him hurted fur me, fur nuthin'! I ain't keerin' now fur what he said. Let him be, — let him be."

She had smarted under the sense of indignity. She had wanted their sympathy, and perhaps their idle anger. She was dismayed by the revengeful passion she had roused.

"No, no!" she reiterated, as one of the younger men, her brother Peter, stepped swiftly out from the shadow, seized her hand with the knife trembling in it, and, catching the moonlight on the barrel of the rifle, guided upon it, close to the muzzle, the mark of a cross.

The moon had weighed anchor at last, and dropped down behind the mountain summit, leaving the bay with a melancholy waning suffusion of light, and the night very dark.

II.

The summer days climbed slowly over the Great Smoky Mountains. Long the morning lingered among the crags, and chasms, and the dwindling shadows. The vertical noontide poised motionless on the great balds. The evening dawdled along the sunset slopes, and the waning crimson waited in the dusk for the golden moonrise.

So little speed they made that it seemed to Rick Tyler that weeks multiplied while they loitered.

It might have been deemed the ideal of a sylvan life, — those days while he lay hid out on the Big Smoky. His rifle brought him food with but the glance of the eye and a touch on the trigger. "Ekal ter the prophet's raven, ef the truth war knowed," he said sometimes, while he cooked the game over a fire of dead-wood gathered by the wayside. A handful of blackberries gave it a relish, and there were the ice-cold, never-failing springs of the range wherever he might turn.

But for the unquiet thoughts that followed him from the world, the characteristic sloth of the mountaineer might have spared him all sense of tedium, as he lay on the bank of a mountain stream, while the slow days waxed and waned. Often he would see a musk-rat — picturesque little body — swimming in a muddy dip. And again his listless gaze was riveted upon the quivering diaphanous wings of a snake-doctor, hovering close at hand, until the grotesque, airy thing would flit away. The arrowy sunbeams shot into the dense umbrageous tangles, and fell spent to earth as the shadows swayed. Farther down the stream two huge cliffs rose on either side of the channel, giving a narrow view of far-away blue mountains as through a gate. In and out stole the mist, uncertain whither. The wind came and went, paying no toll. Sometimes, when the sun was low, a shadow — an antlered shadow — slipped through like a fantasy.

But when the skies would begin to darken and the night come tardily on, the scanty incidents of the day lost their ephemeral interest. His human heart would assert itself, and he would yearn for the life from which he was banished, and writhe with an intolerable anguish under his sense of injury.

"An' the law holds me the same ez 'Bednego Tynes, who killed Joel Byers, jes' ter keep his hand in, — hevin' killed another man afore, — an' I never so much ez lifted a finger agin him!"

He pondered much on his past, and the future that he had lost. Sometimes he gave himself to adjusting, from the meagre circumstances of their common lot on Big Smoky, the future of those with whose lives his own had heretofore seemed an integrant part, and from which it should forevermore be dissevered. All the pangs of penance were in that sense of irrevocability. It was done, and here was his choice: to live the life of a skulking wolf, to prowl, to flee, to fight at bay, or to return and confront an outraged law. He experienced a frenzy of rage to realize how hardily his world would roll on without him. Big Smoky would not suffer! The sun would shine, and the crops ripen, and the harvest come, and the snows sift down, and the seasons revolve. The boys would shoot for beef, and there was to be a gander-pulling at the Settlement when the candidates should come, "stumpin' the Big Smoky" for the midsummer elections. And when, periodically, "the mountings" would awake to a sense of sin, and a revival would be instituted, all the people would meet, and clap their hands, and sing, and pray, and that busy sinner, D'rindy, might find time to think upon grace, and perhaps upon the man whom she likened to the prophets of old.

Then Rick Tyler would start up from his bed of boughs, and stride wildly about among the bowlders, hardly pausing to listen if he heard a wolf howling on the lonely heights. An owl would hoot derisively from the tangled laurel. And oh, the melancholy moonlight in the melancholy pines, where the whip-poor-will moaned and moaned!

"I'd shoot that critter ef I could make out ter see him!" cried the harassed fugitive, his every nerve quivering.

It all began with Dorinda; it all came back to her. He drearily foresaw that she would forget him; and yet he could not know how the alienation was to commence, how it should progress, and the process of its completion. "All whilst I'm a-roamin' off with the painters an' sech!" he exclaimed, bitterly.

And she, — her future was plain enough. There was a little log-cabin by the grist-mill: the mountains sheltered it; the valley held it as in the palm of a hand. Hardly a moment since, his jealous heart had been racked by the thought of the man she likened to the prophets of old, and now he saw her spinning in the door of Amos James's house, in the quiet depths of Eskaqua Cove.

This vision stilled his heart. He was numbed by his despair. Somehow, the burly young miller seemed a fitter choice than the religious enthusiast, whose leisure was spent in praying in the desert places. He wondered that he should ever have felt other jealousy, and was subacutely amazed to find this passion so elastic.

With wild and haggard eyes he saw the day break upon this vision. It came in at the great gate, — a pale flush, a fainting star, a burst of song, and the red and royal sun.

The morning gradually exerted its revivifying influence and brought a new impulse. He easily deceived himself, and disguised it as a reason.

"This hyar powder is a-gittin' mighty low," he said to himself, examining the contents of his powder-horn. "An' that thar rifle eats it up toler'ble fast sence I hev hed ter hunt varmints fur my vittles. Ef that war the sher'ff a-ridin' arter me the day I war at Cayce's, he's done gone whar he b'longs by this time, — 't war two weeks ago; an' ef he ain't gone back he would n't be layin' fur me roun' the Settle*mint*, nohow. An' I kin git some powder thar, an' hear 'em tell what the mounting air a-doin' of. An' mebbe I won't be so durned lonesome when I gits back hyar."

He mounted his horse, later in the day, and picked his way slowly down the banks of the stream and through the great gate.

The Settlement on a spur of the Big Smoky illustrated the sacrilege of civilization. A number of trees, girdled years ago, stretched above the fields their gigantic skeletons, suggesting their former majesty of mien and splendid proportions. Their forlorn leafless branches rattled together with a dreary sound, as the breeze stirred among the gaunt and pallid assemblage. The little log-cabins, five or six in number, were so situated among the stumps which disfigured the clearing that if a sudden wind should bring down one of the monarchical spectres of the forest it would make havoc only in the crops. The wheat was thin and backward. A little patch of cotton in a mellow dip served to show the plant at its minimum. There was tobacco, too, placed like the cotton where it was hoped it would take a notion to grow. Sorghum flourished, and the tasseled Indian corn, waving down a slope, had aboriginal suggestions of plumed heads and glancing quivers. A clamor of Guinea fowls arose, and geese and turkeys roved about in the publicity of the clearing with the confident air of esteemed citizens. Sheep were feeding among the ledges.

It was hard to say what might be bought at the store except powder and coffee, and sugar perhaps, if " long-sweetenin' " might not suffice ; for each of the half dozen small farms was a type of the region, producing within its own confines all its necessities. Hand-looms could be glimpsed through open doors, and as yet the dry-goods trade is unknown to the homespun-clad denizens of the Settlement. Beeswax, feathers, honey, dried fruit, are bartered here, and a night's rest has never been lost for the perplexities of the currency question on the Big Smoky Mountains.

The proprietor of the store, his operations thus limited, was content to grow rich slowly, if needs were to grow rich at all. In winter he sat before the great wood fire in the store and smoked his pipe, and his crony, the blacksmith, often came, hammer in hand and girded with his leather apron, and smoked with him. In the summer he sat all day, as now, in front of the door, looking meditatively at the scene before him. The sunlight slanted upon the great dead trees; their forms were imposed with a wonderful distinctness upon the landscape that stretched so far below the precipice on which the little town was perched. They even touched, with those bereaved and denuded limbs, the far blue mountains encircling the horizon, and with their interlacing lines and curves they seemed some mysterious scripture engraven upon the world.

It was just six o'clock, and the shadow of a bough that still held a mass of woven sticks, once the nest of an eagle, had reached the verge of the cliff, when the sound of hoofs fell on the still air, and a man rode into the clearing from the encompassing woods.

The storekeeper glanced up to greet the newcomer, but did not risk the fatigue of rising. Women looked out of the windows, and a girl on a porch, reeling yarn, found a reason to stop her work. A man came out of a house close by, and sat on the fence, within range of any colloquy in which he might wish to participate. The whole town could join at will in a municipal conversation. The forge fire showed a dull red against the dusky brown shadows in the recesses of the shop. The blacksmith stood in front of the door, his eyes shielded with his broad blackened right hand, and looked critically at the steed. Horses were more in his line than men. He was a tall, powerfully built fellow of thirty, perhaps, with the sooty aspect peculiar to his calling, a swarthy complexion, and a remarkably well-knit, compact, and muscular frame. He often said in pride, "Ef I hed hed the forgin' o' myself, I would n't hev welded on a pound more, or hammered out a leader differ."

Suddenly detaching his attention from the horse, he called out, "Waal, sir! Ef thar ain't Rick Tyler!" This was addressed to the town at large. Then, "What ails ye, Rick? I hearn tell ez you-uns war on yer way ter Shaftesville along o' the sher'ff." He had a keen and twinkling eye. He cast it significantly at the man on the fence. "Ye kem back, I reckon, ter git yer hand-cuffs mended at my shop. Gimme the bracelets." He held out his hand in affected anxiety.

"I ain't a-wearin' no bracelets now." Rick Tyler's hasty impulse had its impressiveness. He leveled his pistol. "Ef ye hanker ter do enny mendin', I'll gin ye repairs ter make in them cast-iron chit'lings o' yourn," he said, coolly.

He was received at the store with a distinct accession of respect. The blacksmith stood watching him, with angry eyes, and a furtive recollection of the reward offered by the governor for his apprehension.

The young fellow, with a sudden return of caution, did not at once venture to dismount; and Nathan Hoodendin, the storekeeper, rose for no customer. Respectively seated, for these diverse reasons, they transacted the negotiation.

"Hy're, Rick," drawled the storekeeper, languidly. "I hopes ye keeps yer health," he added, politely.

The young man melted at the friendly tone. This was the welcome he had looked for at the

Settlement. Loneliness had made his sensibilities tender, and "hiding out" affected his spirits more than dodging the officers in the haunts of men, or daring the cupidity roused, he knew, by the reward for his capture. The blacksmith's jeer touched him as cruelly as an attempt upon his liberty. "Jes' toler'ble," he admitted, with the usual rural reluctance to acknowledge full health. "I hopes ye an' yer fambly air thrivin'," he drawled, after a moment.

A whiff came from the storekeeper's pipe; the smoke wreathed before his face, and floated away.

"Waal, we air makin' out, — we air makin' out."

"I kem over hyar," said Rick Tyler, proceeding to business, "ter git some powder out'n yer store. I wants one pound."

Nathan Hoodendin smoked silently for a moment. Then, with a facial convulsion and a physical wrench, he lifted his voice.

"Jer'miah!" he shouted in a wild wheeze. And again, "Jer'miah!"

The invoked Jer'miah did not materialize at once. When a small tow-headed boy of ten came from a house among the stumps, with that peculiar deftness of tread characteristic of the habitually barefoot, he had an alert, startled expression, as if he had just jumped out of a bush. His hair stood up in front; he had wide pop-eyes, and long ears, and a rabbit-like aspect that was not diminished as he scudded round the heels of Rick Tyler's horse, at which he looked apprehensively.

"Jer'miah," said his father, with a pathetic cadence, "go into the store, bub, an' git Rick Tyler a pound o' powder."

As Jeremiah started in, the paternal sentiment stirred in Nathan Hoodendin's breast.

"Jer'miah," he wheezed, bringing the forelegs of the chair to the ground, and craning forward with unwonted alacrity to look into the dusky interior of the store, "don't ye be foolin' round that thar powder with no lighted tallow dip nor nuthin'. I'll whale the life out'n ye ef ye do. Jes' weigh it by the winder."

Whether from fear of a whaling by his active parent, or of the conjunction of a lighted tallow dip and powder, Jeremiah dispensed with the candle. He brought the commodity out presently, and Rick stowed it away in his saddlebags.

"Can't ye 'light an' sot a while 'an talk, Rick?" said the storekeeper. "We-uns hev done hed our supper, but I reckon they could fix ye a snack yander ter the house."

Rick said he wanted nothing to eat, but, although he hesitated, he could not finally resist the splint-bottomed chair tilted against the wall of the store, and a sociable pipe, and the countryside gossip.

"What's goin' on 'round the mounting?" he asked.

Gid Fletcher, the blacksmith, came and sat in another chair, and the man on the fence got off and took up his position on a stump hard by. The great red sun dropped slowly behind the purple mountains; and the full golden moon rose above the corn-field that lay on the eastern slope, and hung there between the dark woods on either hand; and the blades caught the light, and tossed with burnished flashes into the night; and the great ghastly trees assumed a ghostly whiteness; and the mystic writing laid on the landscape below had the aspect of an uninterpreted portent. The houses were mostly silent; now and then a guard-dog growled at some occult alarm; a woman somewhere was softly and fitfully singing a child to sleep, and the baby crooned too, and joined in the vague, drowsy ditty. And for aught else that could be seen, and for aught else that could be heard, this was the world.

"Waal, the Tempter air fairly stalkin' abroad on the Big Smoky, — leastwise sence the summer season hev opened," said Nathan Hoodendin. His habitual expression of heavy, joyless pondering had been so graven into his face that his raised grizzled eyebrows, surmounted by a multitude of perplexed wrinkles, his long, dismayed jaw, his thin, slightly parted lips, and the deep grooves on either side of his nose were not susceptible of many gradations of meaning. His shifting eyes, cast now at the stark trees, now at the splendid disk of the rising moon, betokened but little anxiety for the Principle of Evil aloose in the Big Smoky. "Fust, — lemme see, — thar war Eph Lowry, ez got inter a quar'l with his wife's half-brother's cousin, an' a-tusslin' 'roun' they cut one another right smart, an' some say ez Eph 'll never hev his eyesight right good no more. Then thar war Baker Teal, what the folks in Eskaqua Cove 'low let down the bars o' the milk-sick pen, one day las' fall, an' druv Jacob White's red cow in; an' his folks never knowed she hed grazed thar till they hed milked an' churned fur butter, when she lay down an' died o' the milk-sick. Ef they hed drunk her milk same ez common, 't would hev sickened 'em, sure, 'an mebbe killed 'em. An' they've been quar'lin' 'bout'n it ever sence. Satan's a-stirrin', — Satan's a-stirrin' 'roun' the Big Smoky."

"Waal, I hearn ez some o' them folks in Eskaqua Cove 'low ez the red cow jes' hooked down the bars, bein' a turrible hooker," spoke up the man on the stump, unexpectedly.

"Waal, White an' his folks won't hear ter no sech word ez that," said the blacksmith; "an' arter jowin' an' jowin' back an' fo'th they went t'other day an' informed on Teal 'fore the jestice, an' the Squair fined him twenty-five dollars, 'cordin' ter the law o' Tennessee fur them ez m'liciously lets down the bars o' the milk-sick pen. An' Baker Teal hed ter pay, an' the county treasury an' the informers divided the money 'twixt 'em."

"What did I tell you-uns? Satan's a-stirrin',— Satan's a-stirrin' 'roun' the Big Smoky," said the storekeeper, with a certain morbid pride in the Enemy's activity.

"The constable o' this hyar deestric'," recommenced Gid Fletcher, who seemed as well informed as Nathan Hoodendin, "he advised 'em ter lay it afore the jestice; he war mighty peart 'bout'n that thar job. They 'low ter me ez he hev tuk up a crazy fit ez he kin beat Micajah Green fur sher'ff, an' he's a-skeetin' arter law-breakers same ez a rooster arter a Juny-bug. He 'lows it 'll show the kentry what a peart sher'ff he 'd make."

"Shucks!" said the man on the stump. "I 'll vote fur 'Cajah Green fur sher'ff agin the old boy; he hev got a nose fur game."

"He hain't nosed you-uns out yit, hev he, Rick?" said the blacksmith, with feigned heartiness and a covert sneer.

"Ho! ho! ho!" laughed Nathan Hoodendin. "What war I a-tellin' you-uns? Satan's a-stirrin', — Satan's surely a-stirrin' on the Big Smoky."

Rick sat silent in the moonlight, smoking his pipe, his brown wool hat far back, the light full on his yellow head. His face had grown a trifle less square, and his features were more distinctly defined than of yore; he did not look ill, but care had drawn a sharp line here and there.

"One sher'ff's same ter you-uns ez another, ain't he, Rick?" said the man on the stump. "Any of 'em 'll do ter run from."

"They tell it ter me," said the storekeeper, with so sudden a vivacity that it seemed it must crack his graven wrinkles, " ez the whole Cayce gang air a-goin' ter vote agin 'Cajah Green, 'count o' the way he jawed at old Mis' Cayce an' D'rindy, the day he run you-uns off from thar, Rick."

"I ain't hearn tell o' that yit," drawled Rick, desolately, " bein' hid out."

"Waal, he jawed at D'rindy, an' from what I hev hearn D'rindy jawed back; an' I dunno ez that's s'prisin', — the gal-folks ginerally do.

Leastwise, I know ez he sent word arterward ter D'rindy, by his dep'ty, — ez war a-scoutin' 'roun' hyar, arter you-uns, I reckon, Rick, — ez he would be up some day soon ter 'lectioneer, an' he war a-goin' ter stop ter thar house an' ax her pardin'. An' she sent him word, fur God's sake ter bide away from thar."

A long pause ensued; the stars were faint and few; the iterative note of the katydid vibrated monotonously in the dark woods; dew was falling; the wind stirred.

"What ailed D'rindy ter say that word?" asked Rick, mystified.

"Waal, I dunno," said Hoodendin, indifferently. "I hev never addled my brains tryin' ter make out what a woman means. Though," he qualified, "I *did* ax the dep'ty an' Amos Jeemes from down yander in Eskaqua Cove, — the dep'ty hed purtended ter hev summonsed him ez a posse, an' they war jes' rollickin' 'roun' the kentry like two chickens with thar heads off, — I axed 'em what D'rindy meant; an' they 'lowed they did n't know, nor war they takin' it ter heart. They 'lowed ez she never axed *them* ter bide away from thar fur God's sake. An' then they snickered an' laffed, like single men do. An' I up an' tole 'em ez the Book sot it down ez the laffter o' fools is like the cracklin' o' bresh under a pot."

Rick Tyler was eager, his eyes kindling, his breath quick. He looked with uncharacteristic alertness at the inexpressive face of the leisurely narrator.

"They capered like a dunno-what-all on the Big Smoky, them two, — the off'cer o' the law an' his posse! Thar goin's on war jes' scandalous: they played kyerds, an' they consorted with the moonshiners over yander," nodding his head at the wilderness, "an' got ez drunk ez two fraish biled ow*els;* an' they sung an' they hollered. An' they went ter the meetin'-house over yander whilst they war in liquor, an' the preacher riz up an' put 'em out. He's toler'ble tough, that thar Pa'son Kelsey, an' kin hold right smart show in a fight. An' the dep'ty, he straightened hisself, an' 'lowed he war a off'-cer o' the law. An' Pa'son Kelsey, he 'lowed *he* war a off'cer o' the law, an' he 'lowed ez his law war higher 'n the law o' Tennessee. An'·· with that he barred up the door. They hed a cornsider'ble disturba*mint* at the meetin'-house yander at the Notch, an' the saints war tried in thar temper."

"The dep'ty 'lows ez Pa'son Kelsey air crazy in his mind," said the man on the stump. "The dep'ty said the pa'son talked ter him like ez ef he war a onregenerate critter. An' he 'lowed he war baptized in Scolacutta River two year ago an' better. The dep'ty say these hyar mounting preachers hain't got no doctrine like the valley folks. He called Pa'son Kelsey a ignorant cuss!"

"Laws-a-massy!" exclaimed Nathan Hoodendin, scandalized.

"He say it fairly makes him laff ter hear Pa'son Kelsey performin' like he hed a cut-throat mortgage on a seat 'mongst the angels. He say ez he thinks Pa'son Kelsey speaks with more insurance 'n enny man he ever see."

"I reckon, ef the truth war knowed, the dep'ty ain't got no religion, an' never war in Scolacutta River, 'thout it war a-fishin'," said the blacksmith, meditatively.

The fugitive from justice, pining for the simple society of his world, listened like a starveling thing to these meagre details, so replete with interest to him, so full of life and spirit. The next moment he was sorry he had come.

"That thar Amos Jeemes air a comical critter," said the man on the stump, after an interval of cogitation, and with a gurgling reminiscent laugh. "He war a-cuttin' up his shines over thar ter Cayce's the t'other day; he war n't drunk *then*, ye onderstan'" —

"I onderstan'. He war jes' fool, like he always air," said the blacksmith.

"Edzactly," assented the man on the stump.

"An' he fairly made D'rindy laff ter see what the critter would say nex'. An' D'rindy always seemed ter me a powerful solemn sorter gal. Waal, she laffed at Amos. An' whilst him an' the dep'ty war a-goin' down the mounting — I went down ter Jeemes's mill ter leave some grist over night ter be ground — the dep'ty, he run Amos 'bout'n it. The dep'ty he 'lowed ez no gal hed ever made so much fun o' him, an' Amos 'lowed ez D'rindy *did n't* make game o' him. She thunk too much o' him fur that. An' that bold-faced dep'ty, he 'lowed he thought 't war *him* ez hed fund favior. An' Amos, — we war mighty nigh down in Eskaqua Cove then, — he turned suddint an' p'inted up the mounting. 'What kin you-uns view on the mounting?' he axed. The dep'ty, he stopped an' stared; an' thar, mighty nigh ez high ez the lower e-end o' the bald, war a light. 'That shines fur me ter see whilst I'm 'bleeged ter be in Eskaqua Cove,' sez Amos. An' the dep'ty said, 'I think it air a star!' An' Amos sez, sez he, 'Bless yer bones, I think so, too, — sometimes!' But 't war n't no star. 'T war jes' a light in the roof-room window o' Cayce's house; an' ye could see it, sure enough, plumb to the mill in Eskaqua Cove!"

Rick rose to go. Why should he linger, and wring his heart, and garner bitterness to feed upon in his lonely days? Why should he look upon the outer darkness of his life, and dream of the star that shone so far for another man's sake into the sheltered depths of Eskaqua Cove? He had an impulse which he scorned, for his sight was blurred as he laid his hand on the pommel of his saddle. He did not see that one of the other men rose, too.

An approach, stealthy, swift, and the sinewy blacksmith flung himself upon his prisoner with the supple ferocity of a panther.

"Naw — naw!" he said, showing his strong teeth, closely set. "We can't part with ye yit, Rick Tyler! I'll arrest you-uns, ef the sher'ff can't. The peace o' Big Smoky an' the law o' the land air ez dear ter me ez ter enny other man."

The young fellow made a frantic effort to mount; then, as his horse sprang snorting away, he strove to draw one of his pistols. There was a turbulent struggle under the great silver moon and the dead trees. Again and again the swaying figures and their interlocked shadows reeled to the verge of the cliff; one striving to fall and carry the other with him, the other straining every nerve to hold back his captive.

Even the storekeeper stood up and wheezed out a remonstrance.

"Look-a-hyar, boys"—he began; then,

"Jer'miah," he broke off abruptly, as the hopeful scion peered shyly out of the store door, "clar out'n the way, sonny; they hev got shootin'-irons, an' some o' em mought go off."

He himself stepped prudently back. The man on the stump, however, forgot danger in his excitement. He sat and watched the scene with an eager relish which might suggest that a love of bull-fights is not a cultivated taste.

"Be them men a-wrastlin'?" called out a woman, appearing in the doorway of a neighboring house.

"'Pears like it ter me," he said, dryly.

The strength of despair had served to make the younger man the blacksmith's equal, and the contest might have terminated differently had Rick Tyler not stumbled on a ledge. He was forced to his knees, then full upon the ground, his antagonist's grasp upon his throat. The blacksmith roared out for help; the man on the stump slowly responded, and the storekeeper languidly came and overlooked the operation, as the young fellow was disarmed and securely bound, hand and foot.

"Waal, now, Gid Fletcher, ye hev got him," said Nathan Hoodendin. "What d' ye want with him?"

The blacksmith had risen, panting, with wild eyes, his veins standing out in thick cords, perspiring from every pore, and in a bounding fury.

"What do I want with him? I want ter put his head on my anvil thar, an' beat the foolishness out'n it with my hammer. I want ter kick him off'n this hyar bluff down ter the forge fires o' hell. That air what *I* want. An' the State o' Tennessee ain't wantin' much differ."

"Gid Fletcher," said the man who had been sitting on the stump, — he spoke in an accusing voice, — "ye ain't keerin' nuthin' fur the law o' the land, nor the peace o' Big Smoky, nuther. It air jes' that two hunderd dollars blood money ye air cottonin' ter, an' ye knows it."

The love of money, the root of evil, is so rare in the mountains that the blacksmith stood as before a deep reproof. Then, with a moral hardihood that matched his physical prowess, he asked, "An' what ef I be?"

"What war I a-tellin' you-uns? Satan's a-stirrin', — Satan's a-stirrin' on the Big Smoky!" interpolated old Hoodendin.

"Waal, I'd never hev been hankerin' fur sech," drawled the moralist.

A number of other men had come out from the houses, and a discussion ensued as to the best plan to keep the prisoner until morning. It was suggested that the time-honored expedient in localities without the civilization of a jail — a wagon-body inverted, with a rock upon it — would be as secure as the state prison.

"But who wants ter go ter heftin' rocks?" asked Nathan Hoodendin, pertinently.

For the sake of convenience, therefore, they left the prisoner bound with a rope made fast around a stump, that he might not, in his desperation, roll himself from the crag, and deputing a number of the men to watch him by turns, the Settlement retired to its slumbers.

The night wore on; the moon journeyed toward the mountains in the west; the mists rose to meet it, and glistened like a silver sea. Some lonely, undiscovered ocean, this; never a sail set, never a pennant flying; all the valley was submerged; the black summits in the distance were isolated and insular; the moonlight glanced on the sparkling ripples, on the long reaches of illusive vapor.

At intervals cocks crew; a faint response, like farthest echoes, came from some neighboring cove; and then silence, save for the drone of the nocturnal insects and the far blast of a hunter's horn.

"Jer'miah," said Rick Tyler, suddenly, as the boy crouched by one of the stumps and watched him with dilated, moonlit eyes, —

when Nathan Hoodendin's vigil came the little factotum served in his stead, — "Jer'miah, git my knife out 'n the store an' cut these hyar ropes. I'll gin ye my rifle ef ye will."

The boy sprang up, scudded off swiftly, then came back, and crouched by the stump again.

The moon slipped lower and lower; the silver sea had turned to molten gold; the stars that had journeyed westward with the moon were dying out of a dim blue sky. Over the corn-field in the east was one larger than the rest, burning in an amber haze, charged with an unspoken poetical emotion that set its heart of white fire aquiver.

"I'll gin ye my horse ef ye will."

"I dassent," said Jer'miah.

The morning star was burned out at last, and the prosaic day came over the corn-field.

III.

TWILIGHT was slipping down on the Big Smoky. Definiteness was annihilated, and distance a suggestion. Mountain forms lay darkening along the horizon, still flushed with the sunset. Eskaqua Cove had abysmal suggestions, and the ravines were vague glooms. Fireflies were aflicker in the woods. There might be a star, outpost of the night.

Dorinda, hunting for the vagrant "crumply cow," paused sometimes when the wandering path led to the mountain's brink, and looked down those gigantic slopes and unmeasured depths. She carried her milk-piggin, and her head was uncovered. Now and then she called with long, vague vowels, "Soo — cow! Soo!" There was no response save the echoes and the vibrant iteration of the katydid. Once she heard an alien sound, and she paused to listen. From the projecting spur where she stood, looking across the Cove, she could see, above the forests on the slopes, the bare, uprising dome, towering in stupendous proportions against the sky. The sound came again and yet again, and she recognized the voice of the man who was wont to go and pray in the desert places on the " bald " of the mountain, and whom she had likened to the prophets of old. There was something indescribably wild and weird in those appealing, tempestuous tones, now rising as in frenzy, and now falling as with exhaustion, — beseeching, adjuring, reproaching.

"He hev fairly beset the throne o' grace!" she said, with a sort of pity for this insistent piety. A shivering, filmy mist was slipping down over the great dome. It glittered in the last rays of the sunlight, already vanished from the world below, like an illuminated silver gauze. She was reminded of the veil of the temple, and she had a sense of intrusion.

"Prayer, though, air free for all," she remarked, as self-justification, since she had paused to hear.

She did not linger. His voice died in the distance, and the solemnity of the impression was gradually obliterated. As she went she presently began to sing, sometimes interpolating, without a sense of interruption, her mellow call of "Soo — cow! Soo!" until it took the semblance of a refrain, with an abrupt crescendo. The wild roses were flowering along the paths, and the pink and white azaleas, — what perfumed ways, what lavish grace and beauty! The blooms of the laurel in the darkling places were like a spangling of stars. Dew was falling, — it dashed into her face from the boughs that interlaced across the unfrequented path, — and still the light lingered, loath to leave. She heard the stir of some wild things in the hollow of a great tree, and then a faint, low growl. She fancied she saw a pair of bright eyes looking apprehensively at her.

"We-uns hev got a baby at our house, too, an' we don't want yourn, ma'am; much obleeged, all the same," she said, with a laugh. But she looked back with a sort of pity for that alert maternal fear, and she never mentioned to the youngest brother, a persistent trapper, the little family of raccoons in the woods.

She had forgotten the voice raised in importunate supplication on the "bald," until, pursuing the path, she was led into the road, hard by a little bridge, or more properly culvert, which had rotted long ago; the vines came up through the cavities in the timbers, and a blackberry bush, with a wren's nest, flourished in their midst. The road was fain to wade through the stream; but the channel was dry now, — a narrow belt of yellow sand lying in a long curving vista in the midst of the dense woods. A yoke of oxen, drawing a rude slide, paused to rest in the middle of the channel, and beside them was a man, of medium height, slender but sinewy, dressed in brown jeans, his trousers thrust into the legs of his boots, a rifle on his shoulder, and a broad-brimmed old wool hat surmounting his dark hair, that hung down to the collar of his coat. Her singing had prepared him for her advent, but he barely raised his eyes. That quick glance was incongruous with his dullard aspect; it held a spark of fire, inspiration, frenzy, — who can say ?

He spoke suddenly, in a meek, drawling way, and with the air of submitting the proposition : —

"I hev gin the beastises a toler'ble hard day's work, an' I 'm a-favorin' 'em goin' home."

A long pause ensued. The oxen hung down their weary heads, with the symbol of slavery upon them. The smell of ferns and damp mould was on the air. Rotting logs lay here and there, where the failing water had stranded them. The grape-vine, draping the giant oaks, swayed gently, and suggested an observation to break the silence.

"How air the moral vineyard a-thrivin'?" she asked, solemnly.

He looked downcast. "Toler'ble, I reckon."

"I hearn tell ez thar war a right smart passel o' folks baptized over yander in Scolacutta River," she remarked, encouragingly.

"I baptized fourteen."

She turned the warm brightness of her eyes upon him. "They hed all fund grace!" she exclaimed.

"They 'lowed so. I hopes they 'll prove it by thar works," he said, without enthusiasm.

"Ye war a-prayin' fur 'em on the bald?" she asked, apprehending that he accounted these converts peculiarly precarious.

"Naw," he replied, with moody sincerity; "I war a-prayin' for myself."

There was another pause, longer and more awkward than before.

"What work be you-uns a-doin' of?" asked Dorinda, timidly. She quailed a trifle before the uncomprehended light in his eyes. It was not of her world, she felt instinctively.

"I hev ploughed some, holpin' Jonas Trice, an' hev been a-haulin' wood. I tuk my rifle along," he added, "thinkin' I mought see suthin' ez would be tasty fur the old men's supper ez I kem home, but I forgot ter look around keen."

There was a sudden sound along the road,— a sound of quick hoof-beats. Because of the deep sand the rider was close at hand before his approach was discovered. He drew rein abruptly, and they saw that it was Gid Fletcher, the blacksmith of the Settlement.

"Hev you-uns hearn the news?" he cried, excitedly, as he threw himself from the saddle.

The man, leaning on the rifle, looked up, with no question in his eyes. There was an almost monastic indifference to the world suggested in his manner.

"Thar's a mighty disturbamint at the Settle*mint*. Las' night this hyar Rick Tyler,— what air under indictment fur a-killin' o' Joel Byers,— he kem a-nosin' 'roun' the Settle*mint* a-tryin' ter buy powder"—

Dorinda stretched out her hand; the trees were unsteady before her; the few faint stars, no longer pulsating points of light, described a circle of dazzling gleams. She caught at the yoke on the neck of the oxen; she leaned upon the impassive beast, and then it seemed that every faculty was merged in the sense of hearing. The horse had moved away from the blacksmith, holding his head down among the bowlders, and snuffing about for the water he remembered here with a disappointment almost pathetic.

"War he tuk?" demanded the preacher.

"Percisely so," drawled the blacksmith, with a sub-current of elation in his tone.

There was a sudden change in Kelsey's manner. He turned fiery eyes upon the blacksmith. Light and life were in every line of his face. He drew himself up tense and erect; he stretched forth his hand with an accusing gesture.

" 'T war you-uns, Gid Fletcher, ez tuk the boy!"

" Lord, pa'son, how 'd you-uns know that?" exclaimed the blacksmith. His manner combined a deference, which in civilization we reccognize as respect for the cloth, with the easy familiarity, induced by the association since boyhood, of equals in age and station. " I hed n't let on a word, hed I, D'rindy?"

The idea of an abnormal foreknowledge, mysteriously possessed, had its uncanny influences. The lonely woods were darkening about them. The stars seemed very far off. A rotting log in the midst of the débris of the stream, in a wild tangle of underbrush and shelving rocks, showed fox-fire and glowed in the glooms.

"I knowed," said Kelsey, contemptuously waiving the suggestion of miraculous forecast, " bekase the sher'ff hain't been in the Big Smoky for two weeks, an' that thar danglin' shadder o' his'n rid off las' Monday from Jeemes's Mill in Eskaqua Cove. An' the constable o' the deestric air sick abed. So I 'lowed 't war you-uns."

" An' why air it me more 'n enny other man

at the Settle*mint?*" The blacksmith's blood was rising; his sensibilities descried a covert taunt which as yet his slower intelligence failed to comprehend.

" An' ye hev rid with speed fur the sher'ff — or mebbe ter overhaul the dep'ty — ter come an' jail the prisoner afore he gits away."

" An' why me, more 'n the t'others ? " demanded the blacksmith.

" Yer heart air ez hard ez yer anvil, Gid Fletcher," said the mind-reader. " Thar ain't another man on the Big Smoky ez would stir himself ter gin over ter the gallus or the pen'tiary the frien' ez trested him, who hev done no harm, but hev got tangled in a twist of a unjest law. Ef the law tuk him, that's a differ."

" 'T ain't fur we-uns ter jedge o' the law ! " exclaimed Gid Fletcher, his logic sharpened by the anxiety of his greed and his prideful self-esteem. " Let the law jedge o' his crime."

" Jes' so; let the law take him, an' let the law try him. The law is ekal ter it. Ef the sher'ff summons me with his posse, I 'll hunt Rick Tyler through all the Big Smoky " —

" Look-a-hyar, Hi Kelsey, the Gov'nor o' Tennessee hev offered a reward o' two hunderd dollars " —

" Blood money," interpolated the parson.

"Ye kin call it so, ef so minded; but ef it war right fur the Gov'nor ter offer it, it air right fur me ter yearn it."

He had come very close. It was his nature and his habit to brook no resistance. He subdued the hard metals upon his anvil. His hammer disciplined the iron. The fire wrought his will. His instinct was to forge this man's opinion into the likeness of his own. His conviction was the moral swage that must shape the belief of others.

"It air lawful fur me ter yearn it," he repeated.

"Lawful!" exclaimed the parson, with a tense, jeering laugh. "Judas war a law-abidin' citizen. He mos' lawfully betrayed *his* Frien' ter the law. Them thirty pieces o' silver! Sech currency ain't out o' circulation yit!"

Quick as a flash the blacksmith's heavy hand struck the prophet in the face. The next moment his sudden anger was merged in fear. He stood, unarmed, at the mercy of an assaulted and outraged man, with a loaded rifle in his hands, and all the lightnings of heaven quivering in his angry eyes.

Gid Fletcher had hardly time to draw the breath he thought his last, when the prophet slowly turned the other cheek.

"In the name of the Master," he said, with all the dignity of his calling.

As the blacksmith mounted his horse and rode away, he felt that the parson's rifle-ball would be preferable to the gross slur that he had incurred. His reputation, moral and spiritual, was annihilated; and he held this dear, for piety, or its simulacrum, on the primitive Big Smoky, is the point of honor. What a text! What an illustration of iniquity he would furnish for the sermons, foretelling wrath and vengeance, that sometimes shook the Big Smoky to its foundations! He was cast down, and indignant too.

"Fur Hi Kelsey ter be a-puttin' up sech a pious mouth, an' a-turnin' the t'other cheek, an' sech, ter me, ez hev seen him hold his own ez stiff in a many a free-handed fight, an' hev drawed his shootin'-irons on folks agin an' agin! An' he fairly tuk the dep'ty, at that thar disturbamint at the meet'n'-house, by the scruff o' the neck, an' shuck him ez ef he hed been a rat or suthin', an' drapped him out'n the door. An' now ter be a-turnin' the t'other cheek! An' thar's that thar D'rindy, a-seein' it all, an' a-lookin' at it ez wide-eyed ez a cat in the dark."

Dorinda went home planning a rescue. Against the law this probably was, she thought. "Ef it air — it ought n't ter be," she concluded, arbitrarily. "It don't hurt nobody." How serious it was — a felony — she did not know, nor did she care. She went on sturdily, debating within herself how best to tell the news. With an intuitive knowledge of human nature, she reckoned on the prejudice aroused by the recital of the blacksmith's assault upon the preacher and the forbearance of the man of God. She began to count those who would be likely to attempt the enterprise when it should be suggested. There were the five men at home, all bold, reckless, antagonistic to the law, and at odds with the sheriff. She paused, with a frightened face and a wild gesture as if to ward off an unforeseen danger. Send them to meet him! Never, never would she lift her hand or raise her voice to aid in fulfilling that grimly prophesied death on the muzzle of the old rifle-barrel. She trembled at the thought of her precipitancy. His life was in her hand. With a constraining moral sense she felt that it was she who had placed it in jeopardy, and that she held it in trust.

She was cold, shivering. There was a change in the temperature; perhaps hail had fallen somewhere near, for the rare air had icy suggestions. She was seldom out so late, and was glad to see, high on the slope, the light that was wont to shine like a star into the dark depths of Eskaqua Cove. The white mists gathered around it; a circle of pearly light encompassed it, like Saturn's ring. As she came nearer, the roof of the house defined itself, with its oblique ridge-pole against the sky, and its clay and stick chimney, also built in defiance of rectangles, and its little porch, the curtaining hop-vines, dripping, dripping, with dew. In the corner of the rail fence was the "crumply cow," chewing her cud.

The radiance of firelight streamed out through the open door, around which was grouped a number of shadows, of intent and wistful aspect. These were the hounds, and they crowded about her ecstatically as she came up on the porch.

She paused at the door, and looked in with melancholy eyes. The light fell on her face, still damp with the dew, giving its gentle curves a subdued glister, like marble; the dark blue of her dress heightened its fairness. A sudden smile broke upon it as she leaned forward. There were three men, Ab, Pete, and Ben, seated around the fire; but she was looking at none of them, and they silently followed her gaze. Only one pair of eyes met hers,— the eyes of a fat young person, wonderfully muscular for the tender age of three, who sat in the chimney-corner in a little wooden chair, and preserved the important and impassive air of a domestic magnate. This was hardly impaired by his ill-defined, infantile features, his large tow-head, his stolid blue eyes, his feminine garb of blue-checked cotton, short enough to disclose sturdy white calves and two feet with the usual complement of toes. He looked at her in grave recognition, but made no sign.

"Jacob," she softly drawled, "why n't ye go ter bed?"

But Jacob was indisposed for conversation on this theme; he said nothing.

"Why n't you-uns git him ter bed?" she asked of the assemblage at large. "He'll git stunted, a-settin' up so late in the night."

"Waal," said one of the huge jeans-clad mountaineers, taking his pipe from his mouth, and scrutinizing the subject of conversation, "I 'low it takes more 'n three full-grown men ter git that thar survigrus buzzard ter bed when he don't want ter go thar, an' we war n't a-goin' ter resk it."

"I did ax him ter go ter bed, D'rindy," said another of the bearded giants, "but he 'lowed he *would n't*. I never see a critter so pompered ez Jacob; he ain't got no medjure o' respec' fur nobody."

The subject of these strictures gazed unconcernedly first at one speaker, then at the other.

Dorinda still looked at him, her face transfigured by its tender smile. But she was fain to exert her authority. "Waal, Jacob," she said, decisively, "ye mus' gin yer cornsent ter go ter bed, arter a while."

Jacob calmly nodded. He expected to go to bed some time that night.

The hounds had taken advantage of Dorinda's entrance to creep into the room and adjust themselves among the family group about the fire. One of them, near Jacob, lured by the tempting plumpness, put out a long red tongue, and gave a furtive lick to his fat white leg. The little mountaineer promptly doubled his plucky fist, and administered a sharp blow on the black nose of the offender, whose yelp of repentant pain attracted attention to the canine intruders. Ab Cayce rose to his feet with an oath. There was a shrill chorus of anguish as he actively kicked them out with his great cowhide boots.

"Git out'n hyar, ye dad-burned beastises! I hev druv ye out fifty times sence sundown; now *stay* druv!"

He emphasized the lesson with several gratuitous kicks after the room and the porch were fairly cleared. But before he was again seated the dogs were once more clustered about the door, with intent bobbing heads and glistening eyes that peered in wistfully, with a longing for the society of their human friends, and a pathetic anxiety to be accounted of the family circle.

There was more stir than usual in the interval between supper and bedtime. During the three memorable days that Dorinda had sojourned in Tuckaleechee Cove Miranda Jane's ineffective administration had resulted in domestic chaos in several departments. The lantern by which the cow was to be milked was nowhere to be found. The filly-like Miranda Jane, with her tousled mane and black forelock hanging over her eyes, was greatly distraught in the effort to remember where it had been put and for what it had been last used, and was "plumb beat out and beset," she declared, as she cantered in and cantered out, and took much exercise in the search, to little purpose. One of the men rose presently, and addressed himself to the effort. He found it at last, and handed it to Dorinda without a word. He did not offer to milk the cow, as essentially a feminine task, in the mountains, as to sew or knit. When she came back she sat down among them in the chair usually occupied by her grandmother, — who had in her turn gone on a visit to "Aunt Jerushy" in Tuckaleechee Cove, — and as she busied herself in putting on her needles a sizable stocking for Jacob she did not join in the fragmentary conversation.

Ab Cayce, the eldest, talked fitfully as he smoked his pipe, — a lank, lantern-jawed man, with a small, gleaming eye and a ragged beard. The youngest of the brothers, Solomon, was like him, except that his long chin, of the style familiarly denominated jimber-jawed, was still smooth and boyish, and, big-boned as he was, he lacked in weight and somewhat in height the proportions of the senior. Peter was the contentious member of the family. He was wont to bicker in solitary disaffection, until he seemed to disprove the adage that it takes two to make a quarrel. He was afflicted with a stammer, and at every obstruction his voice broke out with startling shrillness, several keys higher than the tone with which the sentence commenced. He was loose-jointed and had a shambling gait; his hair seemed never to have outgrown the bleached, colorless tone so common among the children of the mountains, and it hung in long locks of a dreary drab about his sun-embrowned face. His teeth were irregular, and protruded slightly. "Ez hard-favored ez Pete Cayce," was a proverb on the Big Smoky. His wrangles about the amount of seed necessary to sow to the acre, and his objurgation concerning the horse he had been ploughing with that day, filled the evening.

"Thar ain't a durned fool on the Big Smoky ez dunno that thar sayin' 'bout 'n the beastises: —

> 'One white huff — buy him ;
> Two white huffs — try him ;
> Three white huffs — deny him ;
> Four white huffs an' a white nose —
> Take off his hide an' feed him ter the crows.'"

Outside, the rising wind wandered fitfully through the Great Smoky, like a spirit of unrest. The surging trees in the wooded vastness on every side filled the air with the turbulent sound of their commotion. The fire smouldered on the hearth. The room was visible in the warm glow: the walls, rich and mellow with the alternate dark shade of the hewn logs and the dull yellow of the "daubin';" the great frame of the warping-bars, hung about with scarlet and blue and saffron yarn ; the brilliant strings of red pepper, swinging from the rafters. The spinning-wheel, near the open door, revolved slightly, with a stealthy motion, when the wind touched it, as though some invisible woodland thing had half a mind for uncanny industrial experiments.

Dorinda told her news at last, in few words and with what composure she could command. As the listeners broke into surprised ejaculations and comments, she sat gazing silently at the fire. Should she speak the thought nearest her heart? Should she suggest a rescue? She was torn by contending terrors, — fears for them, for the man in his primitive shackles at the Settlement, for the enemy whose life she felt she had jeopardized. She had a wild vision — half in hope, half in anguish — of her brothers, in the saddle, armed to the teeth and riding like the wind. They had not moved of their own accord. Should she urge them to go?

Oh, never had the long days on the Big Smoky, never had all the years that had visibly rolled from east to west with the changing seasons, brought her so much of life as the last few hours, — such intensity of emotion, such swiftness of thought, such baffling perplexity, such woe!

IV.

KELSEY trudged on with his slide and his oxen, elated by his moral triumph. He glorified himself for his meekness. He joyed, with all the turbulent impulses of victory, in the blacksmith's discomfiture.

Yet he was cognizant of his own deeper, subtler springs of action. There was that within him which forbade him to take the life of an unarmed man, but he piqued himself that he forbore. He had withheld even the return of the blow. But he knew that in refraining he had struck deeper still. He dwelt upon the scene with the satisfaction of an inventor. He, too, could foresee the consequences: the bloodcurdling eloquence; the port and pose of a martyr; the far-spread distrust of the blacksmith's professions of piety, under which that doughty religionist already quaked.

And as he reflected he replied, tartly, to the monitor within, "Be angry and sin not."

And the monitor had no text.

Because of the night drifting down, perhaps, — drifting down with a chilling change; because of the darkened solemnity of the dreary woods; because of the stars shining with a splendid aloofness from all that is human; because of the melancholy suggestions of a will-o'-the-wisp glowing in a marshy tangle, his exultant mood began to wane.

"Thar it is!" he cried, suddenly, pointing at the mocking illusion, — "that's my religion: looks like fire, an' it's fog!"

His mind had reverted to his wild supplications in the solitudes of the "bald," — his unanswered prayers. The oxen had paused of their own accord to rest, and he stood looking at the spectral gleam.

"I'd never hev thunk o' takin' up with religion," he said, in a shrill, upbraiding tone, "ef I hed been let ter live along like other men be, or ef me an' mine could die like other folks be let ter die! But it 'peared ter me ez religion war 'bout all ez war lef', arter I hed gin the baby the stuff the valley doctor hed lef' fur Em'ly, — bein' ez I could n't read right the old critter's cur'ous scrapin's with his pencil, — an' gin Em'ly the stuff fur the baby. An' it died. An' then Em'ly got onsettled an' crazy, an' tuk ter vagrantin' 'roun', an' fell off'n the bluff. An' some say she flunged herself off'n it. And I knows she flunged herself off'n it through bein' out'n her mind with grief."

He paused, leaning on the yoke, his dreary

eyes still on the *ignis fatuus* of the woods. "An' then Brother Jake Tobin 'lowed ez religion war fur sech ez me. I hed no mind ter religion. But the worl' hed in an' about petered out for me. An' I tuk up with religion. I hev sarved it five year faithful. An' now" — he cast his angry eyes upward — "ye let me believe that thar is no God!"

So it was that Satan hunted him like a partridge on the mountains. So it was that he went out into the desert places to upbraid the God in whom he believed because he believed that there was no God. There was a tragedy in his faith and his unfaith. That this untrained, untutored mind should grope among the irreconcilable things, — the problems of a merciful God and his afflicted people, foreordained from the beginning of the world and free agents! That to the ignorant mountaineer should come those distraught questions that vex polemics, and try the strength of theologies, and give the wise men an illimitable field for the display of their agile and ingenious solutions and substitutions! He knew naught of this; the wild Alleghanies intervened between his yearning, empty despair and their plenished fame, the splendid superstructure on the ruins of their faith. He thought himself the only unbeliever in a Christian world, the only inherent infidel; a mysteriously accursed creature, charged with the discovery of the monstrous fallacy of that beneficent comfort, assuaging the grief of a stricken world, and called an overruling Providence. Again his flickering faith would flare up, and he would reproach God who had suffered its lapse. This was his secret and his shame, and he guarded it. And so when he preached his wild sermons with a certain natural eloquence; and prayed his frantic prayers, instinct with all the sincerities of despair; and sang with the people the mournful old hymns in the little meeting-house on the notch, or on the banks of the Scolacutta River, where they went down to be baptized, his keen introspection, his moral dissent, which he might not forbear, yet would not avow, were an intolerable burden, and his spiritual life was the throe of a spiritual anguish.

Often there was no intimation in those sermons of his of the quaint doctrines which delight the simple men of his calling in that region, who are fain to feel learned. His Christ, to judge from this mood, was a Paramount Emotion: not the Christ who confuted the wise men in the temple, and read in the synagogues, and said dark allegories; but he who stilled the storm, and healed the sick, and raised the dead, and wept, most humanly, for the friend whom he loved. Kelsey's trusting heart contended with his doubting mind, and the simple humanities of these sermons comforted him. Sometimes he sought consolation otherwise; he would remember that he had never been like his fellows. This was only another manifestation of the dissimilarity that dated from his earliest recollections. He had from his infancy peculiar gifts. He was learned in the signs of the weather, and predicted the mountain storms; he knew the haunts and habits of every beast and bird in the Great Smoky, every leaf that burgeons, every flower that blows. So deep and incisive a knowledge of human nature had he that this faculty was deemed supernatural, and akin to the gift of prophecy. He himself understood, although perhaps he could not have accurately limited and defined it, that he exercised unconsciously a vigilant attention and an acute discrimination; his forecast was based upon observation so close and unsparing, and a power of deduction so just, that in a wider sphere it might have been called judgment, and, reinforced by education, have attained all the functions of a ripened sagacity.

Crude as it was, it did not fail of recognition. In many ways his "word" was sought and heeded. His influence yielded its richest effect when his *confrère* of the pulpit would call on him to foretell the fate of the sinner and the wrath of God to the Big Smoky. And then Brother Jake Tobin would accompany the glowing picture by a slow rhythmic clapping of hands and a fragmentary chant, " That dreadful Day air a-comin' along!"— bearing all the time a smiling and beatific countenance, as if he were fireproof himself, and brimstone and flame were only for his friends.

Rousing himself from his reverie with a sigh, Hiram Kelsey urged the oxen along the sandy road, which had here and there a stony interval threatening the slide with dissolution at every jolt. They began presently to quicken their pace of their own accord. The encompassing woods and the laurel were so dense that no gleam of light was visible till they brought up suddenly beside a rail fence, and the fitful glimmer of firelight from an open door close at hand revealed the presence of a double log cabin. There was an uninclosed passage between the two rooms, and in this a tall, gaunt woman was standing.

" Thar be Hi now, with the steers," she said, detecting the dim bovine shadows in the flickering gleams.

" Tell Hiram ter come in right now," cried a chirping voice, like a superannuated cricket. " I hev a word ter ax him."

"Tell Hiram ter feed them thar steers fust," cried out another ancient voice, keyed several tones lower, and also with the ring of authority.

"Tell Hiram," shrilly piped the other, "ter hustle his bones, ef he knows what air good fur 'em."

"Tell Hiram," said the deeper voice, sustaining the antiphonal effect, "I want them thar steers feded foreshortly."

Then ensued a muttered wrangle within, and finally the shriller voice was again uplifted: "Tell Hiram what my word air."

"An' ye tell Hiram what *my* word air."

The woman, who was tall as a grenadier, and had a voice like velvet, looked meekly back into the room, upon each mandate, with a nod of mild obedience.

"Ye hearn 'em," she said softly to Kelsey. Evidently she could not undertake the hazard of discriminating between these coequal authorities.

"I hearn 'em," he replied.

She sat down near the door, and resumed her occupation of monotonously peeling June apples for "sass." Her brown calico sunbonnet, which she habitually wore, in doors and out, obscured her visage, except her chin and absorbed mouth, that now and then moved in unconscious sympathy with her work. There was a piggin on one side of her to receive the quartered fruit, and on the other a white oak splint basket, already half full of the spiral parings. On the doorstep her husband sat, a shaggy-headed, full-bearded, unkempt fellow, in brown jeans trousers reaching almost to his collar-bone in front, and supported by the single capable suspender so much affected in the mountains. His unbleached cotton shirt was open at the throat, for there was fire enough in the huge chimney-place to make the room unpleasantly warm, despite the change of temperature without. Now and then he stretched out his hand for an apple already pared, which his wife gave him with an adroit back-handed movement, and which he ate in a mouthful or two. He made way for Kelsey to enter, and asked him a question, almost inarticulate because of the apples, but apparently of hospitable intent, for Kelsey said he had had a bite and a sup at Jonas Trice's, and did not want the supper which had been providently saved for him.

Kelsey did not betray which command he had thought best to obey.

"I hed ter put my rifle on the rack in the t'other room, gran'dad," he observed meekly, addressing one of two very old men who sat on either side of the huge fireplace. There were cushions in their rude arm-chairs, and awkward little three-legged footstools were placed in front of them. Their shoes and clothing, although coarse to the last degree, were clean and carefully tended. They had each long ago lived out the allotted threescore years and ten, but they had evidently not worn out their welcome. One had suffered a paralytic attack, and every word and motion was accompanied with a convulsive gasp and jerk. The other old man was saturnine and lymphatic, and seemed a trifle younger than his venerable associate.

"What war ye a-doin' of with yer rifle?" mumbled "gran'dad," in wild, toothless haste.

"I tuk it along ter see, when I war a-comin' home, ef I mought shoot suthin' tasty for supper."

"What did ye git?" demanded gran'dad, with retrospective greed; for supper was over, and he had done full justice to his share.

"I never got nuthin'," said Kelsey, a trifle shamefacedly.

"Waal, waal, waal! These hyar latter times gits cur'ouser ez they goes along. The stren'th an' the seasonin' hev all gone out'n the lan'. Whenst I war young, folks ez kerried rifles ter git suthin' fur supper never kem home a-suckin' the bar'l. Folks ez kerried rifles in them days did n't tote 'em fur—fur—a ornamint.

Folks in them days lef' preachin' an' prophecy an' sech ter thar elders, an' hunted the beastis an' the Injun', — though sinners is plentier than the t'other kind o' game on the Big Smoky these times. No man, in them days, jes' turned thirty sot hisself down ter idlin', an' preachin', an' convictin' his elders o' sin."

Kelsey bore himself with the deferential humility characteristic of the mountaineers toward the aged among them.

"What war the word ez ye war a-layin' off ter say ter me, gran'dad?" he asked, striving to effect a diversion.

"Waal, waal, look-a-hyar, Hiram!" exclaimed the old man, remembering his question in eager precipitancy. "This hyar 'Cajah Green, ye know, ez air a-runnin' fur sher'ff — air — air he Republikin or Dimmycrat?"

"Thar's no man in these hyar parts smart enough ter find that out," interpolated Obediah Scruggs in the door, circumspectly taking the apple seeds out of his mouth. He was the son of one of the magnates, and the son-in-law of the other; his matrimonial venture had resulted in doubling his filial obligations. His wife had brought, instead of a dowry, her aged father to the fireside.

"'Cajah Green," continued the speaker, "run ez a independent las' time, an' thar war so many bolters an' sech they split the vote, an' he war 'lected. An' now he air a-runnin' agin."

The old man listened to this statement, his eye blazing, his chin in a quiver, his lean figure erect, and the pipe in his palsied hand shaking till the coal of fire on top showed brightening tendencies.

" Waal, sir! waal! " exclaimed the aged politician, with intense bitterness. " The stren'th an' the seasonin' hev *all* gone out'n the lan'! Whenst I war young," he declared dramatically, drawing the pitiable contrast, " folks knowed what they war, an' they let other folks know, too, ef they hed ter club it inter 'em. But them was Old Hickory's times. Waal, waal, we ain't a-goin' ter see Old Hickory no more — no — more! "

" I hopes not," said the other old man, with sudden asperity. " I hopes we 'll never see no sech tormentin' old Dimmycrat agin. But law! I need n't fret my soul. Henry Clay shook all the life out'n him five year afore he died. Henry Clay made a speech agin Andrew Jackson in 1840 what forty thousan' people kem ter hear. *Thar* war a man fur ye! He hed a tongue like a bell; 'pears like ter me I kin hear it yit, when I listens right hard. By Gum! " triumphantly, " that day he tuk the stiffenin' out'n Old Hickory! Surely, surely, he did! Ef I thought I war never a-goin' ter hear Old Hickory's name agin I'd tune up my ears fur the angel's quirin'. I war born a Republikin, I grow'd ter be a good Whig, an' I'll die a Republikin. Ef that ain't religion I dunno what air! That's the way I hev lived an' walked afore the Lord. An' hyar in the evenin' o' my days I hev got ter set alongside o' this hyar old consarn, an' hear him jow 'bout'n Old Hickory from mornin' till night. Ef I hed knowed how he war goin' ter turn out 'bout'n Old Hickory in his las' days, I would n't hev let my darter marry his son, thirty five year ago. I knowed he war a Dimmycrat, but I never knowed the stren'th o' the failin' till I war called on ter 'speriunce it."

"Ye 'lowed t'other day, gran'dad," said Kelsey, addressing the aged paralytic in a propitiatory manner, " ez ye war n't a-goin' ter talk 'bout'n Old Hickory no more. It 'pears like ter me ez ye oughter gin yer 'tention ter the candidates ez ye hev got ter vote fur in August, — 'Cajah Green, an' sech."

But it must be admitted that Micajah Green was not half the man that Old Hickory was, and the filial remonstrance had no effect. The acrimonies of fifty years ago were renewed across the hearth with a rancor that suggests that an old grudge, like old wine, improves with time. No one ventured to interrupt, but Obediah Scruggs, still lounging in the door, commented in a low tone: —

"The law stirs itself ter sot a time when a man air old enough ter vote an' meddle with politics ginerally. 'Pears like ter me it ought ter sot a time when he hev got ter quit."

"Waal, Obediah!" exclaimed the soft-voiced woman, the red parings hanging in concentric circles from her motionless knife. "That ain't religion. Ye talk like a man would hev ter be ez sensible an' solid fur politics ez fur workin' on the road. They don't summons the old men fur sech jobs ez that. They mought ez well enjye the evenin' o' thar days with this foolishness o' politics ez enny other."

"Shucks!" said Obediah, who had the courage of his convictions. "These hyar old folks hev hed ter live in the same house an' ride in the same wagin thirty-five year, jes' 'kase, when we war married, they agreed ter put what they hed tergether; an' they hev been a-fightin' over thar dead an' gone politics ev'y minit o' the time sence. Thar may be some good Dimmycrats, an' thar may be some good Republikins; but they make a powerful oneasy team, yoked tergether. An' when it grows on 'em so, the law oughter step in, an' count 'em over age, an' shet 'em up. 'Specially ez dad hev voted fur

Andy Jackson fur Presi*dint*, outer respec' fur his mem'ry, ev'y 'lection sence the tormentin' old critter died."

But he said all this below his breath, and presently fell silent, for his wife's face had clouded, and her soft drawling voice had an intimation of a depression of spirit.

"The kentry hev kem ter its ruin," exclaimed the paralytic, "when men — brazen-faced buzzards — kin go an' git 'lected ter office 'thout no party ter boost 'em! Look-a-hyar," — he turned to his grandson, — "ye air always a-prophesyin'. Prophesy some now. Air 'Cajah Green a-goin' ter be 'lected?"

He thumped the floor with his stick, and fixed his imperative eye upon Hiram Kelsey's face.

"Naw, gran'dad. He won't be 'lected," said the prophet.

The old man's face was scarlet because of this contradiction of his own dismal vaticinations.

"'Cajah Green *will* be 'lected," he cried. "The kentry's ruined. Folks dunno whether they air Republikins or Dimmycrats! Lor' A'mighty, ter think o' that! The kentry's ruined! An' yer prophesyin' don't tech it. They hed false prophets in the old days, an' the tribe holds out yit."

He struck the floor venomously with his stick.

Its defective aim once or twice brought it upon a rough black bundle that lay rolled up in front of the fire like a great dog. A slow head was lifted inquiringly, with an offended mien, from the rolls of fat and fur. Twinkling small eyes glared out. When another blow descended, with a wild disregard of results, there was a whimper, a long low growl, a flash of white teeth, and with claw and fang the pet cub caught at the stick. The old man dropped it in a panic.

"Look a-yander at the bar!" he shrieked.

But the cub had crouched on the floor since the stick had fallen, and was whimpering again, and looking about in cowardly appeal.

The old man rallied, "What d'ye bring the savage beastis home fur, Hiram, out'n the woods whar they b'long?" he vociferated.

"Kase he 'lowed he hed killed the dam, an' the young 'un war bound ter starve," put in the other old man actuated, perhaps, by some sympathy for the grandson, whose strength and youth counted for naught against this adversary.

"What air ye a-aimin' ter do with it? Ter kill sech chillen ez happen ter make game o' ye? That's what the prophets of old cited thar bars ter do, — ter kill the little laffin' chillen."

Kelsey winced. The cruelties of the old chronicles bore hard upon his wavering faith.

The old man saw his advantage, and with the wantonness of tyranny followed it up: "That's it, — that's it! That would suit Hiram, like the prophets, — ter kill the innercent chillen!"

The young man recoiled suddenly. The patriarch, a wild terror on his pallid, aged face, recognized the significance of his words. He held up his shaking hands as if to recall them, to clutch them. He had remembered the domestic tragedy: the humble figure of the little mountain child, all gayety and dimples and gurgling laughter, who had known no grief and had wrought such woe, who had left a rude, empty cradle in the corner, a mound — such a tiny mound! — in the graveyard, and an imperishable anguish of self-reproach, unquenchable as the fires of hell.

"I furgot, — I furgot!" shrieked the old man. "I furgot the baby! When war she buried? — las' week or year afore las'? The only one, — the only great-gran'child I ever hed. The frien'liest baby! Knowed me jes' ez well!" He burst into senile tears. "Don't ye go, Hiram. What did the doctor say ye gin her? Laws-a-massy! 'Pears like 't war jes' yestiddy she war a-crawlin' 'roun' the floor, stiddier that heejus beastis ez I wisht war in the woods — laffin' — Lord A'mighty! laffin' an' takin' notice ez peart. Hiram, don't ye go, — don't ye go! Peartes', pretties' chile I ever see — an' I had six o' my own — an' the frien'lies'! An' I hed planned fur sech a many pleasures when she hed got some growth an' hed l'arned ter talk. I wanted ter hear what she hed ter say, — the only great-grandchild I ever hed, — an' now the words will never be spoke. 'Pears like ter me ez the Lord shows mighty little jedgmint ter take her, an' leave me a-cumberin' the groun'."

Then he began once more to wring his hands and sob aloud, — that piteous weeping of the aged! — and to mumble brokenly, " The frien'lies' baby!"

The woman left her work and took off her bonnet, showing her gray hair drawn into a skimpy knot at the back of her head, and leaving in high relief her strong, honest, candid features, on which the refinements of all benign impulses effaced the effects of poverty and ignorance. She crossed the room to the old man's chair; her velvety voice soothed him. He suffered himself to be lifted by his son and grandson, and carried away bodily to bed in the room across the passage. In the mean time the woman filled a tin cup with lard, placing in its midst a button tied in a bit of cloth to serve as a wick, and lighted it at the fire, while the cub presided with sniffling curiosity at the unusual proceeding, pressing up close against her as she knelt on the hearth, well knowing that she was not to be held in fear nor in any special respect by young bears.

"I'm goin' ter gin him a button-lamp ter sleep by, bein' ez he hev tuk the baby in his head agin," she said to her father in explanation; "he won't feel so lonesome ef he wakes up."

He had looked keenly after his venerable compeer as the paralytic was borne across the uninclosed passage between the two rooms.

"He's breaking some. He's aging," he said critically; not without sympathy, but with a stalwart conviction that his own feebleness was as strength to the other's weakness. "He's breaking some," he repeated, with a physical vanity that might have graced a prize-fighter.

The next moment there came sharp and shrill through the open door the old man's voice, high and glib in cheerful forgetfulness, conversing with his attendants as they got him to bed.

"Whenst I war young," he cried, "I went down to Sevierville wunst. 'T war when they war a-runnin' of Old Hickory."

"Thar it is again!" exclaimed the ancient Republican. "Old Hickory war bad enough when he war alive; but I b'lieves he's wusser now that he is dead, with this hyar old critter a-moanin' 'bout him night and day. I'd feel myself called ter fling him off'n the bluff, ef it war n't that he hev got the palsy, an' I gits sorry fur him wunst in a while. An' then, I b'lieves that ennybody what is a Dimmycrat air teched in the head, an' ain't 'sponsible fur thar foolishness, 'kase sensible folks ain't Dimmycrats. That's been my 'speriunce fur eighty year, an' I hev hed no call ter change my mind. So I hev to try my patience an' stan' this hyar old critter's foolishness, but it air a mighty tough strain."

V.

The shadows of the great dead trees in the midst of the Settlement were at their minimum in the vertical vividness of the noontide. They bore scant resemblance to those memorials of gigantic growths which towered, stark and white, so high to the intensely blue sky; instead, they were like some dark and leafless underbrush clustering about the sapless trunks. The sandy stretch of the clearing reflected the sunlight with a deeply yellow glare, its poverty of soil illustrated by frequent clumps of the woolly mullein-weeds. The Indian corn and the sparse grass were crudely green in the inclosures about the gray, weather-beaten loghouses, which stood distinct against the dark, restful tones of the forest filling the background. The mountains with each remove wore every changing disguise of distance: shading from sombre green to a dull purple; then overlaid with a dubious blue; next showing a true and turquoise richness; still farther, a delicate transient hue that has no name; and so away to the vantage-ground of illusions, where the ideal poises upon the horizon, and the fact and the fantasy are undistinguishably blended. The intermediate valleys appeared in fragmentary glimpses here and there: sometimes there was only the verdure of the tree-tops; one was cleft by a canary-colored streak which betokened a harvested wheatfield; in another blazed a sapphire circle, where the vertical sun burned in the waters of a blue salt "lick."

The landscape was still, — very still; not the idle floating of a cloud, not the vague shifting of a shadow, not the flutter of a wing. But the Settlement on the crags above had known within its experience no similar commotion. There were many horses hitched to the fences, some girded with blankets in lieu of saddles. Clumsy wagons stood among the stumps in the clearing, with the oxen unyoked and their provender spread before them on the ground. Although the log-cabins gave evidence of hospitable proceedings within, family parties were seated in some of the vehicles, munching the dinner providently brought with them. All the dogs in the Great Smoky, except perhaps a very few incapacitated by extreme age or extreme youth, were humble participants in the outing, having trotted under the wagons many miles from their mountain homes, and now lay with lolling tongues among the wheels.

About the store lounged a number of men, mostly the stolid, impassive mountaineers. A few, however, although in the customary jeans, bore the evidence of more worldly prosperity and a higher culture; and there were two or three resplendent in the " b'iled shirt and store clothes " of civilization, albeit the first was without collar or cravat, and the latter showed antique cut and reverend age. These were candidates, — talkative, full of anecdote, quick to respond, easily flattered, and flattering to the last degree. They were especially jocose and friendly with each other, but amid the fraternal guffaws and exchanges of "chaws o' terbacco" many quips were bandied, barbed with ridicule; many good stories recounted, charged with uncomplimentary deductions; many jokes cracked, discovering the kernel of slander or detraction in the merry shell. The mountaineers looked on, devoid of envy, and despite their stolidity with an understanding of the conversational masquerade. Beneath this motley verbal garb was a grave and eager aspiration for public favor, and it was a matter of no small import when a voter would languidly glance at another with a silent laugh, slowly shake his head with a not-to-be-convinced gesture, and spit profusely on the ground.

In and out of the store dawdled a ceaseless

procession of free and enlightened citizens; always emerging with an aspect of increased satisfaction, wiping their mouths with big bandanna handkerchiefs, and sometimes with the more primitive expedient of a horny hand. Nathan Hoodendin sat in front of the door, keeping store after his usual fashion, except that the melancholy wheeze " Jer'miah " rose more frequently upon the air. Jer'miah's duties consisted chiefly in serving out whiskey and apple-jack, and the little drudge stuck to his work with an earnest pertinacity, for which the privilege of draining the very few drops left in the bottom of the glass after each dram seemed hardly an adequate reward.

The speeches, which were made in the open air, the candidate mounted on a stump in front of the store, were all much alike, — the same self-laudatory meekness, the same inflamed party spirit, the same jocose allusions to opponents, — each ending, " Gentlemen, if I am elected to office I will serve you to the best of my skill and ability. Gentlemen, I thank you for your attention." The crowd, close about, stood listening with great intentness, each wearing the impartial pondering aspect of an umpire.

On the extreme outskirts of the audience, however, there was an unprecedented lapse of attention; a few of the men, seated on stumps or on the wagon-tongues, now and then whispering together, and casting excited glances toward the blacksmith's shop. Sometimes one would rise, approach it stealthily, stoop down, and peer in at the low window. The glare outside made the interior seem doubly dark, and a moment or two was needed to distinguish the anvil, the fireless hearth, the sooty hood. A vague glimmer fell through a crevice in the clapboard roof upon a shock of yellow hair and gleaming eyes, two sullen points of light in the midst of the deep shadows. None of the mountaineers had ever seen a wild beast caged, but Rick Tyler's look of fierce and surly despair, of defiance, of all vain and vengeful impulses, as he sat bound hand and foot in the forge, was hardly more human. The faces multiplied at the window, — stolid, or morbidly curious, awe-struck, or with a grinning display of long tobacco-stained teeth. Many of them were well known to Rick Tyler, and if ever he had liked them he hated them now.

There was a stir outside, a clamor of many voices. The "speaking" was over. Footsteps sounded close to the door of the blacksmith's shop. The sheriff was about to enter, and the crowd pressed eagerly forward to catch a glimpse of the prisoner. Arriving this morning, the sheriff had been glad to combine his electioneering interests with his official duty. The opportunity of canvassing among the assemblage gave him, he thought, an ample excuse for remaining a few hours longer at the Settlement than was necessary; and when he heard of the impending diversion of the gander-pulling he was convinced that his horse required still more rest before starting with his prisoner for Shaftesville jail.

He went briskly into the forge, carrying a pair of clanking handcuffs. He busied himself in exchanging these for the cord with which the young fellow's wrists were bound. It had been drawn brutally tight, and the flesh was swollen and raw. "It seems ter me, ez 't was the blacksmith that nabbed ye, he might hev done better for ye than this, by a darned sight," he said in an undertone.

He had not been reluctant at first that the crowd should come in, but he appreciated unnecessary harshness as an appeal for sympathy, and he called out to his deputy, who had accompanied him on his mission, to clear the room.

"We 're goin' ter keep him shet up fur a hour or so, an' start down the mounting in the cool of the evenin'," he explained; "so ef ye want ter view him the winder is yer chance."

The forge was cleared at last, the broad light vanishing with the closing of the great barn-like doors. Rick heard the lowered voices of the sheriff and deputy gravely consulting without, as they secured the fastenings with a padlock which they had brought with them in view of emergencies. They had taken the precaution, too, to nail strips of board at close intervals across the shutterless window; more, perhaps, to prevent the intrusion of the curious without than the escape of the manacled prisoner. The section of the landscape glimpsed through the bars, — the far blue mountains and a cluster of garnet pokeberries, with a leaf or two of the bush growing close by the wall — sprang into abnormal brilliancy at the end of the dark vista of the interior. It was a duskier brown within for that fragment of vivid color and dazzling clearness in the window. Naught else could be seen, except a diagonal view of the porch of one of the log-cabins and the corn-field beyond.

Curiosity was not yet sated; now and then a face peered in, as Rick sat bound, securely, the cords still about his limbs and feet and the clanking handcuffs on his wrists. These inquisitive apparitions at the window grew fewer as the time went by, and presently ceased altogether. The bustle outside increased: it drowned the drowsy drone of the cicada; it filled the mountain solitudes with a trivial incongruity. Often sounded there the sudden tramp of a horse and a loud guffaw. Rick knew that they were making ready for the gander-pulling, which unique sport had been selected by the long-headed mountain politicians as likely to insure the largest assemblage possible from the surrounding region to hear the candidates prefer their claims.

Electioneering topics were not suspended even while the younger men were saddling and bridling their horses for the proposed festivity. As Micajah Green strolled across the clearing, and joined a group of elderly spectators who in their chairs sat tilted against the walls of the store, which began to afford some shade, he found that his own prospects were under discussion.

" They tell me, 'Cajah," said Nathan Hoodendin, who had hardly budged that day, his conversational activity, however, atoning for his physical inertia, "ez ye air bound ter eend this 'lection with yer finger in yer mouth."

" Don't know why," said Micajah Green, with a sharp, sudden effect as of an angry bark, and lapsing from the smiling mien which he was wont to conserve as a candidate.

" Waal, word hev been brung hyar ter the

Settle*mint* ez this prophet o' ourn in the Big Smoky, he say ye ain't goin' ter be re'lected."

The sheriff laughed scornfully, snapping his fingers as he stood before the group, and whirled airily on his boot-heel.

Nevertheless, he was visibly annoyed. He knew the strength of a fantastic superstition among ignorant people, and their disposition to verify rather than disprove. There were voters in the Big Smoky liable to be controlled by a morbid impulse to make the prophet's word true. It was an unexpected and unmeasured adverse influence, and he chafed under the realization.

" An' what sets Pa'son Kelsey agin me ? " he demanded.

"He ain't in no ways *sot agin you-uns* ez I knows on," discriminated Nathan Hoodendin, studious impartiality expressed among the graven wrinkles of his face. " Not ez it war *sot agin* ye ; but he jes' 'lows ez that air the fac'. Ye ain't goin' ter be 'lected agin."

" The pa'son hev got a gredge agin the old man, hyar," said the deputy. He was a stalwart fellow of about twenty-five years of age. He had sandy hair and mustache, a broad freckled face, light gray eyes, and a thin-lipped, defiant mouth. He bore himself with an air of bravado, which conveyed as many degrees of insult as one felt disposed to take up. "He lit out on me fust, — I war with Amos Jeemes thar, — an' the pa'son put us out'n the meet'n'-house. He did! He don't want no sorter sher'ffs in the Big Smoky. An' he called Gid Fletcher, the blacksmith, 'Judas' fur arrestin' that lot o' bacon yander in the shop, when he kem hyar ter the Settle*mint* fur powder, ter keep him able ter resis' the law! Who sold Rick Tyler that powder, Mister Hoodendin?" he added, turning his eyes on the proprietor of the store.

Old Hoodendin hesitated. "Jer'miah," he wheezed feebly.

His anxious eyes gleamed from out their perplexed wrinkles like a ray of sunlight twinkling through a spiderweb.

There was an interchange of glances between the sheriff and his deputy, and the admonished subordinate continued:

"'T war jes' the boy, eh; an' I reckon he war afeard o' Rick's shootin'-irons an' sech."

"'T war Jer'miah," repeated the storekeeper, his discreet eyes upon the bosom of his bluechecked homespun shirt.

"Waal, the pa'son, ez I war sayin', he called the blacksmith 'Judas' fur capturin' the malefactor, an' the gov'nor's reward 'blood money,'" continued the deputy, expertly electioneering, since his own tenure was on the uncertain continuance of the sheriff in office. " An' now he's goin' 'round the kentry prophesyin' ez 'Cajah Green ain't goin' ter be 'lected. Waal, thar war false prophets 'fore his time, an' will be agin, I 'm thinkin'."

There was a sudden clamor upon the air; a vibrant, childish voice, and then a great horse-laugh. An old crone had come out of one of the cabins and was standing by the fence, holding out to Gid Fletcher, who seemed master of ceremonies, a large white gander. The fowl's physiognomy was thrown into bold prominence by a thorough greasing of the head and neck. His wings flapped, he hissed fiercely, he dolorously squawked. A little girl was running frantically by the side of the old woman, clutching at her skirt, and vociferously claiming the "gaynder." Hers it was, since "Mam gin me the las' aig when the gray goose laid her ladder out, an' it war sot under the old Dominicky hen ez kem off'n her nest through settin' three weeks, like a hen will do. An' then 't war put under old Top-knot, an' 't war the fust aig hatched out'n old Top-knot's settin'."

This unique pedigree, shrieked out with a shrill distinctness, mixed with the lament of the prescient bird, had a ludicrous effect. Fletcher took the gander with a guffaw, the old crone chuckled, and the young men laughed as they mounted their horses.

The blacksmith hardly knew which part he preferred to play. The element of domination in his character gave a peculiar relish to the rôle of umpire; yet with his pride in his deftness and strength it cost him a pang to forego the competition in which he felt himself an assured victor. He armed himself with a whip of many thongs, and took his stand beneath a branch of one of the trees, from which the gander was suspended by his big feet, head downward. Aghast at his disagreeable situation, his wild eyes stared about; his great wings flapped drearily; his long neck protruded with its peculiar motion, unaware of the clutch it invited. What a pity so funny a thing can suffer!

The gaping crowd at the store, on the cabin porches, on the fences, watched the competitors with wide-eyed, wide-mouthed delight. There were gallant figures among them, shown to advantage on young horses whose spirit was not yet quelled by the plough. They filed slowly around the prescribed space once, twice; then each made the circuit alone at a break-neck gallop. As the first horseman rode swiftly along the crest of the precipice, his head high against the blue sky, the stride of the steed covering mountain and valley, he had the miraculous effect of Prince Firouz Shah and the enchanted horse in their mysterious aerial journeys. When he passed beneath the branch whence hung the frantic, fluttering bird, the blacksmith, standing sentinel with his whip of many thongs, laid it upon the flank of the horse, and despite the wild and sudden plunge the rider rose in his stirrups and clutched the greased neck of the swaying gander. Tough old fowl! The strong ligaments resisted. The first hardly hoped to pluck the head, and after his hasty convulsive grasp his frightened horse carried him on almost over the bluff. The slippery neck refused to yield at the second pull, and the screams of the delighted spectators mingled with the shrieks of the gander. The mountain colt, a clay-bank, with a long black tail full of cockle-burrs, bearing the third man, reared violently under the surprise of the lash. As the rider changed the balance of his weight, rising in his stirrups to tug at the gander's neck, the colt pawed the air wildly with his fore feet, fell backward, and rolled upon the ground, almost over the hapless wight. The blacksmith was fain to support himself against the tree for laughter, and the hurrahing Settlement could not remember when it had enjoyed anything so much. The man gathered himself up sheepishly, and limped off; the colt being probably a mile away, running through the woods at the height of his speed.

The gander was in a panic by this time. If ever a fowl of that gender has hysterics, that gander exhibited the disease. He hissed; he flapped his wings; he squawked; he stared; he used every limited power of expression with which nature has gifted him. He was so funny one could hardly look at him.

As Amos James was about to take his turn, amid flattering cries of "Amos 'll pull his head!" "Amos 'll git his head!" a man who had suddenly appeared on horseback at the verge of the clearing, and had paused, contemplating the scene, rode swiftly forward to the tree.

"Ye can't pull out'n· turn, — ye can't pull out'n turn, pa'son!" cried half a dozen voices from the younger men. The elders stared in amaze that the preacher should demean his calling by engaging in this public sport.

Kelsey checked his pace before he reached the blacksmith, who, seeing that he was not going to pull, forbore to lay on the lash. The next moment he thought that Kelsey was going to pull; he had risen in his stirrups, with uplifted arm.

"What be you-uns a-goin' ter do?" demanded Gid Fletcher, amazed.

"I 'm a-goin' ter take this hyar critter down."

His words thrilled through the Settlement like a current of electricity. The next phrase was lost in a wild chorus of exclamations.

"Take the gaynder down?"

"What fur?"

"Hi Kelsey hev los' his mind; surely he hev."

Then above the angry, undistinguishable tumult of remonstrance the preacher's voice rose clear and impressive: "The pains o' the beastis he hev made teches the Lord in heaven; fur he marks the sparrow's fall, an' minds himself o' the pitiful o' yearth!" He spoke with the authority appertaining to his calling. "The spark o' life in this fow-*el* air kindled ez fraish ez yourn, — fur hevin' a soul, ye don't ginerally prove it; an' hevin' no soul ter save, this gaynder hain't yearned the torments o' hell, an' I 'm a-goin' ter take the critter down."

"'T ain't yer gaynder!" conclusively argued the blacksmith, applying the swage of his own conviction.

"He air *my* gaynder!" shrieked out a childish voice. "Take him down, — take him down!"

This objection to the time-honored sport seemed hardly less eccentric than an exhibition of insanity. To apply a dignified axiom of humanity to that fluttering, long-suffering tumult of anguish familiarly known as the " gaynder " was regarded as ludicrously inappropriate. To refer to the Lord and the typical sparrow in this connection seemed almost blasphemy. Nevertheless, with the rural reverence for spiritual authority and the superior moral perception of the clergy, the crowd wore a submissively balked aspect, and even the young men who had not yet had their tug at the fowl's neck succumbed, under the impression that the preacher's fiat had put a stop to the gander-pulling for this occasion.

As Kelsey once more lifted his hand to liberate the creator of the day's merriment, the blacksmith, his old grudge reinforced by a new one, gave the horse a cut with his whip. The animal plunged under the unexpected blow, and carried the rider beyond the tree. Reverence for the cloth had no longer a restraining influence on the young mountaineers. They burst into yells of laughter.

" Cl'ar out, pa'son ! " they exclaimed, delightedly. " Ye hev hed yer pull. Cl'ar out ! "

There was a guffaw among the elders about the store. A clamor of commenting voices rose from the cabin porches, where the feminine spectators stood. The gander squawked dolorously. The hubbub was increased by the sudden sharp yelping of hounds that had started game somewhere near at hand. Afterward, from time to time, canine snarls and yaps rose vociferously upon the air, — unheeded, since the inherent interests of a gander-pulling were so enhanced by the addition of a moral discussion and the jeopardy of its conclusion.

The next man in turn, Amos James, put his horse to a canter, and came in a cloud of yellow dust toward the objective point under the tree. In another moment there was almost a collision, for Kelsey had wheeled and ridden back so swiftly that he reined up under the bough where the fowl hung as Amos James, rising in his stirrups, dashed toward it. His horse shied, and carried him past, out of reach, while the blacksmith stepped precipitately toward the bole, exclaiming angrily, " Don't ride me down, Hi Kelsey ! "

He recovered his presence of mind and the use of his whip immediately, and laid a stinging lash upon the parson's horse, as once more the champion of the bird reached up to release it. The next instant Gid Fletcher recoiled suddenly ; there was a significant gesture, a steely glimmer, and the blacksmith was gazing with petrified reluctance down the muzzle of a six-shooter. He dared not move a muscle as he stood, with that limited field of vision, and with more respectful acquiescence in the opinion of another man than he had ever before been brought to entertain. The horseman looked at his enemy in silence for a moment, the broad-brimmed hat shading his face, with its melancholy expression, its immobile features, and its flashing eyes.

"Drap that lash," Kelsey said.

Gid Fletcher's grasp relaxed ; then the parson with his left hand reached up and contrived to unloose the fluttering gander. He handed the bird down to the little girl, who had been fairly under the horse's heels at the tree since the first suggestions of its deliverance. She clutched it in great haste, wrapped her apron about it, and carrying it, baby-wise, ran fleetly off, casting apprehensive glances over her shoulder.

So the gander was saved, but in its fright, its woe, and the frantic presage in whatever organ may serve it for mind, the fowl had a pretty fair case against the Settlement for exemplary damages.

The sport ended in great disaffection and a surly spirit. Several small grievances among the younger men promised to result in a disturbance of the peace. The blacksmith, held at bay only by the pistol, flared out furiously when relieved of that strong coercion. His pride was roused in that he should be publicly balked and terrorized.

"I'll remember this," he said, shaking his fist in the prophet's face. "I'll save the gredge agin ye."

But he was pulled off by his brethren in the church, who thought it unwise to have a member in good standing again assault the apostle of peace.

Amos James — a tall, black-eyed fellow of twenty three or four, with black hair, slightly powdered with flour, and a brown jeans suit, thus reminiscent also of the mill — sighed for the sport in which he had hoped to be victorious.

"Pa'son talked like the gaynder war his blood relation, — own brothers, I'm a-thinkin'," he drawled, disconsolately.

The sheriff was disposed to investigate prophecy. "I've heard, pa'son," he said, with a smile ill-concealing his vexation, "ye have foreseen I ain't goin' ter be lucky with this here 'lection; goin' ter come out o' the leetle eend o' the horn."

The prophet, too, was perturbed and out of sorts. The sustaining grace of feeling a martyr was lacking in the event of to-day, in which he himself had wielded the coercive hand. He marked the covert aggressiveness of the sheriff's manner, and revolted at being held to account and forced to contest. He fixed his gleaming eyes upon the officer's face, but said nothing.

"I 'm a-hustlin' off now," said Micajah Green, "an' ez I won't be up in the Big Smoky agin afore the 'lection, I 'lowed ez I 'd find out what ails ye ter set sech a durned thing down as a fac'. Why ain't I goin' ter be 'lected?" he reiterated, his temper flaring in his face, his eyes fierce. But for the dragging block and chain of his jeopardized prospects he could not have restrained himself from active insult. With his peculiar qualifications for making enemies, and the opportunities afforded by the difficult office he had filled for the past two years, he illustrated at this moment the justice of the prophecy. But his evident anxiety, his eagerness, even his fierce intolerance, had a touch of the pathetic to the man for whom earth held so little and heaven nothing. It seemed useless to suggest, to admonish, to argue.

"I say the word," declared the prophet. "I can't ondertake ter gin the reason."

"Ye won't gin the reason?" said the sheriff, between his teeth.

"Naw," said the prophet.

"An' I won't be 'lected, hey?"

"Ye won't be 'lected."

The deputy touched the sheriff on the shoulder. "I want ter see ye."

"In a minute," said the elder man, impatiently.

"I want ter see ye."

Something in the tone constrained attention. The sheriff turned, and looked into a changed face. He suffered himself to be led aside.

"Ye *ain't* goin' ter be 'lected," said the deputy, grimly, "an' for a damned good reason. Look-a-thar!"

They had walked to the blacksmith's shop. The deputy motioned to him to look into the window.

"Damn ye, what is it?" demanded Micajah Green, mystified.

The other made no reply, and the officer stooped, and looked into the dusky interior.

VI.

THREE sides of the blacksmith shop, the door, and the window were in full view from the little hamlet; the blank wall of the rear was close to a sheer precipice. The door was locked, and the key was in the sheriff's pocket. The prisoner, bound with cords around his ankles and limbs, and with his wrists manacled, was gone!

Every detail was as it had been left, except that at the rear, the only point secure from observation, there were traces of burrowing in the earth. In the cavity thus made between the lowest log and the "dirt floor" a man's body might with difficulty have been compressed, — but a man so shackled! Undoubtedly he had had assistance. This was a rescue.

Only a moment elapsed before the great barn-like doors were widely flaring and the anxious care of the officers and the eager curiosity of the crowd had explored every nook and cranny within. The ground was dry, and there was not even a footprint to betoken the movements of the fugitive and his rescuers; only in the freshly upturned earth where he effected escape were the distinct marks of the palms of his hands, significantly close together. Evidently he was still handcuffed when he had crawled through.

"He's a-wearin' my bracelets yit!" exclaimed the sheriff, excitedly. "Him an' his friends warn't able ter cut them off, like they done the ropes."

A search was organized in hot haste. Every cabin, the corn-fields, the woods near at hand, were ransacked. Parties went beating about through the dense undergrowth. They climbed the ledges of great crags. They hovered with keen eyes above dark abysses. They pursued for hours a tortuous course down a deep gorge, strewn with gigantic bowlders, washed by the wintry torrents into divers channelings, overhung by cliffs hundreds of feet high, honeycombed with fantastic niches and rifts. What futile quest! What vastness of mountain wilderness!

The great sun went down in a splendid suffusion of crimson color and a translucent golden haze, with a purple garb for the mountains and a glamourous dream for the sky, and bestowing far and near the gilded license of imagination.

The searchers were hard at it until late into the night; never a clew to encourage them, never a hope to lure them on. More than once they flagged, these sluggish mountaineers, who had passed the day in unwonted excitement, and had earned their night's rest. But the penalties of refusing to aid the officer of the law spurred them on. Even old Hoodendin — not so old as to be exempt from this duty, for the sheriff had summoned every available man at the Settlement to his assistance — hobbled from stone to stone, from one rotting log to another, where he sat down to recuperate from his exertions. The search degenerated into a mere form, an aimless beating about in the brush, before Micajah Green could be induced to relinquish the hope of capture, and blow the horn as a signal for reassembling. The bands of fagged-out men, straggling back to the Settlement toward dawn, found reciprocal satisfaction in expressing the opinion that 'Cajah Green had "keerlessly let Rick git away, an' warn't a-goin' ter mend the matter by incitin' the mounting ter bust 'round the woods like a lot o' crazy deer all night, ter find a man ez warn't nowhar."

They wore surly enough faces as they gathered about the door of the store, or lounged on the stumps and the few chairs, waiting for a mounted party that had been ordered to extend the search down in the adjacent coves and along the spurs. The agile Jer'miah scudded about, furnishing such consolation as can be contained in a jug. Had the quest resulted differently, they would have laughed and joked and caroused till daybreak. As it was, their talk was fragmentary; slight and innuendo were in every word. The sheriff had supplemented his own negligence by a grievous disregard of their comfort, and the sense of defeat, so bitter to an American citizen, completed the æsthetic misery of the situation.

The wagons still stood about in the clearing; here and there the burly dark steers lay ruminant and half asleep among the stumps. Among them, too, were the cattle of the place; the cows, milked late the evening before, had not yet roamed away. Against a dark background of blackberry bushes a white bull stood in the moonlight, motionless, the lustre gilding his horns and touching his great sullen eyes with a spark of amber light. In his imperious stillness he looked like a statue of a masquerading Jupiter.

A sound. "Hist!" said the sheriff.

The moon, low in the west, was drawing a seine of fine-spun gold across the dark depths of the valley. In that enchanted enmeshment were tangled all the fancies of the night; the vague magic of dreams; vagrant romances, dumb but for the pulses; the gleams of a poetry, too delicately pellucid to be focused by a pen. The mountains maintained a majesty of silence. All the world beneath was still. The wind was laid. Far, far away, once again, a sound.

So indistinct, so undistinguishable, — they hardly knew if they had heard aright. There was a sudden scuffle near at hand. Over one of the rail fences, gleaming wet with dew, and rich with the loan of a silver beam, there climbed a long, lean old hound; with an anxious aspect he ran to the verge of the crag. Once more that sound, alien alike to the mountain solitudes and the lonely sky; then the deep-mouthed baying broke forth, waking all the echoes, and rousing all the dogs in the cove as well as the canine visitors and residents at the Settlement.

"Dod-rot that critter!" exclaimed the sheriff, angrily. "We can't hear nuthin' now but his long jaw."

"Jes' say 'Silence in court!'" suggested Amos James from where he lay at length in the grass.

The sheriff nimbly kicked the dog instead, and the night was filled with wild shrieks of pain and anger. When his barking was renewed it was punctuated with sharp, reminiscent yelps, as the injustice of his treatment ever and anon recurred to his mind. The sound of human voices grew very distinct when it could be heard at all, and the tramp of approaching horses shook the ground.

Every eye was turned toward the point at which the road came into the Settlement, between the densities of the forest and the gleaming array of shining, curved blades and tossing plumes, where the corn-field spread its martial suggestions. When an equestrian shadow suddenly appeared, the sheriff saluted it in a tremor of excitement.

"Hello!" he shouted. "Did ye ketch him?"

The foremost of the party rode slowly forward: the horse was jaded; the rider slouched in the saddle with an aspect of surly exhaustion.

"Ketch him!" thundered out Gid Fletcher's gruff voice. "Ketch the devil!"

The bold-faced deputy was brazening it out. He rode up with as dapper a style as a man may well maintain who has been in the saddle ten hours without food, sustained only by the strength of a "tickler" in his pocket, whose prospects are jeopardized and whose official prestige is ruined. The demeanor of the other riders expressed varying degrees of injured disaffection as they threw themselves from their horses.

The blacksmith dismounted in front of the cumbersome doors of his shop, on which still hung the sheriff's padlock, and with tne stiff gait of one who has ridden long and hard he strode across the clearing, and stopped before the group in front of the store.

He looked infuriated. It might have been a matter of wonder that so tired a man could nourish so strong and active a passion.

" Look-a-hyar, 'Cajah Green!" he exclaimed, with an oath, " folks 'low ter me ez I ain't got no right ter my reward fur ketchin' that thar greased peeg, — ez ye hed ter leave go of, — kase he warn't landed in jail or bailed. That air the law, they tells me."

" That's the law," replied the sheriff. His chair was tilted back against the wall of the store, his hat drawn over his brow. He spoke with the calmness of desperation.

" Then 'pears-like ter me ez I hev hed all my trouble fur nuthin', an' all the resk I hev tuk," said the blacksmith, coming close, and mechanically rolling up the sleeve of his hammer-arm.

" Edzac'ly."

The blacksmith turned on him a look like that of a wounded bear. " An' ye sit thar ez peaceful ez skim-milk, an' 'low ez ye hev let my two hunderd dollars slip away?" he demanded. " Dadburn yer greasy soul!"

" I hopes it air all I hev let slip," said the sheriff, quietly. There was so much besides which he had cause to fear that it did not occur to him to be afraid of the blacksmith.

Perhaps it was the subacute perception that he shared the officer's attention with more engrossing subjects which had the effect of tempering Gid Fletcher's anger.

The rim of the moon was slipping behind the purple heights of Chilhowee. Day was suddenly upon them, though the sun had not yet risen, — when did the darkness flee ? — the day, cool, with a freshness as of a new creation, and with an atmosphere so clear that one might know the ash from the oak in the deep green depths of the wooded valley. The hour had not yet done with witchery : the rose-red cloud was in the east, and the wild red rose had burst its bud; a mocking-bird sprang from its nest in a dogwood-tree, with a scintillating wing and a soaring song, and a ray of sunlight like a magic wand fell athwart the landscape.

Gid Fletcher sat vaguely staring. Presently he lifted his hand with a sudden gesture demanding attention.

" Ye ain't goin' ter be 'lected, air ye, 'Cajah Green ? "

The sheriff stirred uneasily. His ambition, a little and a selfish thing, was the index to his soul. Without it he himself would not be able to find the page whereon was writ all that there was of the spiritual within him. He writhed to forego it.

"Naw," he said, desperately, " I s'pose I ain't." He pushed his hat back nervously.

He heard, without marking, the sudden rattling of one of the wagons that had left some time ago: it was crossing a rickety bridge near the foot of the mountain; the hollow reverberations rose and fell, echoed and died away. One of the cabin doors opened, and a man came out upon the porch. He washed his face in a tin pan which stood on a bench for the public toilet, treated his head to a refreshing souse, and then, with the water dripping from his long locks upon the shoulders of his shirt, the bold-faced deputy, much refreshed by a snack and his ablutions, came lounging across the clearing to join them.

Suddenly Micajah Green noted that the blacksmith was looking at him, with a significant gleam in his black eyes and a flush on his swarthy face.

"Who said ye warn't goin' ter be 'lected?"

"Why, this hyar prophet o' yourn on the Big Smoky."

"Why did he 'low ez that warn't comin' ter pass?"

"He wouldn't gin no reason."

"He lef' ye ter find that out. An' ye fund it out?"

The sheriff said nothing. He was breathlessly intent.

"An' he met me in the woods, an' 'lowed ez Rick Tyler ought n't ter be tuk, an' hed done no wrong; an' he called the gov'nor's reward blood money, an' worked hisself nigh up ter the shoutin' p'int; an' called me 'Judas' fur takin' the boy, sence me an' him hed been frien'ly, an' 'lowed ez them thar thirty pieces o' silver warn't out o' circulation yit."

"An' then," the bold-faced deputy struck in, "he rode up yestiddy, a-raisin' a great wonderment over a gaynder-pullin', ez if thar 'd never been one before; purtendin' 't war wicked, like he 'd never killed an' eat a fowel, an' drawin' pistols, an' raisin' a great commotion an' excitin' an' *destractin'* the Settlemint, so a man handcuffed, an' with a rope twisted round his arms an' legs, gits out of a house right under thar nose, an' runs away. Rick Tyler could n't hev done it 'thout them ropes war cut, an' he war gin a chance ter sneak out. Now, I ain't a prophet by natur, but I kin say who cut them ropes, an' who raised a disturbament outside ter gin him a chance ter mosey."

"Whar's he now?" demanded the sheriff, rising from his chair and glancing about.

"He was a-huntin' with the posse, las' night," said the deputy. "He never lef' till 'bout an hour ago. He never wanted nobody ter 'spicion nuthin', I reckon. Mebbe that's him now."

He pointed to a road in the valley, a tawny streak elusively appearing upon a hilltop or skirting a rocky spur, soon lost in a sea of foliage. Beside a harvested wheat-field it was again visible, and a tiny moving object might be discerned by eyes trained to the long stretches of mountain landscape. The sun was higher, the dew exhaled in warm and languishing perfume, the mocking-bird filled the air with ecstasy. The men stood among their elongated shadows on the crag staring at the moving object until it reached the dense woods, and so passed out of sight.

VII.

DOWN a precipitous path, hardly more civilized of aspect than if it were trodden by the deer, filled with interlacing roots, barricaded by long briery tangles, overhung by brush and overshadowed by trees, — down this sylvan way Dorinda, followed by Jacob and one or two of the companionable old hounds, was wont to go to the spring under the crag.

The spot had its fascinations. The great beetling cliff towered far above, the jagged line of its summit serrating the zenith. Its rugged face was seamed with many a fissure, and here and there were clumps of ferns, a swaying vine, a huckleberry bush that fed the birds of the air. Below surged the tops of the trees. There was a shelving descent from the base of the crag, and Jacob must needs have heed of the rocky depths beneath in treading the narrow ledge that led to a great cavernous niche in the face of the rock. Here in a deep cleft welled the never-failing spring. It always reminded Dorinda of that rock which Moses smote; although, of course, when she thought of it, she said, she knew that Mount Horeb was in Jefferson

County, because a man who had married her brother's wife's cousin had an aunt who lived there. And when she had abandoned that unconscious effort to bring the great things near, she would sit upon the rock and look with a sigh of pleasure at that pure, outgushing limpidity, unfailing and unchanging, and say it reminded her of the well-springs of pity.

One day, as she sat there, her dreaming head thrown back upon her hands clasped behind it, there sounded a sudden step close by. The old hounds, lying without the cavernous recess, could see along the upward vista of the path, and their low growl was rather in surly recognition than in active defiance. Dorinda and Jacob, within the great niche, beheld naught but the distant mountain landscape framed in the rugged arch above their heads. The step did not at once advance; it hesitated, and then Amos James came slowly into view. Dorinda looked up dubiously at him, and it occurred to him that this was the accepted moment to examine the lock of his gun.

" Howdy," he ventured, as he turned the rifle about.

She had assumed a more constrained attitude, and had unclasped her hands from behind her head. The seat was a low one, and the dark blue folds of her homespun dress fell about her with simple amplitude. Her pink calico sunbonnet lay on the rock under her elbow. The figure of the pudgy Jacob in the foreground had a callow grotesqueness. He, too, undertook the demeanor he had learned to discriminate as "manners." Outside, the old dog snapped at the flies.

Amos James seemed to think an account of himself appropriate.

"I hev been a-huntin'," he said, his grave black eyes on the rifle and his face in the shadow of his big white hat. "I happened ter pass by the house, an' yer granny said ez ye hed started down hyar arter a pail o' water, an' I 'lowed ez I 'd kem an' fetch it fur ye."

Dorinda murmured that she was "much obleeged," and relapsed into silent propriety.

Extraordinary gun! It really seemed as if Amos James would be compelled to take it to pieces then and there, so persistently did it require his attention.

Jacob, whose hearing was unimpaired, but whose education in the specious ways of those of a larger growth was as yet incomplete, got up briskly. Since Amos had come to fetch the pail he saw no reason in nature why the pail should not be fetched, and he imagined that the return was in order. He paused for a moment in surprise; then seeing that no one else moved, he sat down abruptly. But for her manners Dorinda could have laughed. Amos James's cheek flushed darkly as he still worked at the gun.

"I s'pose ez you-uns hev hearn the news?" he remarked, presently. As he asked the question he quickly lifted his eyes.

Ah, what laughing lights in hers, — what radiant joys! She did not look at him. Her gaze was turned far away to the soft horizon. Her delicate lips had such dainty curves. Her pale cheek flushed tumultuously. She leaned her head back against the rock, the tendrils of her dark hair spreading over the unyielding gray stone, which, weather-shielded, was almost white. In its dead, dumb finality — the memorial of seas ebbed long ago, of forms of life extinct — she bore it a buoyant contrast. She looked immortal!

"I hev hearn the news," she said, her long lashes falling, and with quiet circumspection, at variance with the triumph in her face.

He looked at her gravely, breathlessly. A new idea had taken possession of him. The rescue, — it was a strange thing! Who in the Great Smoky Mountains had an adequate temptation to risk the penalty of ten years in the state-prison for rescuing Rick Tyler from the officers of the law? His brothers? —

they were step-brothers. His father was dead.
Affection could not be accounted a factor.
Venom might do more. Some reckless enemy
of the sheriff's might thus have craftily compassed his ruin. Then there suddenly came
upon Amos James a recollection of the Cayces'
grudge against Micajah Green, and of the fact
that they had already actively bestirred themselves to electioneer against him. Once, before
it all happened, Rick Tyler had hung persistently about Dorinda, and perhaps the "men-
folks" approved him. Amos remembered too
that a story was current at the gander-pulling
that the reason the Cayces had absented themselves and were lying low was because a party
of revenue raiders had been heard of on the
Big Smoky. Who had heard of them, and
when did they come, and where did they go?
It seemed a fabrication, a cloak. And Dorinda, — she was the impersonation of delighted
triumph.

"Agged the men-folks on, I reckon," he
thought, — "agged 'em on, fur the sake o'
Rick Tyler!"

A sense of despair, quiet, numbing, was
creeping over him.

"'T ain't no reg'lar ail, I know," he said to
himself, "but I b'lieve it'll kill me."

Conversation in the mountains is a leisurely

procedure, time being of little value. The ensuing pause, however, was of abnormal duration, and at last Amos was fain to break it, albeit irrelevantly.

"This hyar weather is gittin' mighty hot," he observed, taking off his hat and fanning himself with it. "I feel like I hed been dragged bodaciously through the hopper."

From the shaded coolness of the grotto the girl admitted that it was "middlin' warm."

Despite the slumberous sunshine here, all the world was not so quiet. Over the valley a cloud was hovering, densely black, but with a gray nebulous margin; now and then it was rent by a flash of lightning in swift zigzag lines, yet the mountains beyond were a tender blue in the golden glow of a sunshine yet more tender.

"'Pears like they air gittin' a shower over yander, at the furder eend o' the cove," Dorinda remarked, encouragingly. "Ef it war ter storm right smart, mebbe the thunder would cool the air some."

"Mebbe so," he assented.

Then he marked again the new beauty abloom in her face, and his heart sank within him. His pride was touched, too. He was a man well to do for the "mountings," with his own grist-mill, and a widowed mother whose plaint it was, night and day, that Amos was "sech a slowly boy ter git married, an' the Lord knows thar oughter be somebody roun' the house spry'r 'n a pore old woman mighty nigh fifty year old, — yes, sir ! a-goin' on fifty. An' I want ter live down ter Emmert's Cove along o' Malviny, my married darter," she would insist, " whar thar air chillen, an' babies ter look arter, an' not sech a everlastin' gang o' men, a-lopin' 'round the mill. But I dunno *what* Amos would do ef I lef' him."

Evidently it was a field for a daughter-in-law. Amos felt in his secret soul that this was not the only attraction. He was well favored and tall and straight, and had a good name in the county, despite his pranks, which were leniently regarded. He honestly thought that Dorinda might do worse. - Whether it was tact or whether it was delicacy, he did not allude to the worldly contrast with the fugitive from justice.

"I s'pose they won't ketch Rick agin," he hazarded.

" I reckon not," she said, demurely, her long black lashes again falling.

He leaned uneasily on his gun, looked down at his great boots drawn over his brown jeans trousers to his knees, adjusted his leathern belt, and pulled his hat a trifle farther over his eyes.

"D'rindy," he said, suddenly, "ye set a heap o' store on Rick Tyler."

Then he was doubtful, and feared he had offended her.

Her sapphire eyes, with their leaping blue lights and dark clear depths, all blended and commingled in the softest brilliancy, shone upon him. The bliss of the event was supreme.

"Mebbe I do," she said.

He turned and looked away at the storm, seeming ineffective as it surged in the distance. The trees in the cove were tossed by a wind that raged on a lower level, as if it issued from Æolian caverns in the depths of the range. It was a wild, aerial panorama, — the black clouds, and the rain, and the mist rolling through the deep gorge, veined with lightnings and vocal with thunder, and the thunderous echoes among the rocks.

Not a leaf stirred on the mountain's brow, and the great "bald" lifted its majestic crest in a sunshine all unpaled, and against the upper regions of the air, splendidly blue. There was an analogy in the scene with his mood and hers.

A moment ago he had been saying to himself that he did not want to be "turned off" in favor of a man who was hunted like a wild animal through the woods; who, if his luck and his friends should hold out, and he could evade capture, might look forward to naught but uncertainty and a fearful life, like others in the Big Smoky, who dared not open their own doors to a summons from without, skulking in their homes like beasts in their den.

The dangers, misfortunes, and indignities suffered by his preferred rival were an added slur upon him, who had all the backing of propitious circumstance. Since there was nothing to gain, why humble himself in vain?

This was his logic, — sound, just, approved by his judgment; and as it arranged itself in his mind with all the lucidity of pure reason, he spoke from the complex foolish dictates of his unreasoning heart.

"I hev hoped ter marry ye, D'rindy, like I hev hoped fur salvation," he said, abruptly.

He looked at her now, straight and earnestly, with his shaded, serious black eyes. Her rebuking glance slanted beyond him from under her half-lifted lashes.

"I thought ye war a good church member," she said, unexpectedly.

"I am. But that don't make me a liar ez I knows on. I'd ruther hear ye a-singin' 'roun' the house in Eskaqua Cove, an' a-callin' the chickens, an' sech, 'n ter hear all the angels in heaven a-quirin' tergether."

"That ain't religion, Amos Jeemes," she said, with cool disapproval.

"Waal," he rejoined, with low-spirited obstinacy, "mebbe 't ain't."

There was a delicate odor of ferns on the air; the cool, outgushing water tinkled on the stones like a chime of silver bells; his shadow fell athwart the portal as he leaned on his rifle, and his wandering glance mechanically swept the landscape. The sudden storm had passed, the verge of the cloud hovering so near that they could hear the last heavy raindrops pattering on the tops of the trees in Eskaqua Cove. Vapors were rising from the ravine; the sun shone upon them, throwing a golden aureola about the opposite mountains, and all the wreathing mists that the wind whirled down the valley had elusive, opalescent effects. The thunder muttered in the distance; the sharp-bladed lightnings were sheathed; a rainbow girdled the world, that had sprung into a magic beauty as if cinctured by the zone of Venus. The arch spanned the blue sky, and on the dark mountains extended the polychromatic reflection. The freshened wind came rushing up the gorge, and the tree-tops bent.

"Look-a-hyar, D'rindy," said Amos James, sturdily, "I want ye ter promise me one thing."

Dorinda had risen in embarrassment. She looked down at Jacob.

"It air about time fur we-uns ter be a-goin' ter the house, I reckon," she said.

But Jacob sat still. He was apt in "takin' l'arnin'," and he had begun to perceive that his elders did not always mean what they said. He was cool and comfortable, and content to remain.

"I want ye ter promise me that ef ever ye find ez ye hev thunk too well o' Rick Tyler, an' hev sot him up too high in yer mind over other folks, ye'll let me know."

Her cheek dimpled; her rare laughter fell on the air; a fervid faith glowed in her deep, bright eyes.

"I promise ye!"

"Ye think Rick Tyler air mighty safe in that promise," he rejoined, crestfallen.

But Dorinda would say no more.

VIII.

THE disappointment which Amos James experienced found expression in much the same manner as that of many men of higher culture. He went down to his home in Eskaqua Cove, moody and morose. He replied to his chirping mother in discouraging monosyllables. In taciturn disaffection he sat on the step of the little porch, and watched absently a spider weaving her glittering gossamer maze about an overhanging mass of purple grapes, with great green leaves that were already edged with a rusty red and mottled with brown. A mockingbird boldly perched among them, ever and anon, the airy grace of his pose hardly giving, in its exquisite lightness, the effect of a pause. The bird swallowed the grapes whole with a mighty gulp, and presently flew away with one in his bill for the refreshment of his family, whose vibratory clamor in an althea bush hard by mingled with the drone of the grasshoppers in the wet grass, louder than ever since the rain, and the persistent strophe and antistrophe of the frogs down on the bank of the mill-pond.

" Did they git enny shower up in the mounting, Amos?" demanded his mother, as she sat knitting on the porch, — a thin little woman, with a nervous, uncertain eye and a drawling, high-pitched voice.

"Naw 'm," said Amos, "not ez I knows on."

"I reckon ye 'd hev knowed ef ye hed got wet," she said, with asperity. "Ye hain't got much feelin', no ways, — yer manners shows it, — but I 'low ye *would* feel the rain ef it kem down right smart, or ef ye war streck by lightnin'."

There was no retort, and from the subtle disappointment in the little woman's eye it might have seemed that to inaugurate a controversy would have been more filial, so bereft of conversational opportunity was her lonely life, where only a "gang o' men loped 'round the mill."

She knitted on with a sharp clicking of the needles for a time, carrying the thread on a gnarled fourth finger, which seemed unnaturally active for that member, and somehow officious.

"I 'll be bound ye went ter Cayce's house," she said, aggressively.

There was another long pause. The empty dwelling behind them was so still that one could hear the footsteps of an intruding rooster, as he furtively entered at the back door.

"Shoo!" she said, shaking her needles at

him, as she bent forward and saw him standing in the slant of the sunshine, all his red and yellow feathers burnished. He had one foot poised motionless, and looked at her with a reproving side-glance, as if he could not believe he had caught the drift of her remarks. Another gesture, more pronounced than the first, and he went scuttling out, his wings half spread and his toe-nails clattering on the puncheon floor. " Ye went ter Cayce's, I'll be bound, and hyar ye be, with nuthin' ter tell. Ef I war free ter jounce 'round the mounting same ez the idle, shif'less men-folks, who hev got nuthin' ter do but eye a mill ez the water works, I'd hev so much ter tell whenst I got home that ye'd hev ter tie me in a cheer ter keep me from talkin' myself away, like somebody happy with religion. An' hyar ye be, actin' like ye hed no mo' gift o' speech 'n the rooster. Shoo! Shoo! Whar did ye go, ennyhow, when ye war on the mounting?"

" A-huntin'," said Amos.

" Huntin' D'rindy Cayce, I reckon. An' ye never got her, ter jedge from yer looks. An' I ain't got the heart ter blame the gal. Sech a lonesome, say-nuthin' husband ye'd make!"

The sharp click of her knitting-needles filled the pause. But her countenance had relaxed. She was in a measure enjoying the conversation, since the spice of her own share atoned for the lack of news or satisfactory response.

"Air old Mis' Cayce's gyarden-truck suff'rin' fur rain?"

There was a gleam of hopeful expectation behind her spectacles. With her reeking "gyarden-spot" dripping with raindrops, and the smell of thyme and sage and the damp mould on the air, she could afford some pity as an added flavor for her pride.

"Never looked ter see," murmured her son, between two long whiffs from his pipe.

His mother laid her knitting on her lap. "I'll be bound, Amos Jeemes, ez ye never tole her how 'special our'n war a-thrivin' this season."

"Naw'm," said Amos, a trifle more promptly than usual, "I never. 'Fore I'd go a-crowin' over old Mis' Cayce 'bout'n our gyarden-truck I'd see it withered in a night, like Jonah's gourd."

"It's the Lord's han'," said his mother quickly, in self-justification. "I ain't been prayin' fur no drought in Mis' Cayce's gyarden-spot."

Another long pause ensued. The sun shining through a bunch of grapes made them seem pellucid globes of gold and amber and crimson among others darkly purple in the shadow. The mocking-bird came once more a-foraging. A yellow and red butterfly flickered around in the air, as if one of the tiger-lilies there by the porch had taken wings and was wantoning about in the wind. On the towering bald of the mountain a cloud rested, obscuring the dome, — a cloud of dazzling whiteness, — and it seemed as if the mountain had been admitted to some close communion with the heavens. Below, the color was intense, so deeply green were the trees, so clear and sharp a gray were the crags, so blue were the shadows in the ravines. Amos was looking upward. He looked upward much of the time.

"See old Groundhog?" inquired his mother, suddenly.

"Whar?" he demanded with a start, breaking from his reverie.

"Laws-a-massy, boy!" she exclaimed, in exasperation. "Whenst ye war up ter the Cayces', this mornin'."

"Naw 'm," said Amos. He had never admitted, save by indirection, that he had been to the Cayces'.

"War he gone ter the still?"

"I never axed."

"I s'pose not, bein' ez ye never drinks nuthin' but buttermilk, do ye?" — this with a scathing inflection.

She presently sighed deeply. "Waal, waal. The millinium an' the revenue will git thar rights one of these days, I hopes an' prays. I'm a favorin' of ennythink ez 'll storp sin an' a-swillin' o' liquor. Tax 'em all, I say! Tax the sinners!"

She had assumed a pious aspect, and spoke in a tone of drawling solemnity, with a vague idea that the whiskey tax was in the interest of temperance, and the revenue department was a religious institution. The delusions of ignorance!

"Thar ain't ez much drunk nohow now ez thar useter war. I 'members when I war a gal whiskey war so cheap that up to the store at the Settlemint they'd hev a bucket set full o' whiskey an' a gourd, free fur all comers, an' another bucket alongside with water ter season it. An' the way that thar water lasted war surprisin', — that it war! Nowadays ye ain't goin' ter find liquor so plenty nowhar, 'cept mebbe at old Groundhog's still."

Amos made no reply. His eyes were fixed on the road. A man on an old white horse had emerged from the woods, and was slowly ambling toward the mill. The crazy old structure was like a caricature; it seemed that only by a lapse of all the rules of interdependent timbers did it hang together, with such oblique disregard of rectangles. Its doors and windows were rhomboidal; its supports tottered in the water. The gate was shut. The whir was hushed. A sleep lay upon the pond, save where the water fell like a silver veil over the dam. Even this motion was dreamy and somnambulistic. On the other side of the stream the great sandstone walls of the channel showed the water-marks of flood and fall of past years, cut in sharp levels and registered in the rock. They beetled here and there, and the verdure on the summits looked over and gave the deep waters below the grace of a dense and shady reflection. Above the dark old roof on every hand the majestic encompassing mountains rose against the sky, and the cove nestled sequestered from the world in this environment.

The man on the gaunt white horse suddenly paused, seeing the mill silent and lonely; his eyes turned to the little house farther down the stream.

"Hello!" he yelled. "I kem hyar ter git some gris' groun'."

"Grin' yer gris' yerse'f," vociferated the miller, cavalierly renouncing his vocation. "I hev no mind ter go a-medjurin o' toll."

Thus privileged, the stranger dismounted, went into the old mill, himself lifted the gate, and presently the musical whir broke forth. It summoned an echo from the mountain that was hardly like a reflection of its simple, industrial sound, so elfin, so romantically faint, so fitful and far, it seemed! The pond awoke, the water gurgled about the wheel, the tail-race was billowy with foam.

Presently there was silence. The gate had fallen; the farmer had measured the toll, and was riding away. As he vanished Amos James rose slowly, and began to stretch his stalwart limbs.

"I'm glad ye ain't palsied with settin' so long, Amos," said his mother. "Ye seem ter hev los' interes' in everythink 'ceptin' the doorstep. Lord A'mighty! I never thunk ez ye'd grow up ter be sech pore comp'ny. No wonder ez D'rindy hardens her heart! An' when ye war a baby, — my sakes! I could set an' list'n ter yer jowin' all day. An sech comp'ny ye war, when ye could n't say a word an' hed n't a tooth in yer head!"

He lived in continual rivalry with this younger self in his mother's affections. She was one of those women whose maternal love is expressed in an idolatry of infancy. She could not forgive him for outgrowing his babyhood, and regarded every added year upon his head as a sort of affront and a sorrow.

He strode away, still gloomily downcast, and

when the woman next looked up she saw him mounted on his bay horse, and riding toward the base of the mountain.

"Waal, sir!" she exclaimed, taking off her spectacles and rubbing the glasses on her blue-checked apron, "D'rindy Cayce'll hev ter marry that thar boy ter git shet o' him. I hev never hearn o' nobody ridin' up that thar mounting twict in one day 'thout they hed suthin' 'special ter boost 'em, — a-runnin' from the sher'ff, or sech."

But Amos James soon turned from the road, that wound in long, serpentine undulations to the mountain's brow, and pursued a narrow bridle-path, leading deep into the dense forests. It might have seemed that he was losing his way altogether when the path disappeared among the bowlders of a stream, half dry. He followed the channel up the rugged, rock-girt gorge for perhaps a mile, emerging at length upon a slope of outcropping ledges, where his horse left no hoof-print. Soon he struck into the laurel, and pressed on, guided by signs distinguishable only to the initiated: some grotesque gnarling of limbs, perhaps, of the great trees that stretched above the almost impenetrable undergrowth; some projecting crag, visible at long intervals, high up and cut sharply against the sky. All at once, in the midst of the dense laurel, he came upon a cavity in the side of the mountain. The irregularly shaped fissure was more than tall enough to admit a man. He stood still for a moment, and called his own name. There was no response save the echoes, and, dismounting, he took the bridle and began to lead the horse into the cave. The animal shied dubiously, protesting against this unique translation to vague subterranean spheres. The shadow of the fissured portal fell upon them; the light began to grow dim; the dust thickened. As Amos glanced over his shoulder he could see the woods without suffused with a golden radiance, and there was a freshness on the intensely green foliage as if it were newly washed with rain. The world seemed suddenly clarified, and tiny objects stood out with strange distinctness; he saw the twigs on the great trees and the white tips of the tail-feathers of a fluttering bluejay. Far down the aisles of the forest the enchantment held its wonderful sway, and he felt in his own ignorant fashion how beautiful is the accustomed light. When the horse's stumbling feet had ceased to sound among the stones, the wilderness without was as lonely and as unsuggestive of human occupation or human existence as when the Great Smoky Mountains first rose from the sea.

IX.

Amos and his steed made their way along a narrow passage, growing wider, however, and taller, but darker and with many short turns, — an embarrassment to the resisting brute's physical conformation.

Suddenly there was a vague red haze in the dark, the sound of voices, and an abrupt turn brought man and horse into a great subterranean vault, where dusky distorted figures, wreathing smoke, and a flare of red fire suggested Tartarus.

" Hy're, Amos! " cried a hospitable voice.

A' weird tone repeated the words with precipitate promptness. Again and again the abrupt echoes spoke; far down the unseen blackness of the cave a hollow whisper announced his entrance, and he seemed mysteriously welcomed by the unseen powers of the earth. He was not an imaginative man nor observant, but the upper regions were his sphere, and he had all the acute sensitiveness incident to being out of one's element. Even after he had seated himself he noted a far, faint voice crying, " Hy're, Amos! " in abysmal depths explored only by the sound of his name.

And here it was that old Groundhog Cayce evaded the law, and ran his still, and defied the revenue department, and maintained his right to do as he would with his own.

"Lord A'mighty, air the corn mine, or no?" he would argue. "Air the orchard mine or the raiders'? An' what ails me ez I can't make whiskey an' apple-jack same ez in my dad's time, when him an' me run a sour mash still on the top o' the mounting in the light o' day, up'ards o' twenty year, an' never hearn o' no raider? Tell me that 's agin the law, nowadays! Waal, now, who made that law? I never; an' I ain't a-goin' ter abide by it, nuther. Ez sure ez ye air born, it air jes' a Yankee trick fotched down hyar by the Fed'ral army. An' ef I hed knowed they war goin' ter gin tharse'fs ter sech persecutions arter the war, I dunno how I 'd hev got my consent ter fit alongside of 'em like I done fower year fur the Union."

A rude furnace made of fire-rock was the prominent feature of the place, and on it glimmered the pleasing rotundities of a small copper still. The neck curved away into the obscurity. There was the sound of gurgling water, with vague babbling echoes; for the never-failing rill of an underground spring, which rose among the rocks, was diverted to the unexpected purpose of flowing through the tub where the worm was coiled, and of condensing the precious vapors, which dripped monotonously into their rude receiver at the extremity of the primitive fixtures. The iron door of the furnace was open now as Ab Cayce replenished the fire. It sent out a red glare, revealing the dark walls; the black distances; the wreaths of smoke, that were given a start by a short chimney, and left to wander away and dissipate themselves in the wide subterranean spaces; and the uncouth, slouching figures and illuminated faces of the distillers. They lounged upon the rocks or sat on inverted baskets and tubs, and one stalwart fellow lay at length upon the ground. The shadows were all grotesquely elongated, almost divested of the semblance of humanity, as they stretched in unnatural proportions upon the rocks. Amos James's horse cast on the wall an image so gigantic that it seemed as if the past and the present were mysteriously united, and he stood stabled beside the grim mastodon whom the cave had sheltered from the rigors of his day long before Groundhog Cayce was moved to seek a refuge. The furnace door clashed; the scene faded; only a glittering line of vivid white light, emitted between the ill-fitting door and the unhewn rock, enlivened the gloom. Now and then, as one of the distillers moved, it fell upon him, and gave his face an abnormal distinctness in the surrounding blackness, like some curiously cut onyx.

"Waal, Amos," said a voice from out the darkness, "I'm middlin' glad ter see you-uns. Hev a drink."

A hand came out into the gleaming line of light, extending with a flourish of invitation a jug of jovial aspect.

"Don't keer ef I do," said Amos, politely. He lifted the jug, and drank without stint. The hand received it back again, shook it as if to judge of the quantity of its contents, and then, with a gesture of relish, raised it to an unseen mouth.

"Enny news 'round the mill, Amos?" demanded his invisible pot companion.

"None ez I knows on," drawled Amos.

"Grind some fur we-uns ter-morrer?" asked Ab.

"I'll grind yer bones, ef ye'll send 'em down," said Amos, accommodatingly. "All's grist ez goes ter the hopper. How kem you-uns ter git the nightmare 'bout'n the raiders? I waited fur Sol an' the corn right sharp time Wednesday mornin'; jes' hed nuthin' ter do but ter sot an' suck my paws, like a b'ar in winter, till 't war time ter put out an' go ter the gaynder-pullin'."

"Waal" — there was embarrassment in the

tones of the burly shadow, and all the echoes were hesitant as Groundhog Cayce replied in Ab's stead: " Mirandy Jane 'lowed ez she hed seen a strange man 'bout'n the spring, an' thought it war a raider, — though he'd hev been in a mighty ticklish place fur a raider, all by himself. Mirandy Jane hev fairly got the jim-jams, seein' raiders stiddier snakes; we-uns can't put no dependence in the gal. An' mam, she drempt the raiders hed camped on Chilhowee Mounting. An' D'rindy, she turned fool: fust she 'lowed ez we-uns would all be ruined ef we went ter the gaynder-pullin', an' then she war powerful interrupted when we 'lowed we would n't go, like ez ef she wanted us ter go most awful. I axed this hyar Pa'son Kelsey, ez rid by that mornin', ef he treed enny raiders in his mind. An' he 'lowed, none, 'ceptin' the devil a-raidin' 'roun' his own soul. But 'mongst 'em we-uns jest bided away that day. I would n't hev done it, 'ceptin' D'rindy tuk ter talkin' six ways fur Sunday, an' she got me plumb catawampus, so ez I did n't rightly know what I wanted ter do myself."

It was a lame story for old Groundhog Cayce to tell. Even the hesitating echoes seemed ashamed of it. Mirandy Jane's mythical raider, and mam's dream, and D'rindy's folly, — were these to baffle that stout-hearted old soldier?

Amos James said no more. If old Cayce employed an awkward subterfuge to conceal the enterprise of the rescue, he had no occasion to intermeddle. Somehow, the strengthening of his suspicions brought Amos to a new realization of his despair. He sought to modify it by frequent reference to the jug, which came his way at hospitably short intervals. But he had a strong head, and had seen the jug often before; and although he thought his grief would be alleviated by getting as drunk as a "fraish b'iled o*wel*," that consummation of consolation was coy and tardy. He was only mournfully frisky after a while, feeling that he should presently be obliged to cut his throat, yet laughing at his own jokes when the moonshiners laughed, then pausing in sudden seriousness to listen to the elfin merriment evoked among the lurking echoes. And he sang, too, after a time, a merry catch, in a rich and resonant voice, with long, dawdling, untutored cadences and distortions of effect, — sudden changes of register, many an abrupt crescendo and diminuendo, and "spoken" interpolations and improvisations, all of humorous intent.

The others listened with the universal greedy appetite for entertainment which might have been supposed to have dwindled and died of inanition in their serious and deprived lives.

Pete Cayce first revolted from the strain on his attention, subordination, and acquiescence. It was not his habit to allow any man to so completely absorb public attention.

"Look-a-hyar, Amos, fur Gawd's sake, shet up that thar foolishness!" he stuttered at last. "Thar's n-no tellin' how f-f-fur yer survigrus bellerin' kin be hearn. An' besides, ye'll b-b-bring the rocks down on to we-uns d-d'rectly. They tell me that it air dangerous ter f-f-f-fire pistols an' jounce 'round in a cave. Bring the roof down."

"That air jes' what I'm a-aimin' ter do, Pete," said Amos, with his comical gravity. "I went ter meetin' week 'fore las', an' the pa'son read 'bout Samson; an' it streck my ambition, an' I'm jes' a-honin' ter pull the roof down on the Philistine."

"Look-a-hyar, Amos Jeemes, ye air the b-b-banged-est critter on this hyar m-mounting! Jes' kem hyar ter our s-still an' c-c-call me a Ph-Ph-Philistine!"

The jug had not been stationary, and as Pete thrust his aggressive face forward the vivid quivering line of light from the furnace showed that it was flushed with liquor and that his eyes were bloodshot. His gaunt head, with long, colorless hair, protruding teeth, and homely, prominent features, as it hung there in the isolating effect of that sharp and slender gleam,— the rest of his body canceled by the darkness, — had a singularly unnatural and sinister aspect. The light glanced back with a steely glimmer. The drunken man had a knife in his hand.

"Storp it, now," his younger brother drawlingly admonished him. "Who be ye a-goin' ter cut?"

"Call m-m-me a Philistine! I'll bust his brains out!" asseverated Pete.

"Ye're drunk, Pete," said old Grounhog Cayce, in an explanatory manner. There was no move to defend the threatened guest. Perhaps Amos James was supposed to be able to take care of himself.

"Call me a Ph-Philistine — a Philistine!" exclaimed Pete, steadying himself on the keg on which he sat, and peering with wide, light eyes into the darkness, as if to mark the whereabouts of the enemy before dealing the blow. "Jes' got insurance — c-c-c-call me a Philistine!"

"Shet up, Pete. I'll take it back," said Amos, gravely. "*I'm* the Philistine myself; fur pa'son read ez Samson killed a passel o' Philistines with the jawbone of an ass, an' ez long ez ye be talkin' I feel in an' about dead."

Amos James had bent close attention to the sermon, and had brought as much accurate information from meeting as was consistent with hearing so sensational a story as Samson's for the first time. In the mountains men do not regard church privileges as the opportunity of a quiet hour to meditate on secular affairs, while a gentle voice drones on antiquated themes. To Amos, Samson was the latest thing out.

Pete did not quite catch the full meaning of this sarcasm. He was content that Amos should seem to recant. He replaced his knife, but sat surly and muttering, and now and then glancing toward the guest.

Meantime that vivid white gleam quivered across the dusky shadows; now and then the horse pawed, raising martial echoes, as of squadrons of cavalry, among the multitudinous reverberations of the place, while his stall-companion, that the light could conjure up, was always noiseless; the continuous fresh sound of water gurgling over the rocks mingled with the monotonous drip from the worm; occasionally a gopher would scud among the heavily booted feet, and the jug's activity was marked by the shifting for an interval of the red sparks which indicated the glowing pipes of the burly shadows around the still.

The stories went on, growing weird as the evening outside waned, in some unconscious sympathy with the melancholy hour, — for in these sunless depths one knew nor day nor night, — stories of bloody vendettas, and headless ghosts, and strange previsions, and unnamed terrors. And Amos James recounted the fable of a mountain witch, interspersed with a wild vocal refrain: —

Cu-vo! Cu-vo! Kil-dar! Kil-dar! Kil-dar!

Thus she called her hungry dogs, that fed on human flesh, while the winds were awhirl, and the waning moon was red, and the Big Smoky lay in densest gloom.

The white line of light had yellowed, deepened, grown dull. The furnace needed fuel. Ab suddenly leaned down and threw open the door. The flare of the pulsing coals resuscitated the dim scene and the long, dun-colored shadows. Here in the broad red light were the stolid, meditative faces of the distillers, each with his pipe in his mouth and his hat on his head; it revealed the dilated eye and unconsciously dramatic gesture of the story-teller, sitting upon a barrel in their midst; the horse was distinct in the background, now dreaming and now lifting an impatient fore-foot, and his gigantic stall-mate, the simulacrum of the mastodon, moved as he moved, but softly, that the echoes might not know, — the immortal echoes, who were here before him, and here still.

And behind all were the great walls of the vault, with its vague apertures leading to unexplored recesses; with many jagged ledges, devoted to shelf-like usage, and showing here a jug, and here a shot-pouch, and here a rat — fat and sleek, thanks to the plenteous waste of mash and grain — looking down with a glittering eye, and here a bag of meal, and here a rifle.

Suddenly Amos James broke off. "Who's that?" he exclaimed, and all the echoes were sharply interrogative.

There was a galvanic start among the moonshiners. They looked hastily about, — perhaps for the witch, perhaps for the frightful dogs, perhaps expecting the materialization of Mirandy Jane's raider.

Amos had turned half round, and was staring intently beyond the still. The man lying on the ground had shifted his position; his soft brown hat was doubled under his head. The red flare showed its long, tawny, tangled hair, of a hue unusual enough to be an identification. His stalwart limbs were stretched out at length; the hands he thrust above his head were unmanacled; as he moved there was the jingle of spurs.

"Why, thar be Rick Tyler!" exclaimed Amos James.

"Hev ye jes' fund that out?" drawled the man on the ground, with a jeering inflection.

"W-w-w-why n't ye lie low, Rick?" demanded Pete, aggressively. "Ef ever thar war a empty cymblin', it's yer head. Amos an' that thar thin-lipped sneak ez called hisself a dep'ty air thick 'n thieves."

There was no hesitation in Amos James's character. He leaned forward suddenly, and clutched Pete by the throat, and the old man and Solomon were fain to interfere actively to prevent that doughty member of the family from being throttled on the spot. Pending the interchange of these amenities, Rick Tyler lay motionless on the ground; Ab calmly continued his task of replenishing the fire; and Ben asked, in a slow monotone, the favor of leaving the furnace door open for a "spell, whilst I unkiver the kag in the corner, an' fill the jug, an' kiver the kag agin, keerful, 'kase I don't want no rat in mine."

When Pete, with a scarlet face and starting eyes and a throat full of complicated coughs and gurgles, was torn out of the young miller's strong hands, old Groundhog Cayce remonstrated: —

"Lord A'mighty, boys! Can't ye set an' drink yer liquor sociable, 'thout clinchin' that-a-way? What did Pete do ter ye, Amos?"

" Nuthin'; he dassent," said the panting Amos.

"Did he hurt yer feelin's?" asked the old man, with respectful sympathy.

" Yes, he did," said Amos, admitting vulnerability in that tender æsthetic organ.

" Never none — now — koo — koo!" coughed Pete. " He hev got no f-f-f-feelin's, koo — koo! I hev hearn his own m-mam say so a-many a time."

" He 'lowed," said Amos, his black eyes flashing indignantly, his face scarlet, the perspiration thick in his black hair, " ez I 'd tell the dep'ty — kase he war toler'ble lively hyar, an' I got sorter friendly with him when I hed ter sarve on the posse — ez I seen Rick Tyler hyar. Mebbe ye think I want two hunderd dollars — hey!" He made a gesture as if to seize again his late antagonist.

" A-koo, koo, koo!" coughed Pete, moving cautiously out of reach.

All the echoes clamored mockingly with the convulsive sound, and thus multiplied they gave a ludicrous suggestion of the whooping cough.

"I dunno, Mr. Cayce," said Amos, with some dignity, addressing the old man, " what call ye hev got ter consort with them under indictment for murder, an' offenders agin the law. But hevin' seen Rick Tyler hyar in a friendly way along o' you-uns, he air ez safe from me ez ef he war under my own roof."

Rick Tyler drew himself up on his elbow, and turned upon the speaker a face inflamed by sudden passion.

"Go tell the dep'ty!" he screamed. "I'll take no faviors from ye, Amos Jeemes. Kem on! Arrest me yerse'f!" He rose to his feet, and held out his bruised and scarred hands, smiting them together as if he were again handcuffed. The light fell full on his clothes, tattered by his briery flight, the long dishevelment of his yellow hair, his burning face, and the blazing fury in his brown eyes. "Kem on! Arrest me yerse'f, — ye air ekal ter it. I kin better bide the law than ter take faviors from you-uns. Kem on! Arrest me!"

Once more he held his free hands as if for the manacles.

Their angry eyes met. Then, as Amos James still sat silent and motionless on the barrel, Rick Tyler turned, and with a gesture of desperation again flung himself on the ground.

There was a pause. Two of the moonshiners were arranging to decant some liquor into a keg, and were lighting a tallow dip for the purpose. In the dense darkness of the recess where they stood it took on a large and lunar aspect. A rayonnant circle hovered attendant upon it;

the shadows about it were densely black, and in the sharp and colorless contrasts the two bending figures of the men handling the keg stood out in peculiar distinctness of pose and gesture. The glare of the fire in the foreground deepened to a dull orange, to a tawny red, even to a dusky brown, in comparison with the pearly, luminous effect of the candle. The tallow dip was extinguished when the task was complete. Presently the furnace door clashed, the group of distillers disappeared as with a bound, and that long, livid line of pulsating light emitted by the ill-fitting door cleft the gloom like a glittering blade.

"I s'pose ye don't mean ter be sassy in 'special, Amos, faultin' yer elders, talkin' 'bout consortin' with them under indictment," said old Groundhog Cayce's voice. "But I dunno ez ye hev enny call ter sot yerse'f up in jedgmint on my actions."

"Waal," said Amos, apologetic, "I never went ter say nuthin' like faultin' nohow. Sech ez yer actions I leaves ter you-uns."

"Ye mought ez well," said the elder, unconsciously satiric. "The Bible 'lows ez every man air a law unto hisself. An' I hev fund I gits peace mos'ly in abidin' by the law ez kems from within. An' I kin see no jestice in my denyin' a rifle an' a lot o' lead an' powder ter a half-starvin' critter ter save his life. Rick war bound ter starve, hid out, ef he hed nuthin' ter shoot deer an' wild varmints with, bein' ez his rifle war tuk by the sher'ff. I knows no law ez lays on me the starvin' o' a human. An' when that boy kem a-cropin' hyar ter the still this evenin', he got ez fair-spoke a welcome, an' ez much liquor ez he' d swaller, same ez enny comer on the mounting. I dunno ez he air a offender agin the law, an' 't ain't my say-so. I ain't a jedge, an' thar ain't enough o' me fur a jury."

This lucid discourse, its emphasis doubled by the iterative echoes, had much slow, impersonal effect as it issued from the darkness. It was to Amos James, accustomed to rural logic, as if reason, pure and simple, had spoken. His heart had its own passionate protest. Not that he disapproved the loan of the rifle, but he distrusted the impulse which prompted it. To find the hunted fugitive here among the distillers added the force of conviction to his suspicions of a rescue and its instigation.

The personal interest which he had in all this annulled for a moment his sense of the becoming, and defied the constraints of etiquette.

"How 'd Rick Tyler say he got away from the sher'ff, ennyhow?" he demanded, bluntly.

"He war n't axed," said old Groundhog Cayce, quietly.

A silence ensued, charged with all the rigors of reproof.

"An' I dunno ez ye hev enny call ter know, Amos Jeemes," cried out Rick, still prone upon the ground. "That won't holp the sher'ff none now. Ye 'd better be studyin' 'bout settin' him on the trail ter ketch me agin."

The line of light from the rift in the furnace door showed a yellow gleam in the blackness where his head lay. Amos James fixed a burning eye upon it.

"I 'll kem thar d'rec'ly an' tromp the life out'n ye, Rick Tyler. I 'll grind yer skull ter pieces with my boot-heel, like ez ef ye war a copperhead."

"Laws-a-massy, boys, sech a quar'lin', fightin' batch ez ye be! I fairly gits gagged with my liquor a-listenin' ter ye, — furgits how ter swaller," said Groundhog Cayce, suddenly fretful.

"Leave Rick be, Amos Jeemes," he added, in an authoritative tone. And then, with a slant of his head toward Rick Tyler, lying on the ground, "Hold yer jaw down thar!"

And the two young men lapsed into silence.

The spring, rising among the barren rocks, chanted aloud its prescient sylvan song of the woodland ways, and the glancing beam, and the springing trout, and the dream of the drifting leaf, as true of tone and as delicately keyed to the dryadic chorus in the forest without as if the waters that knew but darkness and the cavernous sterilities were already in the liberated joys of the gorge yonder, reflecting the sky, wantoning with the wind, and swirling down the mountain side. The spirits dripped from the worm, the furnace roared, the men's feet grated upon the rocks as they now and then shifted their position.

"Waal," said Amos at last, rising, "I'd better be a-goin'. 'Pears like ez I hev wore out my welcome hyar."

He stood looking at the line of light, remembering desolately Dorinda's buoyant, triumphant mood. Its embellishment of her beauty had smitten him with an afflicted sense of her withdrawal from all the prospects of his future. He had thought that he had given up hope, but he began to appreciate, when he found Rick Tyler in intimate refuge with her kindred, how sturdy an organism was that heart of his, and to realize that to reduce it to despair must needs cost many a throe.

"I hev wore out my welcome, I reckon," he repeated, dismally.

"I dunno what ails ye ter say that. Ye hev jes' got tired o' comin' hyar, I reckon," said old man Cayce. "Wore out yer welcome, — shucks!"

"Mighty nigh wore me out," said Pete, remembering to cough.

"Waal," said Amos, slightly salved by the protestations of his host, "I reckon it air time I war a-puttin' out, ennyhow. Jes' set that thar furnace door on the jar, Pete, so I kin see ter lay a-holt o' the beastis."

The door opened, the red glow flared out, the figures of the moonshiners all reappeared in a semicircle about the still, and as Amos James took the horse's bridle and led him away from the wall the mastodon vanished, with noiseless tread, into the dim distance of the unmeasured past.

The horse's hoofs reverberated down the cavernous depths, echoed, reëchoed, multiplied indefinitely. Even after the animal had been led through the tortuous windings of the passage his tramp resounded through the gloom.

X.

THE displeasure of his fellows is a slight and ephemeral matter to a man whose mind is fixed on a great essential question, charged with moral gravity and imperishable consequence; whose physical courage is the instinct of his nature, conserved by its active exercise in a life of physical hardship.

Kelsey had forgotten the gander-pulling, the impending election, the excitement of the escape, before he had ridden five miles from the Settlement. He jogged along the valley road, the reins on the horse's neck, his eyes lifted to the heights. The fullness of day was on their unpeopled summits. Infinity was expressed before the eye. On and on the chain of mountains stretched, with every illusion of mist and color, with every differing grace of distance, with inconceivable measures of vastness. The grave delight in which their presence steeped the senses stirred his heart. They breathed solemnities. They lent wings to the thoughts. They lifted the soul. Could he look at them and doubt that one day he should see God? He had been near, — oh, surely, He had been near.

Kelsey was comforted as he rode on. Somehow, the mountains had for his ignorant mind some coercive internal evidence of the great truths. In their exalted suggestiveness were congruities: so far from the world were they, — so high above it; so interlinked with the history of all that makes the races of men more than the beasts that perish, that conserves the values of that noble idea, — an immortal soul. On a mountain the ark rested; on a mountain the cross was planted; the steeps beheld the glories of the transfiguration; the lofty solitudes heard the prayers of the Christ; and from the heights issued the great sermon instinct with all the moralities of every creed. How often He went up into the mountain !

.The thought uplifted Kelsey. The flush of strong feeling touched his cheek. His eyes were fired with that sudden gleam of enthusiasm as remote from earthly impulses as the lightnings of Sinai.

"An' I will preach his name!" the parson exclaimed, in a tense and thrilling voice. He checked his horse, drew out of his pocket a thumbed old Bible, clumsily turned the leaves and sought for his text.

No other book had he ever read : only that sublime epic, with its deep tendernesses and its mighty portents; with its subtleties of prophecy in wide and splendid phrase, and their fulfillment in the barren record of the simplest life; with all the throbbing presentment of martyrdom and doom and death, dominated by the miracle of resurrection and the potency of divinity. Every detail was as clearly pictured to his mind as if, instead of the vast, unstoried stretches of the Great Smoky Mountains, he looked upon the sanctities of the hills of Judæa.

He read as he rode along,—slowly, slowly. A bird's shadow would flit across the holy page, and then away to the mountain; the winds of heaven caressed it. Sometimes the pollen of flowering weeds fell upon it; for in the midst of the unfrequented road they often stood in tall rank rows, with a narrow path on either side, trodden by the oxen of the occasional team, while the growth bent elastically under the passing bed of the wagon.

He was almost happy. The clamors of his insistent heart were still. His conscience, his memory, his self-reproach, had loosed their hold. His keen and subtile native intellect stretched its unconscious powers, and discriminated the workings of character, and reviewed the deploying of events, and measured results. He was far away, walking with the disciples.

Suddenly, like an aerolite, he was whirled from high ethereal spaces by the attraction of the earth. A man was peering from between the rails of a fence by the wayside.

"Kin ye read yer book, pa'son, an' ride yer beastis all ter wunst?" he cried out, with the fervor of admiration.

That tree of knowledge, — ah, the wily serpent! Galilee, — it was thousands of miles away across the deep salt seas.

The parson closed his book with a smile of exultation.

"The beast don't hender me none. I kin read ennywhar," he said, proud of the attainment.

"Waal, sir!" exclaimed the other, one of that class, too numerous in Tennessee, who can neither read nor write. "Air it the Good Book?" he demanded, with a sudden thought.

"It air the Holy Bible," said the parson, handing him the book.

The man eyed it with reverence. Then, with a gingerly gesture, he gave it back. The parson was looking down at him, all softened and humanized by this unconscious flattery.

"Waal, pa'son," said the illiterate admirer of knowledge, with a respectful and subordinate air, "I hearn ez ye war a-goin' ter hold fo'th up yander at the meet'n-house at the Notch nex' Sunday. Air that a true word?"

"I 'lows ter preach thar on the nex' Lord's day," replied the parson.

"Then," with the promptness of a sudden resolution, "I 'm a-goin' ter take the old woman an' the chillen an' wagon up the Big Smoky ter hear the sermon. I 'low ez a man what kin ride a beastis an' read a book all ter wunst mus' be a powerful exhorter, an' mebbe ye 'll lead us all ter grace."

The parson said he would be glad to see the family at the meeting-house, and presently jogged off down the road.

One might regard the satisfaction of this simple scene as the due meed of his labors; one might account his pride in his attainments as a harmless human weakness. There have been those of his calling, proud, too, of a finite knowledge, and fain to conserve fame, whose conscience makes no moan, — who care naught for humility, and hardly hope to be genuine.

The flush of pleasure passed in a moment. His face hardened. That fire of a sublimated anger or frenzy touched his eyes. He remembered Peter, the impetuous, and Thomas, the doubter, and the warm generosities of the heart of him whom Jesus loved, and he "reckoned" that they would not have left Him standing in the road for the joy of hearing their learning praised. He rebuked himself as caring less for the Holy Book than that his craft could read it. His terrible insight into motives was not dulled by a personal application. Introverted upon his own heart, it was keen, unsparing, insidiously subtle. He saw his pride as if it had been another man's, except that it had no lenient mediator; for he was just to other men, even gentle. He took pitiless heed of the pettiness of his vanity; he detected pleasure that the man by the wayside should come, not for salvation, but to hear the powerful exhorter speak. He saw the instability of his high mood, of the gracious reawaking of faith; he realized the lapse from the heights of an ecstasy at the lightest touch of temptation.

"The Lord lifts me up," he said, "ter dash me on the groun'!"

No more in Judæa, in the holy mountains; no more among the disciples. Drearily along the valley road, glaring and yellow in the sun, the book closed, the inspiration fled, journeyed the ignorant man, who would fain lay hold on a true and perfected sanctity.

He dispatched his errand in the valley, — a secular matter, relating to the exchange of a cow and a calf. The afternoon was waning when he was again upon the slopes of the Big Smoky; for the roads were rough, and he had traveled slowly, always prone to "favor the beastis." He stopped in front of Cayce's house, where he saw Dorinda spinning on the porch, and preferred a request for a gourd of water. The old woman heard his voice, and came hastily out with hospitable insistence that he should dismount and "rest his bones, sence he hed rid fur, an' tell the news from the Settlemint." There was a cordial contrast between this warm esteem and his own unkind thoughts, and he suffered himself to be persuaded. He sat under the hop-vines, and replied in monosyllables to the old woman's animated questions, and gave little news of the excitements at the Settlement which they had not already heard. Dorinda, her wheel awhirl, one hand lifted holding the thread, the other poised in the air to control the motion, her figure thrown back in a fine, alert pose, looked at him with a freshened pity for his downcast spirit, and with intuitive sympathy. He sorrowed not because of the things of this world, she felt. It was some high and spiritual grief, such as might pierce a prophet's heart. Her eyes, full of the ideality of the sentiment, dwelt upon him reverently.

He marked the look. With his overwhelming sense of his sins, he was abased under it, and he scourged himself as a hypocrite.

"Thar air goin' ter be preachin' at the meetin'-house Sunday, I hearn," she observed presently, thinking this topic more meet for his discussion than the "gaynder-pullin'" and the escape, and such mundane matters. The tempered green light fell upon her fair face, adding a delicacy to its creamy tint; her black hair caught a shifting golden flake of sunshine as she moved back and forth; her red lips were slightly parted. The grasshoppers droned in the leaves an accompaniment to the whir of her wheel. The "prince's feathers" bloomed in great clumsy crimson tufts close by the step. Mirandy Jane, seated on an inverted noggin, listened tamely to the conversation, her wild, uncertain eyes fixed upon the parson's face; she dropped them, and turned her head with a shying gesture, if by chance his glance fell upon her.

From this shadowed, leafy recess the world seen through the green hop-vines was all in a great yellow glare.

"Be you-uns a-goin' ter hold fo'th," demanded the old woman, "or Brother Jake Tobin?"

"It air me ez air a-goin' ter preach," he said.

"Then I'm a-comin'," she declared, promptly. "It do me good ter hear you-uns fairly make the sinners spin. Sech a gift o' speech ye hev got! I fairly see hell when ye talk o' thar doom. I see wrath an' I smell brimstone. Lord be thanked, I hev fund peace! An' I'm jes' a-waitin' fur the good day ter come when the Lord 'll rescue me from yearth!" She threw herself back in her chair, closing her eyes in a sort of ecstasy, and beating her hands on her knees, her feet tapping in rhythm.

"Though ef ye 'll b'lieve me," she added, sitting up straight with an appalling suddenness, and opening her eyes, " D'rindy thar ain't convicted yit. Oh, child," in an enthused tone of reproof, " time is short, — time is short!"

"Waal," said Dorinda, speaking more quickly than usual, and holding up her hand to stop the wheel, "I hev hed no chance sca'cely ter think on salvation, bein' ez the weavin' war hendered some — an'"— She paused in embarrassment.

" That air a awful word ter say, — puttin' the Lord ter wait! Why n't ye speak the truth ter her, pa'son ? Fix her sins on her."

"Sometimes," said the parson, abruptly, looking at her as if he saw more or less than was before him, "I dunno ef I hev enny call ter say a word. I hev preached ter others, an' I 'm like ter be a castaway myself."

The old woman stared at him in dumb astonishment. But he was rising to take leave, — a simple ceremony. He unhitched the horse at the gate, mounted, and, with a silent nod to the group on the porch, rode slowly away.

Old Mrs. Cayce followed him with curious eyes, peering out in the gaps of the hop-vines.

"D'rindy," she said, "that thar Pa'son Kelsey,—we-uns useter call him nuthin' but Hi, —he's got suthin' heavy on his mind. It always 'peared ter me ez he war a mighty cur'ous man ter take up with religion an' sech. A mighty suddint boy he war,—ez good a fighter ez a catamount, an' always 'mongst the evil, bold men. Them he consorted with till he gin his child morphine by mistake, an' its mammy quine-iron; an' she los' her senses arterward, an' flunged herse'f off'n the bluff. 'Pears like ter me ez them war jedgments on him,— though Em'ly war n't much loss; ez triflin' a ch'ice fur a wife ez a man could make. An' now he hev got suthin' on his mind."

The girl said nothing. She stayed her wheel with one hand, holding the thread with the other, and looked over her shoulder at the receding figure riding slowly along the vista of the forest-shadowed road. Then she turned, and fixed her lucent, speculative eyes on her grandmother, who continued: "Calls hisself a castaway! Waal, he knows bes', bein' a prophet an' sech. But it air toler'ble comical talk fur a preacher. Brother Jake Tobin kin hardly hold hisself together, a-waitin' fur his sheer o' the joys o' the golden shore."

"Waal, 'pears like ter me," said Mirandy Jane, whose mind seemed never far from the culinary achievements to which she had been dedicated, " ez Brother Jake Tobin sets mo' store on chicken fixin's than on grace, an' he fattens ev'y year."

" I hopes," proceeded the grandmother, disregarding the interruption, and peering out again at the road where the horseman had disappeared, " ez Hi Kelsey won't sot hisself ter prophesyin' evil at the meetin'; 'pears ter me he ought ter be hendered, ef mought be, 'kase the wrath he foresees mos'ly kems ter pass, an' I'm always lookin' ter see him prophesy the raiders, — though he hev hed the grace ter hold his hand 'bout'n the still. An' I hopes he won't hev nuthin' ter say 'bout it at the meetin' Sunday."

The little log meeting-house at the Notch stood high on a rugged spur of the Great Smoky. Dense forests encompassed it on every hand, obscuring that familiar picture of mountain and cloud and cove. From its rude, glassless windows one could look out on no distant vista, save perhaps in the visionary glories of heaven or the climatic discomforts of hell, according to the state of the conscience, or perchance the liver. The sky was aloof and limited. The laurel tangled the aisles of the woods. Sometimes from the hard benches a weary tow-headed brat might rejoice to mark in the monotony the frisking of a squirrel on a bough hard by, or a woodpecker solemnly tapping. The acorns would rattle on the roof, if the wind stirred, as if in punctuation of the discourse. The pines, mustering strong among the oaks, joined their mystic threnody to the sad-voiced quiring within. The firs stretched down long, pendulous, darkling boughs, and filled the air with their balsamic fragrance. Within the house the dull light fell over a few rude benches and a platform with a chair and table, which was used as pulpit. Shadows of many deep, rich tones of brown lurked among the rafters. Here and there a cobweb, woven to the consistence of a fabric, swung in the air. The drone of a blue-bottle, fluttering in and out of the window in a slant of sunshine, might invade the reverent silence, as Brother Jake Tobin turned the leaves to read the chapter. Sometimes there would sound, too, a commotion among the horses without, unharnessed from the wagons and hitched to the trees; then in more than one of the solemn faces might be descried an anxious perturbation, — not fear because of equine perversities, but because of the idiosyncrasies of callow human nature in the urchins left in charge of the teams. No one ventured to investigate, however, and, with that worldly discomfort contending with the spiritual exaltations they sought to foster, the rows of religionists swayed backward and forward in rhythm to the reader's voice, rising and falling in long, billowy sweeps of sound, like the ground swell of ocean waves.

It was strange, looking upon their faces, and with a knowledge of the limited phases of their existence, their similarity of experience here, where a century might come and go, working no change save that, like the leaves, they fluttered awhile in the outer air with the spurious animation called life, and fell in death, and made way for new bourgeonings like unto themselves, — strange to mark how they differed. Here was a man of a stern, darkly religious conviction, who might either have writhed at the stake or stooped to kindle the flames; and here was an accountant soul that knew only those keen mercantile motives, — the hope of reward and the fear of hell; and here was an enthusiast's eye, touched by the love of God; and here was an unfinished, hardly humanized face, that it seemed as presumptuous to claim as the exponent of a soul as the faces of the stupid oxen out-of-doors. All were earnest; many wore an expression of excited interest, as the details of the chapter waxed to a climax, like the tense stillness of a metropolitan audience before an unimagined *coup de théâtre*. The men all sat on one side, chewing their quids; the women on the other, almost masked by their limp sun-bonnets. The ubiquitous baby — several of him — was there, and more than once babbled aloud and cried out peevishly. Only one, becoming uproarious, was made a public example; being quietly borne out and deposited in the ox-wagon, at the mercy of the urchins who presided over the teams, while his mother creaked in again on the tips of deprecating, anxious toes, to hear the Word.

Brother Jake Tobin might be accounted in some sort a dramatic reader. He was a tall, burly man, inclining to fatness, with grizzled hair roached back from his face. He cast his light gray eyes upward at the end of every phrase, with a long, resonant " Ah ! " He smote the table with his hands at emphatic passages; he rolled out denunciatory clauses with a freshened relish which intimated that he considered one of the choicest pleasures of the saved might be to gloat over the unhappy predicament of the damned. He chose for his reading paragraphs that, applied to aught but spiritual enemies and personified sins, might make a civilized man quake for his dearest foe. He paused often and interpolated his own observations, standing a little to the side of the table, and speaking in a conversational tone. "Ain't that so, my brethren an' sisters! But *we* air saved in the covenant — ah!" Then, clapping his hands with an ecstatic upward look, — "I 'm so happy, I 'm so happy!" — he would go on to read with the unction of immediate intention, "Let death seize them! Let them go down quick into hell!"

He wore a brown jeans suit, the vest much creased in the regions of his enhanced portliness, its maker's philosophy not having taken into due account his susceptibility to "chicken fixin's." After concluding the reading he wiped the perspiration from his brow with his red bandana handkerchief, and placed it around the collar of his unbleached cotton shirt, as he proceeded to the further exertion of "lining out" the hymn.

The voices broke forth in those long, lingering cadences that have a melancholy, spiritual, yearning effect, in which the more tutored church music utterly fails. The hymn rose with a solemn jubilance, filling the little house, and surging out into the woods; sounding far across unseen chasms and gorges, and rousing in the unsentient crags an echo with a testimony so sweet, charged with so devout a sentiment, that it seemed as if with this voice the very stones would have cried out, had there been dearth of human homage when Christ rode into Jerusalem.

Then the sudden pause, the failing echo, the sylvan stillness, and the chanting voice lined out another couplet. It was well, perhaps, that this part of the service was so long; the soul might rest on its solemnity, might rise on its aspiration.

It came to an end at last. Another long pause ensued. Kelsey, sitting on the opposite side of the table, his elbow on the back of his chair, his hand shading his eyes, made no movement. Brother Jake Tobin looked hard at him, with an expression which in a worldly man we should pronounce exasperation. He hesitated for a moment in perplexity. There was a faint commotion, implying suppressed excitement in the congregation. Parson Kelsey's idiosyncrasies were known by more than one to be a thorn in the side of the frankly confiding Brother Jake Tobin.

"Whenst I hev got him in the pul*pit* alongside o' me," he would say to his cronies, "I feel ez onlucky an' weighted ez ef I war a-lookin' over my lef' shoulder at the new moon on a November Friday. I feel ez oncommon ez ef he war a deer, or suthin', ez hev got no salvation in him. An' ef he don't feel the sperit ter pray, he *won't* pray, an' I hev got ter surroun' the throne o' grace by myself. He *kin* pray ef he hev a mind ter, an' he *do* seem ter hev hed a outpourin' o' the sperit o' prophecy; but he hev made me 'pear mighty comical 'fore the Lord a-many a time, when I hev axed him ter open his mouth an' he hev kep' it shut."

Brother Jake did not venture to address him now. An alternative was open to him. " Brother Reuben Bates, will ye lead us in prayer? " he said to one of the congregation.

They all knelt down, huddled like sheep in the narrow spaces between the benches, and from among them went up the voice of supplication, that anywhere and anyhow has the commanding dignity of spiritual communion, the fervor of exaltation, and all the moving humility of the finite leaning upon the infinite. Ignorance was annihilated, so far as Brother Reuben Bates's prayer was concerned. It grasped the fact of immortality, — all worth knowing ! — and humble humanity was presented as possessing the intimate inherent principle of the splendid fruitions of eternity.

He had few words, Brother Reuben, and the aspirated " Ah! " was long drawn often, while he swiftly thought of something else to say. Brother Jake Tobin, after the manner in vogue among them, broke out from time to time with a fervor of assent. "Yes, my Master!" he would exclaim in a wild, ecstatic tone. "Bless the Lord!" "That's a true word!" "I'm so happy!"

Always these interpolations came opportunely when Brother Reuben seemed entangled in his primitive rhetoric, and gave him a moment for improvisation. It was doubtless Hi Kelsey's miserable misfortune that his acute intuition should detect in the reverend tones a vainglorious self-satisfaction, known to no one else, not even to the speaker; that he should accurately gauge how Brother Jake Tobin secretly piqued himself upon his own gift in prayer, never having experienced these stuttering halts, never having needed these pious boosts; that he should be aware, ignorant as he was, of that duality of cerebration by which Brother Jake's mind was divided between the effect on God, bending down a gracious ear, and the impression of these ecstatic outbursts on the congregation; that the petty contemptibleness of it should depress him; that its dissimulations angered him. With the rigor of an upright man, he upbraided himself. He was on his knees: was he praying? Were these the sincerities of faith. Was this lukewarm inattention the guerdon of the sacrifice of the cross? His ideal and himself, himself and what he sought to be, — oh, the gulf! the deep divisions!

He gave his intentions no grace. He conceded naught to human nature. His conscience revolted at a sham. And he was a living, breathing sham — upon his knees.

Ah, let us have a little mercy on ourselves! Most of us do. For there was Brother Jake Tobin, with a conscience free of offense, happily unobservant of his own complicated mental processes and of the motives of his own human heart, becoming more and more actively assistant as Brother Reuben Bates grew panicky, hesitant, and involved, and kept convulsively on through sheer inability to stop, suggesting epilepsy rather than piety.

It was over at last; exhausted nature prevailed, and Brother Bates resumed his seat, wiping the perspiration from his brow and raucously clearing his rasped throat.

There was a great scraping of the rough shoes and boots on the floor as the congregation rose, and one or two of the benches were moved backward with a harsh, grating sound. A small boy had gone to sleep during the petition, and remained in his prayerful attitude. Brother Jake Tobin settled himself in his chair as comfortably as might be, tilted it back on its hind-legs against the wall, and wore the air of having fairly exploited his share of the services and cast off responsibility. The congregation composed itself to listen to the sermon.

There was an expectant pause. Kelsey remembered ever after the tumult of emotion with which he stepped forward to the table and opened the book. He turned to the New Testament for his text, — turned the leaves with a familiar hand. Some ennobling phase of that wonderful story which would touch the tender, true affinity of human nature for the higher things, — from this he would preach to-day. And yet, at the same moment, with a contrariety of feeling from which he shrank aghast, there was skulking into his mind all that grewsome company of doubts. In double file they came: fate and free agency, free will and foreordination, infinite mercy and infinite justice, God's loving kindness and man's intolerable misery, redemption and damnation. He had evolved them all from his own unconscious logical faculty, and they pursued him as if he had, in some spiritual necromancy, conjured up a devil, — nay, legions of devils. Perhaps if he had known how they have assaulted the hearts of men in times gone past; how they have been combated and baffled, and yet have risen and pursued again; how, in the scrutiny of science and research, men have paused before their awful presence, analyzed them, philosophized about them, and found them interesting; how others, in the levity of the world, having heard of them, grudge the time to think upon them, — if he had known all this, he might have felt some courage in numbers.

As it was, there was no fight left in him. He closed the book with a sudden impulse. " My frien's," he said, " I stan' not hyar ter preach ter-day, but fur confession."

There was a galvanic start among the congregation, then intense silence.

"I hev los' my faith!" he cried out, with a poignant despair. " God ez gin it — ef thar is a God — hev tuk it away. You-uns kin go on. You-uns kin b'lieve. Yer paster b'lieves, an' he'll lead ye ter grace, — leastwise ter a better life. But fur me thar's the nethermost depths of hell, ef " — how his faith and his unfaith tried him! — " ef thar be enny hell. Leastwise — Stop, brother," — he held up his hand in deprecation, for Parson Tobin had risen at last, with a white, scared face; nothing like this had ever been heard in all the length and breadth of the Great Smoky Mountains, — " bear with me a little; ye'll see me hyar no more. Fur me thar is shame, ah! an' trial, ah! an' doubt, ah! an' despair, ah! The good things o' life hev not fallen ter me. The good things o' heaven air denied. My name is ter be a by-word an' a reproach 'mongst ye. Ye'll grieve ez ye hev ever hearn the

Word from me, ah! Ye'll be held in derision! An' I hev hed trials, — none like them ez air comin', comin', down the wind. I hev been a man marked fur sorrow, an' now fur shame."

He stood erect; he looked bold, youthful. The weight of his secret, lifted now, had been heavier than he knew. In his eyes shone that strange light which was frenzy, or prophecy, or inspiration; in his voice rang a vibration they had never before heard.

"I will go forth from 'mongst ye, — I that am not of ye. Another shall gird me an' carry me where I would not. Hell an' the devil hev prevailed agin me. Pray fur me, brethren, ez I cannot pray fur myself. Pray that God may yet speak ter me, — speak from out o' the whurlwind."

There was a sound upon the air. Was it the rising of the wind? A thrill ran through the congregation. The wild emotion, evoked and suspended in this abrupt pause, showed in pallid excitement on every face. Several of the men rose aimlessly, then turned and sat down again. Brought from the calm monotony of their inner life into this supreme crisis of his, they were struck aghast by the hardly comprehended situations of his spiritual drama enacted before them. And what was that sound on the air? In the plenitude of their ignorant faith, were they listening for the invoked voice of God?

Kelsey, too, was listening, in anguished suspense.

It was not the voice of God, that man was wont to hear when the earth was young; not the rising of the wind. The peace of the golden sunshine was supreme. Even a tiny cloudlet, anchored in the limited sky, would not sail to-day.

On and on it came. It was the galloping of horse, — the beat of hoofs, individualized presently to the ear, — with that thunderous, swift, impetuous advance that so domineers over the imagination, quickens the pulse, shakes the courage.

It might seem that all the ingenuity of malignity could not have compassed so complete a revenge. The fulfillment of his prophecy entered at the door. All its spiritual significance was annihilated; it was merged into a prosaic material degradation when the sheriff of the county strode, with jingling spurs, up the aisle, and laid his hand upon the preacher's shoulder. He wore his impassive official aspect. But his deputy, following hard at his heels, had a grin of facetious triumph upon his thin lips. He had been caught by the nape of the neck, and in a helpless, rodent-like attitude had been slung out of the door by the stalwart man of God, when he and Amos James had ventured to the meeting-house in liquor; and neither he nor the congregation had forgotten the sensation. It was improbable that such high-handed proceedings could be instituted to-day, but the sheriff had taken the precaution to summon the aid of five or six burly fellows, all armed to the teeth. They too came tramping heavily up the aisle. Several wore the reflection of the deputy's grin; they were the "bold, bad men," the prophet's early associates before "he got religion, an' sot hisself ter consortin' with the saints." The others were sheepish and doubtful, serving on the posse with a protest under the constraining penalties of the law.

The congregation was still with a stunned astonishment. The preacher stood as one petrified, his eyes fixed upon the sheriff's face. The officer, with a slow, magisterial gesture, took a paper from his breast-pocket, and laid it upon the Bible.

"Ye kin read, pa'son," he said. "Ye kin read the warrant fur yer arrest."

The deputy laughed, a trifle insolently. He turned, swinging his hat, — he had done the sacred edifice the reverence of removing it, — and surveyed the wide-eyed, wide-mouthed people, leaning forward, standing up, huddled together, as if he had some speculation as to the effect upon them of these unprecedented proceedings.

Kelsey could read nothing. His strong head was in a whirl; he caught at the table, or he might have fallen. The amazement of it, — the shame of it!

"Who does this?" he exclaimed, in sudden realization of the situation. Already self-convicted of the blasphemy of infidelity, he stood in his pulpit in the infinitely ignoble guise of a culprit before the law.

Those fine immaterial issues of faith and unfaith, — where were they? The torturing fear of futurity, and of a personal devil and a material hell, — how impotent! His honest name, — never a man had borne it that had suffered this shame; the precious dignity of freedom was riven from him; the calm securities of his self-respect were shaken forever. He could never forget the degradation of the sheriff's touch, from which he shrank with so abrupt a gesture that the officer grasped his pistol and every nerve was on the alert. Kelsey was animated at this moment by a pulse as essentially mundane as if he had seen no visions and dreamed no dreams. He had not known how he held himself, — how he cherished those values, so familiar that he had forgotten to be thankful till their possession was a retrospection.

He sought to regain his self-control. He

caught up the paper; it quivered in his trembling hands; he strove to read it. "Rescue!" he cried out in a tense voice. "Rick Tyler! I never rescued Rick Tyler!"

The words broke the long constraint. They were an elucidation, a flash of light. The congregation looked at him with changed eyes, and then looked at each other. Why did he deny? Were not the words of his prophecy still on the air? Had he not confessed himself an evil-doer, forsaken of God and bereft of grace? His prophecy was matched by the details of his experience. Had he done no wrong he could have foreseen no vengeance.

"Rick Tyler ain't wuth it," said one old man to another, as he spat on the floor.

The widow of Joel Byers, the murdered man, fell into hysterical screaming at Rick Tyler's name, and was presently borne out by her friends and lifted into one of the wagons.

"It air jes' ez well that the sher'ff takes Pa'son Kelsey, arter that thar confession o' his'n," said one of the dark-browed men, helping to yoke the oxen. "We could n't hev kep' him in the church arter sech words ez his'n, an' church discipline ain't a-goin' ter cast out no sech devil ez he air possessed by."

Brother Jake Tobin, too, appreciated that the arrest of the preacher in his pulpit was a solution of a difficult question. It was manifestly easier for the majesty of the State of Tennessee to deal with him than for the little church on the Big Smoky.

"Yer sins hev surely fund ye out, Brother Kelsey," he began, with the air of having washed his hands of all responsibility. "God would never hev fursook ye, ef ye hed n't fursook the good cause fust. Ye air ter be cast down, — ye who hev stood high."

There was a momentary silence.

"Will ye come?" said the sheriff, smiling fixedly, "or had ye ruther be fetched?"

The deputy had a pair of handcuffs dangling officiously. They rattled in rude contrast with the accustomed sounds of the place.

Kelsey hesitated. Then, after a fierce internal struggle, he submitted meekly, and was led out from among them.

XI.

It is seldom, in this world at least, that a man who absents himself from church repents it with the fervor of regret which Amos James experienced when he heard of the unexpected proceedings at the Notch.

"Sech a rumpus — dad-burn my luck — I mought never git the chance ter see agin!" he declared, with a pious sense of deprivation. And he thought it had been a poor substitute to sit on the doorstep all the forenoon Sunday, "ez lonesome ez a b'ar in a hollow tree," because his heart was yet so sore and sensitive that he could not see Dorinda's pink sun-bonnet without a rush of painful emotion, or her face without remembering how she looked when he talked of the rescue of Rick Tyler.

The "gang o' men" — actively described by his mother as "lopin' roun' the mill" — lingered long in conclave this morning. Perhaps their views had a more confident and sturdy effect from being propounded at the top of the voice, since the insistent whir of the busy old mill drowned all efforts in a lower tone; but it was very generally the opinion that Micajah

Green had transcended all the license of his official character in making the arrest at the place and time he had selected.

"I knows," commented one of the disaffected, "ez it air the law o' Tennessee ez a arrest kin be made of a Sunday, ef so be it must. But 'pears like ter me 't war nuthin' in this worl' but malice an' meanness ez tuk ch'ice o' the minute the man hed stood up ter preach the Word ter arrest him. 'Cajah Green mus' hev tuk keerful heed o' time, — jes' got thar spang on the minute."

"He w-war n't p-p-preachin' the Word," stuttered Pete Cayce, antagonistically. "He hed jes' 'lowed he w-w-war n't fit ter preach it. No more war he."

He had come down from the still to treat for meal for the mash. He was willing to wait, — nay, anxious, that he might bear his share in the conversation.

He tilted his chair back against the wall, and nodded his long, drab-tinted locks convincingly.

The water whirled around the wheel; the race foamed with prismatic bubbles, flashing opal-like in the sun; the vague lapsing of the calm depths in the pond was like some deep sigh, as of the fullness of happiness or reflective content, — not pain. The water falling over the dam babbled in a meditative undertone. All sounds were dominated by the whir of the mill in its busy, industrial monody, and within naught else could be heard, save the strident voices pitched on the miller's key and roaring the gossip. Through the window could be seen the rocky banks opposite, their summits tufted with huckleberry and sassafras bushes and many a tangle of weeds; the dark shadow in the water below; the slope of the mountain rising above. A branch, too, of the low-spreading chestnut-oak, that hung above the roof of the mill, was visible, swaying close without; it cast a tempered shade over the long cobwebs depending from the rafters, whitened by the dust of the flour. The rough, undressed timbers within were of that mellow, rich tint, intermediate between yellow and brown, so restful to the eye. The floor was littered with bags of corn, on which some of the men lounged; others sat in the few chairs, and Amos James leaned against the hopper.

"Waal, retorted the first speaker, ez fur ez 'Cajah Green could know, he'd hev been a-preachin' then, an' argyfyin' his own righteousness; an' 'Cajah laid off ter kem a-steppin' in with his warrant ter prove him a liar an' convict him o' sinnin' agin the law 'fore his congregation."

"'Pears like ter me ez pa'son war sorter

forehanded," said Pete, captiously. "He hed proved hisself a liar 'fore the sher'ff got thar; saved 'Cajah the trouble."

"I hearn," said another man, "ez pa'son up-ed an' 'lowed ez he did n't b'lieve in the Lord, an' prophesied his own downfall an' his trial 'fore the sher'ff got thar."

"He d-d-did!" shouted Pete. "We never knowed much more arter 'Cajah an' the dep'ty kem 'n we did afore. Pa'son said they 'd gird him an' t-t-take him whar he did n't want ter g-go, — an' so they d-d-d-did."

"D-d-did what?" mockingly demanded Amos James, with unnecessary rancor, it might have seemed.

Pete's infirmity became more pronounced under this cavalier treatment. "T-t-take him w-w-w-whar he did n't w-w-w-want" — explosively — "ter go, ye fool!"

"Whar?"

"D' ye reckon he wanted ter go ter jail in Shaftesville?" demanded Pete, with scathing scorn. His sneering lip exposed his long, protruding teeth, and his hard-featured face was unusually repellant.

"Hev they tuk him ter jail, — the pa'son? — Pa'son Kelsey?" exclaimed Amos James, in a deeply serious tone. He looked fixedly at Pete, as if he might thus express more than he said in words. There was indignation in his black eyes, even reproach. He still leaned on the hopper, but there was nothing between the stones, for he had forgotten to pour in more corn, and the industrious flurry of the unsentient old mill was like the bustle of many clever people, — a great stir about nothing. He wore his broad-brimmed white hat far back on his head. His black hair was sprinkled with flour and meal, and along the curves of his features the snowy flakes had congregated in thin lines, bringing out the olive tint of his complexion, and intensifying the sombre depths of his eyes.

Pete returned the allusion to his defective speech by a comment on the intentness of the miller's gaze.

"Ye look percisely like a ow-*el*, Amos, — percisely like a old horned ho-ho-hooter," he declared, with a laugh. "Ya-as," he continued, "they did take pa'son ter jail, bein' ez the jestice that the sher'ff tuk him afore — old Squair Prine, ye know — h-he couldn't decide ez ter his g-guilt. The Squair air so onsartain in his mind, an' wavers so ez ter his knowledge, that I hev hearn ez ev'y day he counts his toes ter make sure he's got ten. So the old Squair h-hummed and h-h-hawed over the evidence, an' he 'l-lowed ter Pa'son K-Kelsey ez he couldn't b'lieve nuthin' agin him right handy, ez he hed sot under his p-preachin' many a time an' profited by it; but thar war his cur'ous performin' 'bout'n the gaynder whilst Rick got off, an' he hed hearn ez pa'son turned his back on the Lord in a s'prisin' way. Then the Squair axed how he kem ter prophesy his own arrest ef he hed done nuthin' ter bring it on. The Squair 'lowed 't war a serious matter, a pen'- tiary offense; an' he war n't cl'ar in his own mind; an' he up-ed an' down-ed, an' twisted an' turned, an' he did n't know *what* ter do: so the e-end war he jes' committed Pa'son Kelsey ter jail, ter await the action o' the g-g-g-gran' jury."

Pete gave this detail with some humor, wagging his head back and forth to imitate the magisterial treatment of the quandary, and putting up first one hand, then the other, stretching out first one rough boot, then the other, to signify the various points of the dilemma.

Amos James did not laugh. He still gravely gazed at the narrator.

"Why n't he git bail?" he demanded, gruffly.

"Waal, he did n't — 'kase he could n't. The old man, he fixed the bail without so much dilly- dallyin' an' jouncin' 'roun' in his mind ez ye mought expec'. He jes' put on his specs, an' polished his old bald noodle with his red h-h-handkercher, an' tuk a fraish chaw o' terbacco, an' put his nose in his book, an' tuk it out ter brag ez them crazy bugs in N-N-Nashvul sent him a book ev'y time they made a batch o' new laws, — pore, prideful old critter mus' hev been lyin'! — an' then he put his nose in his book agin' like he smelt the law an' trailed it by scent. 'T war n't more 'n haffen hour 'fore he tuk it out, an' say the least bail he could take war a thousand d-d-dollars fur the defendant, an' five hunderd fur each of his sureties, — like it hev been in ev'y sech case 'fore a jestice s-sence the Big Smoky Mountings war made."

Pete laughed, his great fore-teeth, his flexible lip, his long, bony face and tangled mane, giving him something of an equine aspect. His mood was unusually jocular; and indeed a man might experience some elation of spirit to be the only one of the "lopers round" at the mill who had been present at a trial of such significance. The close attention accorded his every word demonstrated the interest in the subject, and the guffaws which greeted his sketch of the familiar character of the old "Squair" was a flattering tribute to his skill as a *raconteur*. The peculiar antagonism of his disposition was manifested only in the delay and digressions by which he thwarted Amos James's eagerness to know why Parson Kelsey had not been admitted to bail. He could not accurately interpret the indignation in the miller's look, and he cared less for the threat it expressed. Cowardice was not predicable of one of the Cayce tribe. Perhaps it might have been agreeable for the community if the discordant Pete could have been more readily intimidated.

"Why n't pa'son gin the bail, then?" demanded Amos, again.

"He *did* gin it," returned Pete, perversely.

"Waal, then, how 'd the sher'ff take him ter jail?"

"Right down the county road, ez ye an' me an' the rest of us hyar in the Big Smoky hev worked on till sech c-c-cattle ez 'Cajah Green an' his buzzardy dep'ty hain't got no sort'n c-chance o' breakin' thar necks over the rocks an' sech."

"Look-a-hyar, Pete Cayce, I'll fling ye bodaciously over that thar bluff!" exclaimed Amos James, darkly frowning.

A rat that had boldly run across the floor a number of times, its whiskers powdered white, its tail white also, and gayly frisking behind it, had ventured so close to the miller's motionless foot that when he stepped hastily forward it sprang into the air with a wonderfully human expression of fright; then, in a sprawling fashion it swiftly sped away to some dark corner, where it might meditate on the escaped danger and take heed of foolhardiness.

" W-w-what would I be a-doin' of, Amos Jeemes, whilst ye war a-flingin' m-me over tho b-b-bluff ? " demanded Pete, pertinently.

" What ails ye, ter git tuk so suddint in yer temper, Amos ? " asked another of the baffled listeners, who desired to promote peace and further the account of Parson Kelsey's examination before the magistrate. " Amos jes' axed ye, Pete, why pa'son war n't admitted ter bail."

" H-h-he never none, now," said Pete. " He axed w-w-why Pa'son Kelsey did n't g-*gin* bail. He did gin it, but 't-t warn't accepted."

" What fur ? " demanded Amos, relapsing into interest in the subject, and leaning back against the hopper.

" Waal," said Pete, preferring, on the whole, the distinction of relating the proceedings before the magistrate to the more familiar diversion of bickering, " pa'son he 'lowed he 'd gin his gran'dad an' his uncle ter go on his bond ; an' the Squair, arter he hed stuck his nose into his book a couple o' times, an' did n't see nuthin' abolishin' gran'dads an' uncles, he tuk it out an' refraished it with a pinch o' snuff, an' 'lowed he 'd take gran'dad an' uncle on the bond. An' then up jumped Gid Fletcher, the blacksmith over yander ter the Settlemint, — him it war ez swore out the warrant, — an' demanded the Squair would hear his testimony agin it. That thar 'Cajah Green, he sick-ed him on, all the time. I seen Gid Fletcher storp suddint wunst, an' wall his eye 'round onsartin' at 'Cajah Green, ez ef ter make sure he war a-sayin' all right. An' 'Cajah Green, he batted his eye, ez much ez ter say, ' Go it, old hoss ! ' Sure ez ye air born them two fixed it up aforehand."

" I do *de*-spise that thar critter, 'Cajah Green ! " exclaimed one of the men, who was sitting on a sack of corn in the middle of the floor. " He fairly makes the trigger o' my rifle itch ! I hope he won't kem out ahead at the August election. The Big Smoky 'll hev ter git him beat somehows; we can't hev him aggervatin' 'roun' hyar another two year."

The fore-legs of Pete Cayce's tilted chair came down with a thump. He leaned forward, and with a marked gesture offered his big horny paw to the man who sat on the bag of corn; they solemnly shook hands as on a compact.

Amos James still leaned against the empty hopper, listening with a face of angry gloom as Pete recommenced : —

"Waal, the Squair, he put his nose inter his book agin, an' then he 'lowed he 'd hear Gid Fletcher's say-so. An' Gid, — waal, he 'll be mighty good metal fur the devil's anvil; I feel it in my bones how Satan will rej'ice ter draw Gid Fletcher down small, — he got up an' 'lowed ez pa'son an' his uncle an' his gran'dad did n't wuth two thousand dollars. They hed what they hed all tergether, an' 't war n't enough, — 't war n't wuth more 'n a thousan', ef that. An' so the Squair, — waal, he looked toler'ble comical, a-nosin' in his book an' a-polishin' off the torp o' his head with his red handkercher, an' he war ez oneasy an' onsartain in his actions ez a man consortin' accidentally with a bumbly bee. He tried 'em all powerful in thar temper, bein' so gin over ter backin' an' fo'thin'; but ez he war the jestice they hed ter sot 'round an' look solemn an' respec'ful. An' at las' he said he could n't accept the bail, ez 't war insufficient. The dep'ty looked like he 'd jump up an' down, an' crack his heels together; 'peared like he war glad fur true. An' the Squair, he 'lowed ez the rescue war a crime ez mought make a jestice keerful how he tuk insufficient bail. Ennybody ez would holp a man ter escape from cust'dy would jump his bond hisself, though he war tol'erble keerful ter explain ter pa'son ez he never ondertook ter charge nuthin' on him, nuther. An' he hed ter bear in mind ez he oc'pied a m-m-mighty important place in the l-law, — though I can't see ez it air so mighty important ter h-h-hev ter say, ' I dunno; let the court decide.' "

Amos James remembered the hopper at last. He turned, and, as he lifted a bag and poured in the corn, he asked, his eyes on the golden stream of grain, —

" An' what did pa'son say when he fund it out ? "

Pete Cayce laughed, his big teeth making the facetious demonstration peculiarly pronounced. He was looking out of the window, through the leafy bough of the overspreading chestnut-oak, at the deep, transparent water in the pond. The dark, lustrous reflection of the sassafras and huckleberry bushes on the summit of the vertical rocky bank was like some mezzotinted landscape under glass. A frog on one of the ledges at the waterside was a picture of amphibious content; sometimes his mouth opened and shut quickly, with an expression, if not beautiful, implying satisfaction. Pete lazily caught up a stick which he had been whittling. The slight missile flew through the air, catching the light as it went. Its aim was accurate, and the next moment the monotony of the placid surface was broken by the elastically widening circles above the spot where the frog jumped in.

"The pa'son," he said languidly, having satisfactorily concluded this exploit, — "at fust it looked like the c-critter could n't make it out, — he 'peared toler'ble peaked an' white-faced, but the way he behaved ter the sher'ff 'minds me o' the tales the old men tell 'bout'n Hangin' Maw an' Bloody Feller, an' them t'other wild Injuns that useter aggervate the white folks in the Big Smoky, — proud an' straight, an' lookin' at 'Cajah Green ez ef he war jes' the dirt under his feet. Waal, pa'son 'lowed, calm an' quiet, ez I 'd be skinnin' a deer or suthin,' ez he 'd ruther be obligated ter his own f-folks fur that holp, but ez that could n't be he 'd git bail from others. 'T war n't m-much matter jes' till he could 'pear 'fore the court, fur nuthin' could be easier'n ter prove ez he hed n't rescued Rick Tyler, nor never gin offense agin the law. An' he turned round ez s-s-sure an' quiet ter Pa'son Tobin, who hed kem along ter see what mought be a-doin', an' sez he, 'B-Brother Jake Tobin, you-uns an' some o' the c-church folks, I know, will be 'sponsible fur the bail.' An' ef ye 'll b'lieve me, Brother Jake Tobin, he got up slanch-wise, an' in sech a hurry the cheer fell over ahint him; an' sez he, 'Naw, brother, — I will call ye brother,' — like that war powerful 'commodatin',— ' I kin not sot my p-people ter do sech, arter yer words yestiddy. We kin lose no money by ye, — the church air pore an' the cause air n-needy. I kin only pray fur the devil ter l-loose his holt on ye, f-fur I perceive the devil in ye.' Waal, sir," continued Pete, drawing a plug of tobacco from his pocket, and gnawing on it with tugging persistence, "Christian perfesser ez I be, I felt sorter 'shamed o' Brother J-Jake Tobin, — he looked s-s-sech a skerry h-half-liver, 'feard o' losin' money! Shucks! I could sca'cely keep my hands off'n him. He looked so — so cur'ous, I wanted ter — ter" — he remembered the reverence due to the cloth — "ter trip him up," he concluded, temperately. "An' then, ez he war a-whurlin' his fat sides around ter pick up the cheer, Pa'son K-Kelsey, — he hed t-turned plumb bleached, like a corpse, — he stood up an' sez, ' The Lord hev fursaken me!' An' Brother Jake Tobin humps around, with the cheer in his hand, an' sez, ' Naw, brother, naw, ye hev fursook the Lord!' "

"Waal," said the man on the bag of corn, gazing meditatively at the dusty floor and at a great yellow cur who had ventured within, as a shelter from the midday heat, and lay at ungainly length asleep near the door, "I dunno ez I kin blame Brother Jake Tobin. 'T would hev made a mighty scandal ter keep Pa'son Kelsey in the church, arter what he said agin the faith. We'll hev ter turn him out; an' ez he air ter be turned out, I dunno ez the church members hev enny call ter go on his bond. He air none o' we-uns, nowadays."

"Leastwise none o' 'em war a-goin' t-ter do it," said Pete, quietly. " They air all mindful o' Brother Jake Tobin's longest ear, ez kin hear a call from the church yander in Cade's Cove ev'y time he g-gits mad at 'em. But I tell ye," added Pete, restoring his plug of tobacco to his pocket, and chewing hard on the bit which his strong teeth had wrenched off, " it did 'pear ter me ez they mought hev stretched a p'int when I see the pa'son ridin' off with them two sneakin' off'cers. He hed so nigh los' his senses with the notion he war a-goin' ter be jailed ez they hed ter hold him up in the saddle, else he'd hev been under the beastis's huffs in a minute."

" Why n't you-uns go on his bond ? " asked Amos James, suddenly.

" Who ? " shouted Pete, in stentorian amaze, above the clamor of the old mill.

" You-uns, — the whole Cayce lay-out," reiterated Amos James.

His blood had risen to his face. All the instincts of justice within him revolted at the picture Pete had drawn, coarsely and crudely outlined, but touched with the vivid realities of nature. It was as a scene present before him: the falsely accused man borne away, crushed with shame, while the true criminal looked on with a lax conscience and an impersonal interest, and thriftily saved his observations to recount to his cronies at the mill. Amos James cared naught for the outraged majesty of the law. The rescue of the prisoner from its fierce talons seemed to him, instead, humane and beneficent. His sense of justice was touched only by the manifest cruelty when one man was forced to bear the consequences of another's act.

"You-uns mought hev done ez much," he said, significantly.

"I reckon they would hev 'lowed ez we war n't wuth it," said Pete, quietly ruminant; "the still can't show up."

"Ye never tried it," said Amos.

"Waal, d-dad, he war n't thar, an' I could n't ondertake ter speak fur the rest. An' I ain't beholden no ways ter Pa'son Kelsey. I hev no call ter b-b-bail him ez I knows on. I hev no hand in his bein' arrested an' sech."

"Hev no hand in his bein' arrested!" retorted Amos, scornfully.

Pete was staring stolidly at him, and the other men assumed an intent, inquiring attitude. Amos James felt suddenly that he had gone too far. He had no wish to fasten this stigma upon the Cayces; he had every reason to avoid it. He did not know how far he had been accounted a confidant in the intimacies of the cave when Rick Tyler had found a refuge there. He could not disregard the trust reposed in him. And yet he could not recall his words.

Pete's blank gaze changed to an amazed comprehension. He spoke out bluntly the thought in the other's mind.

"Ye air a-thinkin', Amos Jeemes, ez 't war we-uns ez cut Rick Tyler a-loose o' the sher'ff!" he exclaimed.

Amos, confronted with his own suspicion, listened with a guilty air.

"Ye air surely the b-b-b-biggest f-f-f-fool"— the words seemed very large with these additional consonants — "in the shadder o' the B-b-b-Big S-s-s-sm-Smoky M-m-Mountings!" Pete spread them out with all the magnifying facilities of his infirmity.

"Waal, then," said Amos, crestfallen, "who done it?"

"Why, P-Pa'son Kelsey, I reckon."

XII.

That memorable arrest in the Big Smoky was the last official act of the sheriff, except the surrender of his books and papers and taking his successor's receipt for the prisoners in the county jail. The defeat had its odious aspects. The race had been amazingly unequal. Had the ground tottered beneath him, as he stood in the grass-fringed streets of Shaftesville, and heard the rumors of the returns from the civil districts, he could hardly have experienced a sensation of insecurity commensurate with this, for all his moral supports were threatened. His self-confidence, his arrogant affinity for authority, his pride, and his ambition keenly barbed the prescience of this abnormal flatness of failure. He was pierced by every careless glance; every casual word wounded him. He had a strange disturbing sense of a loss of identity. This anxious, brow-beaten, humiliated creature, — was this Micajah Green? He did not recognize himself; every throb within him had an alien impulse; he repudiated every cringing mental process. It was his first experience of the rigors of adversity; it did not quell him; he felt effaced.

He feebly sought to goad himself to answer the rough chaff of spurious sympathizers with his old bluff spirit; his retort was like the lisp of a child in defiance of the challenge of a bugle. He saw with faltering bewilderment how the interesting spectacle increased his audience; it resembled in some sort an experiment in vivisection, and where the writhings most suggested an appreciated anguish, each curious scientist most longed to thrust the scalpel.

The coroner held the election, as the sheriff himself was a candidate, and when the result became known the details excited increased comment. In the district of the county town he had a majority, but the unanimity against him in the outlying districts, especially in the Big Smoky and its widespread spurs and coves, was unprecedented in the annals of the county. He had hoped that the election of judge and attorney-general, taking place at the same time, might divert attention from the disastrous completeness of his failure. But their race involved no peculiar phase of popular interest, and the more important results were subordinated, so far as the county was concerned, to the spectacle of 'Cajah Green, " flabbergasted an' flustrated like never war seen." New elements of gossip were added now and then, vivaciously canvassed among the knots of men perched on barrels in the stores, or congregated in the post-office, or sitting on the steps of the court-house, and were ruthlessly detailed to the ex-sheriff, whose starts of rage, unthinking relapses into official speech, jerks of convulsive surprise, prolonged the amusement beyond its natural span.

It ceased suddenly. The adjustment to a new line of thought and to a future under altered conditions was facilitated by the inception of an immediate definite intention and a sentiment coequal with the passion of despair. The idlers of the town might not have been able to accurately define the moment when the drama of defeat, with which he had prodigally entertained them, lost its interest. But there was a moment that differed from all the others of the lazy August hours; the minimum of time charged with disproportionate importance. It might be likened to a symbol of chemistry, which, though the simplest alphabetical character, is significant of an essential element involving life, — perhaps death.

That moment the wind came freshly down from the mountains; the glare of the morning sun rested on the empty, sandy street of the village; the weeds and grass that obscured the curbing of the pavement were still overhung by a glittering gossamer net of dew. A yellow butterfly flitted over it, followed by another so like that it could not be distinguished from its aerial counterpart. The fragrance of new-mown hay somewhere in the rural metropolis was sweet on the air. A blue-bottle, inside the window of the store hard by, droned against the glass, and seemed in some sort an echo to the monotonous drawl of a man who had lately been up in the Big Smoky, and who had gleaned fresh points concerning the recent election.

" What did ye ever do ter the Cayces, 'Cajah, or what did Bluff Peake ever do fur 'em ? " he asked, as preliminary to detailing that the Cayces had turned out and pervaded the Great Smoky Mountains, electioneering against the incumbent. " They rid hyar an' they rid thar, — up in the mountings an' down in the coves; an' some do say thar war one o' 'em in ev'y votin'-place in all the mounting deestric's the day the 'lection kem off, jes' a-stiffenin' up the Peake men, an' a-beggin', an' a-prayin', an' a-wraslin' in argymint with them ez hed gin out they war a-goin' ter vote fur you-uns. Bluff Peake say they fairly 'lected him, though he 'lowed 't war n't fur love o' him. I wonder ye done ez well ez ye did, 'Cajah, though ye could n't hev done much wuss, sure enough. All o' 'em war out, from old Groundhog down ter Sol, when they war 'lectioneerin', an' the whiskey ez war drunk round the Settlemint an' sech war 'sprisin'. Some say old Groundhog furnished it free."

The ex-sheriff made no reply. There was a look in his eye that gave his long, lean head, deeply sunken at the temples, less the aspect of that of a whipped hound than it had worn of late. One might have augured that he was a dangerous brute. And after that, the conversation with the recent election as a theme flagged, and died out gradually.

It was only a few days before he had occasion to go up into the Great Smoky Mountains, on matters, he averred, connected with closing unsettled business of the office which he had held. As he jogged along, he moodily watched the distant mountains, growing ever nearer, and engirdled here and there with belts of white mists, above whose shining silver densities sometimes would tower a gigantic "bald," with a suspended, isolated effect, like some wonderful aerial regions unknown to geography, foreign to humanity. The supreme dignity of their presence was familiar to him. Their awful silence, like the unspeakable impressiveness of some overpowering thought, affected him not. The vastness of the earth which they suggested, beneath the immensities of the sky, which leaned upon them, found no responsive largeness in his emotions. Those barren domes of an intense blue, tinged with purple where the bold rocks jutted out, flushed where the yellow sunshine languished to a blush; those heavily wooded slopes below the balds, sombre and rich in green and bronze and all darkling shades, — touched, too, here and there with a vivid crimson where the first fickle sumach flared; those coves in which shadows lurked and vague sentiments of color were abroad in visionary guise, in unexplained softness of grays and hardly realized blues, in dun browns and sedate yellows, vanishing before the plain prose of an approach, — he had reduced all this to a scale of miles, and the splendors of the landscape were not more seemly or suggestive than the colors of a map on the wall. It was a mental scale of miles, for the law decreeing a sufficiency of mile-posts seemed to weaken in the ruggedness of the advance, and when he was fairly among the coves and ravines they disappeared. He pushed his horse rather hard, as the time wore on, but sunset was on the mountains before he came upon the great silent company of dead trees towering above the Settlement in the reddening light, and tracing their undeciphered hieroglyphics across the valley beneath and upon the heights beyond. The ringing vibrations of the anvil were on the air; the measured alternations of the hand-hammer and the sledge resounded in a clear, metallic fugue; the flare from the forge fire streamed through the great door of the blacksmith's shop, giving fluctuating glimpses of the interior, but fainting and fading into impotent artificiality before the gold and scarlet fires ablaze in the western sky.

A wagon, broken down and upheld by a pole in lieu of one of the wheels, stood in front of the blacksmith's shop, and was evidently the reason of Gid Fletcher's industry at this late hour. Its owner loitered aimlessly about; now looking, with the gloat of acquisition, at his purchases stowed away in the wagon, and now nervously at a little barefoot girl whom he had brought with him to behold the metropolitan glories of the Settlement. He occasionally asked her anxious questions. "Ain't you-uns 'most tired out, Euraliny?" he would say; or, "Don't ye feel wore in yer backbone, hevin' ter wait so long?" or, "Hedn't ye better lay down on the blanket in the wagin an' rest yer bones, bein' ez we-uns started 'fore daybreak?" But the sturdy Euralina shook her sun-bonnet, with her head in it, in emphatic negation at every suggestion, and sat upright on the board laid across the rough, springless wagon, looking about her gravely, with a stalwart determination to see all there was in the famed Settlemint; thinking, perhaps, that her backbone would have leisure to humor its ails in the retirement of home. What an ideal traveler Euralina would be under a wider propitiousness of circumstance! And so the anxious parent could only stroll about as before, and contemplate his purchases, and pause at the door of the blacksmith's shop to say, "Ain't you-uns 'most done, Gid?" in a tone of harrowing insistence, for the fortieth time since the blacksmith's services were invoked.

Gid Fletcher looked up with a lowering brow as Micajah Green entered. The shadows of evening were dense in the ill-lighted place; the fluctuations of the forge fire, now flaring, now fading, intensified the idea of gloom. The redhot iron that the blacksmith held on the anvil threw its lurid reflection into his swarthy face and his eyes; his throat was bare; his athletic figure, girded with his leather apron, demonstrated in its poses the picturesqueness of the simple craft; his sleeve was rolled tightly from his huge, corded hammer-arm. His handhammer seemed endowed with some nice discriminating sense as it tapped here and there with an imperative clink, and the great sledge in the striker's hands came crashing down to execute its sharp behests, while the flakes flew from the metal in jets of golden sparks.

A man is never so plastic to virtuous impulses as when he is doing well his chosen work. Labor was ordained to humanity as a curse; surely God repented him of the evil. What blessing has proved so beneficent!

The suggestions entering with the new-comer were at variance with this wholesome industrial mood. They recalled to the blacksmith his baffled avarice, his revenge, and the malice that had influenced his testimony at the committing trial. More than once, of late, while the anvil sang responsive to the hammer's sonorous clangor, and the sparks flew, emblazoning the twilight of the shop with arabesques of golden flakes, and the iron yielded like wax to fire and force, he had a sudden fear that he had not done well. True, he had sworn to nothing which he did not believe, either in the affidavit for the warrant or at the committing trial; but the widely chartered credulity of an angry man! He said to himself in extenuation that he would not have gone so far but for the sheriff.

He was not glad, with these recollections paramount, to see Micajah Green again. Some concession he made, however, to the dictates of hospitality.

"Hy 're, 'Cajah," he said, albeit gruffly, and the monotonous clinking of the hand-hammer and the clanking of the sledge went on as before.

Micajah Green's knowledge of life had not been wide, but there was space to evolve a cynical reflection that, being down in the world now, he must bite the dust, and he attributed this cavalier treatment to the perverse result of the election.

He had acquired something of the manner of bravado, from his recent experience as a defeated candidate, and he swaggered a little as he strolled about the dirt floor of the shop; glancing at the forge fire, slumberously glowing, at the smoky hood above it, at the window opening upon the purpling mountains and the fading west. He even paused, and turned with his foot the clods of the cavity still yawning below the lowest log, where the escaped man had crawled through.

There was an altercation at this moment between the smith and his assistant; for the work was not so satisfactory as when Gid Fletcher's mind was exclusively bent upon it, and his striker officiated also as scapegoat, although that function was not specified as his duty in their agreement. Gid Fletcher had marked with furtive surprise and doubt every movement of the intruder, and this show of interest in the only trace of the escape by which was lost his rich reward roused his ire.

"Even the dogs hev quit that, 'Cajah," he

said, enigmatically, as he caught up the iron for the new skene and thrust it into the fire, while the striker fell to at the bellows. The long sighing burst forth; the fire flared to redness, to a white heat, every vivid coal edged by a fan of yellow shimmer. The blacksmith's fine stalwart figure was thrown backward; his face was lined with sharp white lights; he was looking over his shoulder, and laughing silently, but with a sneer.

"The dogs?" said Micajah Green, amazed. He did not sneer.

"The dogs tuk ter cropin' in an' out'n that thar hole fur five or six days arter Rick Tyler got away," Gid Fletcher explained. "'Peared ter be nosin' round fur him, too. I dunno what notion tuk 'em, but I never would abide 'em in the shop, an' so I jes' kep' that fur 'em," — he nodded at a leather strap hanging on the rod, — "an' larnt 'em ter stay out o' hyar. But even they hev gin it up now."

"I hain't gin it up, though," said Micajah Green, still turning the clods with his foot. "I'll be held responsible by the court fur the escape, I reckon, ef the gran' jury remembers ter indict me fur it, ez negligence. An' ef I kin lay my hands on Rick Tyler yit I'll be mighty glad ter feel of him."

The blacksmith, without changing his attitude, looked hard at his visitor for a moment. Something rang false in the speech. He could not have said what it was, but his moral sense detected it, as his practiced ear might have discovered by the sound a flaw in the metal under his hammer.

"Ye ain't kem up the Big Smoky a-huntin' fur Rick Tyler," he said at length.

"Naw," admitted Micajah Green; "it's jes' 'bout some onsettled business o' the county. But ef I war ter meet up with Rick in the road I would n't pass him by."

He said this with a satirical half laugh, still turning the clods with his foot, the vivid white light illuminating his figure and his face beneath his straw hat. The next moment the sighing bellows was silent, and Gid Fletcher and his striker had the red-hot metal between them on the anvil, and were once more forging that intricate metallic melody, with its singing echoes, that seemed to endow the little log cabin with a pulsing heart, that flowed from its surcharged chamber out into the gray night, to the deeply purple mountains, to the crescent golden moon, to the first few stars pulsating as if in rhythm to the clinking of the hand-hammer and the clanking of the sledge, — forging this, and as its incident the durable skene which should enable Euralina and her parent to leave the Settlement shortly.

"I hopes ter git home 'fore daybreak, Gid," he said, desperately, standing in the door, and looking wistfully at the iron in process of transformation upon the anvil. He turned out again presently, and Micajah Green paused, leaning against the window, and looking doubtfully from time to time at the striker. This was an ungainly, heavy young mountaineer, with a shock of red hair, a thick neck, and unfinished features which seemed not to have been accounted worthy of more careful moulding. There was a look of humble pain in his face when the blacksmith angrily upbraided him. His perceptions were inefficient to accurately distribute blame; he was only receptive, poor fellow! and we all know that in every sense those who can only take, and cannot return, have little to hope from the world. He was evidently not worth fearing; and Micajah Green disregarded him as completely as the presence of the anvil.

"Talkin' 'bout Rick Tyler, did you-uns go sarchin' that night — the dep'ty's party — ter the still they say old man Cayce runs?"

"Naw," — Gid Fletcher paused, his hammer uplifted, the red glow of the iron on his meditative face and eyes; the striker, both hands upholding the poised sledge, waited in the dusky background, — "naw. We met up with Pete

Cayce, an' he 'lowed ez he hed n't seen nor hearn o' Rick Tyler."

" Ef I hed been along I 'd hev sarched the still, too."

The blacksmith stared in astonishment.

" Pete Cayce's say-so war all I wanted," he declared; "an' I hed the two hunderd dollars ez I hed yearned, an' ye hed flunged away, a-hangin' on ter it," he added.

" I hev a mind ter go thar now, whilst I be on the Big Smoky, an' talk ter the old man 'bout'n it," Green said, reflectively. He had drawn out his clasp knife, and was whittling a piece of white oak which he had picked up from the ground. With the energy of his intention the slivers flew.

The blacksmith glanced in furtive surprise at his downcast face, but for a moment said nothing.

Then, " Hain't you-uns hearn how the Cayces turned out agin ye at the 'lection? Ef they did n't defeat ye, they made it an all-fired sight wuss. Ez fur ez I could hear, me and Tobe Grimes war the only men in the Big Smoky ez voted fur ye. I war plumb 'shamed o' it arterward. I hates ter be beat. I 'm thinkin' they ain't a-hankerin' ter see ye down yander at the still."

The defeated candidate's face turned deeply

scarlet pending this recital. But he said with an off-hand air, " I ain't a-keerin' fur that now; that's 'count o' an old grudge the Cayces hold agin me. All I want now is ter kem up with Rick Tyler, ef so be I kin, afore the gran' jury sits again ; an' I hev talked with ev'ybody on the mountings, mighty nigh, 'ceptin' it be the Cayces. Which fork o' the road is it ye take fur the still, — I furgit, — the lef' or the right ? "

Gid Fletcher burst into a sudden laugh, almost as metallic, as inexpressive of any human emotion, as if it had issued from the anvil. His face flushed, not the reflection from the iron, which had cooled, but with his own angry red blood ; his figure, visible in the sullen illumination of the dull forge fire, was tense and motionless.

" Ye never knew, 'Cajah Green ! " he cried. " Ye don't take nare one o' the forks o' the road. Ye ain't a-goin' ter know, nuther, from me. I ain't a-hankerin' ter be fund dead in the road some mornin', with a big bullet in my skullbone, an' nobody ter know how sech happened. Ef ye hev a mind ter spy out the Cayces fur the raiders, ye air on a powerful cold scent; thar ain't nobody on this mounting ez loves lead well enough ter tell whar old Groundhog holds forth. Them ez he wants ter know — knows 'thout bein' told. Ye ain't smart enough, 'Cajah Green, ter match yer meanness!"

It is difficult for a man, without the hope of deceiving, to maintain a deception, and it was with scant verisimilitude that Micajah Green denied the detection of his clumsy ruse, and swore that he only wanted to come up with Rick Tyler. He went through the motions, however, while the blacksmith looked at him with uncovered teeth, and a demonstration that in a man might be described as a smile, but in a wildcat would be called a snarl. The fierce, surprised glare of the eyes added the complement of expression. Now and then he growled indignant interpolations: " Naw ; ye 'lowed ez I 'd tell ye, an' ye 'd tell the raiders, an' then somehow ye 'd hev shifted the blame on me, an' them Cayces — five of 'em an' all thar kin — would hev riddled me with thar bullets till folks would n't hev knowed which war metal an' which war man."

Still Micajah Green maintained his feint of denial, and the blacksmith presently ceased to contradict.

It was Fletcher's privilege to entertain this visitor at the Settlement, and the behests of hospitality could hardly be served without ignoring the disagreement that had arisen between them. Little, however, was said while

the wagon axle and skene were in process of
completion, and then adjusted to the vehicle
by the light of a lantern. Jer'miah came over
from the store, and presided after the manner
of small boys, regarding each phase of the operation with an interest for which a questioner
would have found no corresponding fullness of
information, — a sort of spurious curiosity, satisfying the eye, but having no connection with
the brain. Euralina, who was small for her
sun-bonnet, a grotesque and top-heavy little figure stood in the door of the forge, — also a wide-eyed and impressed spectator. The blacksmith
was a very good illustration of a rural Hercules,
as he riveted his bolts, and lifted the body of
the ponderous vehicle, and went lightly in and
out of the forge. He did his work well and
quickly too, for a mountaineer, and he had the
artisan's satisfaction in his handicraft, as with
his hammer still in his hand, he watched the
slow vehicle creak along the road between the
cornfield and the woods, and disappear gradually from view. The wheels still sounded assertively on the air; the katydids' iteration rose
in vibrant insistence; the long, vague, pervasive sighing of the woods added to the night its
deep melancholy. The golden burnished blade
of the new moon was half sheathed in invisibility behind a dark mountain's summit. The

blacksmith's house was on the elevated slope beyond the forge, and as he turned on his porch and looked back he noted the one salient change in the landscape as seen from the higher level, — above the distant mountain summit the moon showed its glittering length, as if withdrawn from the scabbard. He glanced at it and shut the door.

Micajah Green had the best that the humble log cabin could afford, and no dearth of fair words as a relish to the primitive feast. It was only the next morning, when his foot was in the stirrup, that his host recurred to the theme of the evening before.

"Look-a-hyar, 'Cajah Green, you-uns jes' let old Groundhog Cayce be. Ye ain't a-goin' ter find out whar his still air a-workin', an' ef he war ter hear ez ye hed been 'quirin' 'round 'bout'n it 't would be ez much ez yer life air wuth."

Micajah Green renewed his hollow protestations, discredited as before, and the blacksmith, shading his eyes from the sun with his broad blackened right hand, watched him ride away. Even when he was out of sight Gid Fletcher stood for a time silently looking at the spot where horse and man had disappeared. Then he shook his head, and went into the forge.

"Zeke," he said to his humble striker, " ye

air a fool, an' ye know it. But ye air a smart man ter that loon, fur the hell of it air he dunno he air a loon."

His warnings, nevertheless, had more effect than he realized. They served as a check on Micajah Green's speech with the few men that he met, — all surly enough, however, to repel confidence, were there no other motive to withhold it. He saw in this another confirmation of the Cayces' enmity, and their activity in weakening his hold on the people. He began to think it hard that he should be thus at their mercy; that his office should be wrested from him; that they should impose unexampled indignities of defeat; that he should not dare to raise his hand against them, — nay, his voice, for even the reckless Gid Fletcher had cautions for so much as a word.

Some trifling errand which he had used as a pretext for his journey brought him several miles along the range, and when he was actually starting down the mountain, his vengeance still muzzled, his ingenuity at fault, his courage faltering, all the intention of his journey merged in its subterfuge, he found himself upon the road which led past the Cayces' house, and in many serpentine windings down the long, jagged slopes to the base. Noontide was near. The shadows were short. He heard the bees droning. The far-away mountains were of an exquisite ethereal azure, discrediting the opaque turquoise blue of the sky. The dark wooded coves had a clear distinctness of tone and definiteness of detail, despite the distance. The harmonies of color that filled the landscape culminated in a crimson sumach growing hard by in a corner of a rail fence. The little house was still. The muffled tread of his horse's hoofs in the deep, dry sand did not rouse the sleeping hounds under the porch. The vines clambering to its roof were full of tiny yellow gourds; he could see through the gaps Dorinda's spinning-wheel against the wall. A hazy curl of smoke wreathed upward from the chimney with a deliberate grace in the sunshine. He smelled the warm fragrance of the apples in the orchard at the rear, stretching along the mountain side. The corn that Dorinda had ploughed on the steep slope was high, and waved above the staked and ridered fence. There were wild blue morning-glories among it, the blossoms still open here and there under a sheltering canopy of blades; and there were trumpet flowers too, boldly facing the blazing sun with a beauty as ardent. He looked up at this still picture more than once, as he paused for his horse to drink at the wayside trough, and then he rode on down the mountain, speculating on his baffled mission.

He hardly knew how far he had gone when he heard voices in loud altercation. He could not give immediate attention, for he was in a rocky section of the road, so full of bowlders and outcropping ledges that it was easy to divine that the overseer had a lenient interpretation of the idea of repair. Once his horse fell, and after pulling the animal up, with an oath of irritation, he came, suddenly, turning sharply around a jutting crag, upon another rider and a recalcitrant steed. This rider was a child, carried on the shoulders of a girl of twelve or so, who had a peculiarly wiry and alert appearance, with long legs, a precipitate and bounding action, a tousled mane, the forelock hanging in her wild, excited eyes. He recognized at once the filly-like Miranda Jane, before either caught a glimpse of him, and he heard enough of her remonstrance to acquaint him with Jacob's tyranny in insisting that his unshod steed should keep straight up the rocky "big road," as he ambitiously called it, in lieu of turning aside in the sandy by-ways of a cow-path.

The expedient flashed through Micajah Green's mind in an instant. He drew up his horse. "I'll give ye a lift, bubby," he said; then, with a mighty effort at recollection, "Howdy, Mirandy Jane!" he cried, jubilantly. His success in recalling the name affected him like an inspiration.

The girl had shied off, according to her custom, with a visible tremor, looking at him with big eyes and a quivering nostril, instantly accounting him a raider. As he called her name she stopped, and stared dubiously at him.

"How 's granny," he asked familiarly, "an' D'rindy?"

"She 's well," Miranda Jane returned, lumping them in the singular number.

Had he inquired for the men folks, she would have been alarmed. As it was, she began to be at ease. She could not at once remember him, it was true, but he was evidently a familiar of the family.

"Come, bubby," he said to Jacob, who had been peering over Miranda Jane's head, sharing her doubts, but sturdily repudiating her fears, "I'll gin ye a ride ter the trough."

Jacob held up his arms, he was swung to the pommel, and the *cortége* started, Miranda Jane nimbly following in the rear.

Such simple things Jacob said, elicited by questions the craft of which he could not divine. Where had he been? He and Mirandy Jane had gone with the apples in the wagon, but the wagon had afterward been driven to the mill, and Mirandy Jane had been charged by D'rindy to "tote" him on the way home if he got tired, and Mirandy Jane wanted to tote him in the cow-path, 'mongst the briers. And where did he say he went with the apples? To the cave.

"To the cave!" exclaimed the querist, astonished.

"Over yander on the backbone," returned the guileless Jacob, reinforcing the information with a stubby forefinger, pointing toward the base of the mountain.

And here was the trough. And Miranda Jane and Jacob stood by the roadside to regretfully watch the big gray horse trot slowly away.

XIII.

THERE came a change in the weather. A vagueness fell upon the landscape. The farthest mountains receded into invisibility, and the horizon was marked by an outline of summits hitherto familiar in the middle distance. The sunshine was languid, slumberous. A haze clothed the air in a splendid garb of translucent, gold-tinted folds, and trailing across the dim blue of the ranges invested them with many a dreamy illusion. Athwart the sky were long sweeps of fibrous white clouds presaging rain. Since dawn they were thickening; silent in the intense stillness of the noontide, they gathered and overspread the heavens and quenched the sun, and bereaved the vapors hanging in the ravines of all the poetic glamours of reflection. A rain-crow was huskily cawing on the trough by the roadside where he had perched. Dorinda heard the guttural note, and went out to gather up the fruit spread to dry on boards that were stretched from stone to stone. Dark clouds were rolling up from the west. She paused to see them submerge Chilhowee, its outline stark and hard beneath their turbulent whirl; toward the south their heavy folds broke into sudden commotion, and they were torn into fringes as the rain began to fall. The mist followed and isolated the Great Smoky from all the rest of the world.

And now the little house was as lonely as the ark on Ararat. The mists possessed the universe. They filled the forests and lay upon the corn and hid the " gyarden-spot," and came skulking about the porch, peering through the vines in a ghostly fashion. Presently they sifted through, and whenever the door was opened it showed them lurking there as if wistfully waiting or with some half humanized curiosity. Night stole on, and the ruddy flare of the fire had heightened suggestions of good cheer and comfort, because of these waifs of the rain and the air shivering in chilly guise about the door. The men came to supper and all went again, except Pete. He was ailing, he declared, and betook himself to bed betimes. The house grew quiet. The grandmother nodded over her knitting, with a limp falling of the lower jaw, occasional spasmodic gestures, and an absorbed, unfamiliar expression of countenance. Dorinda in her low chair sat in the glow of the fire. As it rose and fell it cast a warm light or a dreamy shadow on her delicately rounded cheek and her shining eyes. One

disheveled tress of her dense black hair fell over
the red kerchief twisted around her neck. Her
blue homespun dress lay in lustreless folds about
her. The shadowy and rude interior of the
room — the dark brown of the logs of the wall
and the intervening yellow clay daubing; the
great clumsy warping-bars; the pendent peltry
and pop-corn and strings of red pepper swaying
from the rafters; the puncheon floor gilded by
the firelight; the deep yawning chimney with
its heaps of ashes and its pulsating coals —
all formed in the rich colors and soft blending of detail an harmonious setting for her
vivid, definite face, as she settled herself to
work at her evening "stent." Her reel was
before her; the spokes, worn smooth and dark
and glossy by age and use, reflected with polished lustre the glimmer of the fire. She had
a broche in her hand, just taken from the spindle. For the lack of the more modern brocheholder she thrust a stick through the tunnel of
the shuck on which the yarn was wound, placing
the end of it, to hold it steady, in her low shoe;
catching the thread between her deft fingers she
threw it with a fine free gesture over the periphery of the reel. And then the whirling
spokes were only a rayonnant suggestion, so
swiftly they sped round and round in the light
of the fire, and a musical low whir broke forth.

Now and then the reel ticked and told off another cut, and she would bend forward to tie the thread with a practiced, dextrous hand.

The downpour of the rain had a dreary, melancholy persistence, beating upon the roof and splashing from the eaves into the puddles beneath. At intervals a drop fell down the wide chimney and hissed upon the coals.

Suddenly there was another splash, differing in its abrupt energy; a foot had slipped outside and groping hands were laid upon the wall. Dorinda sprang up with a white face and tense muscles. The old woman was suddenly bolt upright in her corner, although not recognizing the sound.

"Hurry 'long, D'rindy," she said, peremptorily, "you-uns ain't goin' ter reel a hank ef ye don't mosey. What ails the gal?" she broke off, her attention attracted to her granddaughter's changed expression.

"Thar's suthin' out o' doors," said Dorinda, in a tremulous whisper. "I hearn 'em step whenst ye war asleep."

"I ain't batted my eye this night," said her grandmother, with the force of conviction. "I ain't slep' a wink. An' ye never hearn nuthin'."

There was a bolder demonstration outside; a foot-fall sounded on the porch and a hand tried the latch.

"Massy on us! Raiders!" shrieked the old woman, rising precipitately, her knitting falling from her lap, the ball of yarn rolling away and the kitten springing after it.

Dorinda ran to the door — perhaps to put up the bar. But with sudden courage she lifted the latch. Outside were the ghostly vapors, white and visible in the light from within. She peered out doubtfully for a moment. A sudden rush of color surged into her face; she made a feint of closing the door and ran back to her work, looking over her shoulder with radiant eyes; she caught up the broche, sticking it deftly in her shoe, seated herself in her low chair, and with her light free gesture led the thread over the reel.

"Massy on us!" shrilled the old woman aghast. "D'rindy, shet the door! Be ye a-lettin' the lawless ones in on us! raiders an' sech, scoutin' 'roun' in the fog — an' nobody hyar but Pete, ez could n't be waked up right handy with nuthin' more wholesome 'n a bullet — a" —

There was a man's figure in the doorway — a slow, hesitating figure, and Rick Tyler, his face grave and dubious, embarrassed by the complicated effort to look at Dorinda and yet seem to ignore her, trod heavily in, and with a soft and circumspect manner closed the door.

"I kem over hyar, Mis' Cayce," he remarked, "ez I 'lowed mebbe the boys war at the still an 'ye felt lonesome, bein' ez it air rainin' right smart, an'" — he hesitated.

"Howdy, Rick — howdy!" she exclaimed, cordially. He had the benefit of her relief in finding the visitor not a raider. "Jes' sot yer bones down hyar by the fire. Airish out o' doors, ain't it? I'm powerful glad ter see ye. D'rindy ain't much company when she air busy, an' the weavin' ain't done yit."

"I 'lowed ez I mought resk comin' up hyar wunst in a while now," he said, with a covert glance at Dorinda. "I ain't keerin' much fur the new sher'ff, 'kase he air a town man, an' don't know me; an' the new constable, he 'lowed over yander ter the store ez he war a off'cer o' the law, an' not a shootin' mark fur folks ez war minded ter hide out; an' Gid Fletcher hev been told ez he'd hev others ter deal with ef he ondertook ter fool along arrestin' me agin. So I hev got no call ter stay ez close in the bresh ez I hev been, though I ain't a-goin' ter furgit these hyar consarns, nuther."

He glanced down at the glimmer of steel in his belt, where Dorinda recognized her father's pistols.

"Bes' be on the safe side," said the old

woman approvingly, her nimble needles quivering in the light. "But law! I useter know a man over yander on Chilhowee Mounting, whar I lived afore I war married, an' he hed killed fower men,—though I b'lieve one o' 'em war a Injun,—an' he hed no call ter aggervate hisself with sher'ffs' nor shootin'-irons, nuther. He walked 'round ez favored an' free ez my old tur-r-key gobbler. Though some said he hed bad dreams. But ez he war a hearty feeder they mought hev kem from the stummick stiddier the heart."

The young man listened with a doubtful mien. He was thrown back at his ease in the splint-bottomed chair. One stalwart leg, the boot reaching over his trousers to the knee, was stretched out to the fire; from the damp sole the steam was starting in the warm air. On his other knee one of the shooting irons in question rested; he held it lightly with one hand. The other hand was thrust into the belt that girded his brown jeans coat. His tawny yellow hair, the ends of a deeper tint, being wet, hung to his coat collar. His hat, from the broad brim of which rain-drops were still trickling, was deposited beneath the chair, and the kitten was investigating it with a dainty, scornful white mitten. He bore the marks of his trials in his sharpened features; his face took on readily a lowering expression, and a touch of anger kindled the smouldering fire in his brown eyes.

"But I hev killed no man," he said, with emphasis. "I hev hurt nobody. Ef I hed, 't wouldn't be no more 'n I oughter do ter g'long with the sher'ff an' leave it ter men. But I ain't done no harm. An' I don't want ter stay in jail, an' be tried, an' kem ter jedgmint, an' sech, an' mebbe hev them buzzardy lawyers fix suthin' on me ennyways."

All through this speech the old woman tried to interrupt.

"Laws-a-massy, Rick," she said at length, "ye hev got mighty tetchy sence ye hev been hid out. I ain't sayin' nuthin' agin you-uns, ez I knows on — nor agin that man that lived on Chilhowee Mounting, nuther. I can't sot myself ter jedge o' him. He war a perfessin' member, an' he hed a powerful gift in 'quirin'; useter raise the chune reg'lar at all the meetin's ez fur back ez I kin remember."

Her interest in the visit was impaired to some degree by this collision; she would have rejoiced to express her mental estimate of Rick as the "headin'-est critter in the kentry," but her hospitable instincts constrained her, and she nobly swallowed her vexation. His presence, however, "hectored" her, and she seized an excuse to absent herself presently, saying that she had to get her clean plaid coat to mend, "bein' ez when it last hung on the clothes-line that thar fresky young hound named Bose stood on his hind legs ter gnaw it, an' actially chawed a piece out'n it, an' I hev ter put a wedge in it afore I kin wear it."

She creaked away into the next room, and as the door shut he turned his eyes for the first time on Dorinda. The fire-light played on the reel, whirling in a lustrous circle before her, on the broche stuck in the rough little shoe, on her arm, uplifted in a graceful curve as she held the thread. Her brilliant eyes were grave and intent; her dense black hair and her dark blue dress heightened the fairness of her face, and the crimson kerchief about her throat was hardly more vivid than the flush on her cheeks.

The knowledge that her embarrassment was greater than his own made him bolder. They sat, however, some time in silence. Then, his heart waxing soft in the coveted domestic atmosphere and the contemplation of the picture before him, he said, gently, —

"They air all agin me, D'rindy."

She forgot herself instantly. She looked full at him with soft melancholy deprecation.

"They don't hender ye none," she said.

"Ye don't sot no store by me nuther, these

days, D'rindy," he went on, with a thrill of elation in his heart belying the doubt and despair in his speech.

The reel ticked and told off another cut. She leaned forward to tie the thread. She could not lift her eyelids now; still he saw the vivid sapphire iris, half eclipsed by the long black lash.

He patted the pistol on his knee.

"Would ye be afeard, D'rindy, ter marry a man ez would hev ter keep his life, and yourn, mebbe, with this pistol? Would ye be afeard ter live in his house along o' him, a hunted critter, — an' set an' sing in his door, when the muzzle of a rifle or the sher'ff's revolver mought peek through the rails of the fence? Would ye be afeard?"

He put the weapon slowly into his belt. "Would ye be afeard?" he reiterated.

The reel stopped. She turned her eyes, dilated with a splendid boldness, full upon him. How they flouted fear!

Such audacity of courage seemed to him gallant in a man; in a woman, expressing faith in his valiance, it was enchanting. He lost his slow decorum. He caught the hand that held the thread. She could not withdraw it from that strong ecstatic clutch, and as she started, protesting, to her feet, he rose too, overturning the reel; and the kitten made merry confusion in the methodical cuts.

"D'rindy," he exclaimed, catching her in his arms, " thar ain't no need ter be afeard! Word kem up the mounting — I got it from Steve Byers — ez when Abednego Tynes war tried he plead guilty, an' axed ter go on the stand an' make a statement. An' he told the truth at last — at last! An' he war sentenced, an' the case war nolle prosequied agin me! An' ye war n't afeard! Ye would hev married me an' resked it. Ye war n't afeard!"

She was tall, and her agitated upturned face was close to his shoulder. He knew it was simply unpardonable, according to the rigid decorums of their code of manners, but the impetuosity of his joy overbore him, and he bent down and kissed her lips.

Dorinda's courage! — it was gone. She looked so frightened and amazed that he relaxed his clasp. "Ye know, D'rindy," he said, apologetically, "I'm fairly out'n my head with joy."

She stood trembling, her hand pressed to her beating heart, her head whirling. And then, he never forgot it, of her own accord she laid her other hand on his breast. "I always believed ye war *good, good, good!*"

And the wild winds whirled around the Great

Smoky, and the world was given over to the clouds and the night, and the rain fell, and the drops splashed with a dreary sound down from the eaves of the house.

They did not hear. How little they heeded. Within, all the atmosphere was suffused by that wonderful irradiation of love, and happiness, and hope that was confidence. The fire might flare if it listed. The shadows might flicker if they would. It seemed to them at the moment each would never see aught, care for aught, save what was expressed in the other's eyes.

The kitten had waxed riotous in the unprecedented opportunities of the reel, still lying with all its tangled yellow yarn upon the floor. As it sprang tigerishly in the air and fell, fixing its predatory claws in another cut, Dorinda looked down with a startled air.

"Granny 'll be axin' mighty p'inted how that thar spun-truck kem ter be twisted so," she said, crestfallen and prescient. "It looks like a hurrah's nest."

"Tell her ez how 't war the cat," said Rick.

Dorinda shook her head dubiously.

"The cat couldn't hev got it ef the reel hed n't been flunged on the floor."

"Let's wind it inter balls, then," suggested Rick, quick at expedients. "She'll never know it war tangled. I'll hold it fur ye."

It was no great hardship for Rick. She lightly slipped the skeins over the wrists that had known sterner shackles. The task required her to sit near him; her face and head were bent toward him as she absorbed herself in the effort to find the end of the thread; sometimes she lifted her eyes and looked radiantly at him. He had not known how beautiful she was, — because he saw her face more closely, he thought, not averted, nor coy, as always before, — or was it embellished by that ineffable joy that filled her heart? Well for them both, perhaps, that those few moments were so happy, — or is it well to remember a supreme felicity, for this is fleeting. Yellow yarn! she was winding threads of gold. How his pulses thrilled at the lightest flying touch of her fleet hands! He looked at her, — into her eyes if he might, — at her round crimson cheek, at her clearly cut chin, at the long lashes, at the black hair drawn back from her brow, where a curling tendril drooped over the temple. And he held the yarn all awry.

It was no first-class job, for this reason and her haste.

"What ails ye ter hustle 'long so, D'rindy?" he asked at last. "Ye ain't so mighty afeard o' yer granny."

"Naw," Dorinda admitted, "but brother

Pete, he be at home ter-night, an' he air toler'-ble fractious ef he sees his chance, an' I don't want him a-laffin' at we-uns; kase I hev hearn him say ez when young folks gits ter windin' yarn tergether 't ain't fur love o' the spun-truck, but jes' fur one another."

Rick laughed a little, slowly. Then growing grave, " Ef ye 'll b'lieve me, Pete told the word yander ter the still ez Amos Jeemes — a mis'able addled aig he be! — 'lowed ter the men at the mill ez he b'lieved ez 't war the Cayces ez rescued me, the day o' the gaynder-pullin', from the sher'ff."

She paused, the bright thread in her motionless hand, her fire-lit face bent upon him.

"Amos Jeemes hed better be keerful how he tries ter fix it on we-uns!" she cried, with the tense vibration of anger, "tellin' the mill an' sech! I hev hearn the boys 'low ez 't war ten year in the pen'tiary fur rescuing a man from the sher'ff, ef it got fund out."

"Pete say ez how he jes' laffed at him an' named him a fool."

"Pete air ekal ter that," she returned, with some sarcasm.

She was deftly winding the yarn once more, the fire showing a deeper thoughtfulness upon her face. Its flicker gave the room a sense of motion; the festoons of scarlet pepper-pods, the long yellow and red strings of pop-corn, the peltry hanging from the rafters, apparently swayed as the light rose and fell; and the warping-bars, with their rainbow of spun-truck stretched from peg to peg, seemed to be dancing a clumsy measure in the corner. The rocking-chair where granny was wont to sit was occupied now by a shadow, and now was visibly vacant.

She looked up into his face with an absorbed unnoting eye. He was pierced by the knowledge that though she saw him, she was thinking of something else.

" Won't the Court let the pa'son go free now, sence they know ye done no crime?" she asked.

" Naw. The pa'son air accused of a rescue, an' whether the man he rescued air convicted or no it air jes' the same ter the law ez agin him. The *rescue* air the thing he hev got ter answer fur."

She dropped her hands in her lap and threw herself back in her chair.

" Ten year in prison!" she exclaimed. Her face was all the tenderest pity; her voice was full of yearning sympathy; she cast her eyes upward with a look that was reverence itself.

" How good he war! I s'pose he knowed ye never done no harm, an' he war willin' ter suffer stiddier you-uns. I never hearn o' sech a man! 'Pears ter me them old prophets don't tech him! I never hearn o' *them* showin' sech love o' God an' thar feller-man. He rescued ye jes' fur that!"

Rick Tyler looked at her for a moment with a kindling eye. He sprang to his feet, throwing the golden skein — it was only yarn after all, a coarse yellow yarn — upon the floor. He strode across the rude hearth and leaned against the mantel-piece, which was as high as his head. The light fell upon his changed face, the weapons in his belt, his long tawny hair, the flashing fire in his eye. He raised his right hand with an importunate gesture.

"D'rindy Cayce, ye air in love with that man!" he said, in a low passionate voice and between his set teeth. "I hev seen it afore — long ago ; but sence ye hev promised ter marry me, ef ye say his name agin, I'll kill him — I'll shoot him through the heart — dead — dead — do ye hear me — *dead!*"

She was shaken by the spectacle of his sudden anger, and she was angered in turn by his jealous rage. There was a dull aching in her heart in the voids left by the ebbing of her ecstatic happiness. This was too precious to lightly let go. She walked over to him and took hold of his right arm, although his hand was toying nervously with his pistol.

" Ye don't b'lieve no sech word, Rick," she said, " deep down in yer heart, ye don't b'lieve it. An' how kin ye grudge me from thinkin' well o' the man, an' feelin' frien'ly, — oh, mighty frien'ly, — when he will hev ter take ten year in the pen'tiary fur givin' ye yer freedom? He rescued ye! An' I'll thank him an' praise him fur it ev'y day I live. My love, ef ye call it love, will foller him fur that all through the prison, an' the bolts an' bars, an' gyards. An' yer pistols can't holp it."

He put her from him with a mechanical gesture and a perplexed brow. He sat down in the chair he had occupied at first; his hat was still under it, one leg was stretched out to the fire, on the other knee his hand rested; he looked exactly as when he first came into the room, but she had a vague idea, as she stood opposite on the hearth, that it was long ago, so much had happened since.

" D'rindy," he said, " he never done it. The pa'son never rescued me."

She stood staring at him in wide-eyed amaze.

He was silent for a moment, and then he broke into a bitter laugh. " I do declar," he said, " it fairly tickles me ter hear o' one man bein' arrested fur rescuin' me, an' another set bein' s'pected o' the same thing, when not one of 'em in all the Big Smoky, not one, lifted a hand ter holp me. Whether the gallus or a life sentence, 't war all the same ter them. Accusin' yer dad an' the boys at the still — shucks! Old Groundhog loant me a rifle, an' ter hear him talk saaft sawder 'bout'n it ter Amos Jeemes ye'd hev thunk he war the author o' my salvation! An' arrest the pa'son! he war a likely one ter rescue a-body! — too 'feard o' Satan! An' ef all they say air true 'bout'n the word he spoke yander at the meetin' 'fore they tuk him off, he hev got cornsider'ble call ter be afeard o' Satan. Naw, sir! he never rescued nuthin' but the gaynder! Nobody holped me! Nobody on the Big Smoky held out a hand! I ain't goin' ter furgit it, nuther!"

She stood looking intently at his face, with its caustic laugh upon it and his eyes full of bitterness. She knew that he secretly upbraided her as well as her people that they had made no move to save him from the clutches of the sheriff. She involuntarily turned her eyes to the gun-rack where the barrel of "Old Betsy" gleamed, and she remembered the mark it bore to commemorate the foregone conclusion of Micajah Green's death. For this she had held her hand. She felt humble and guilty, since she had acted in the interests of peace. And yet that shrewd sense, that true conscience, which coexisted with the idealistic tendencies of her nature, demanded how could she justify herself in asking the sacrifice of ten years of other men's liberty that her lover might escape the consequences of his own act; how could she dare to precipitate a collision with the sheriff, while their grievance was still fresh in their minds? Fortunately she did not lay this train of thought bare before Rick Tyler. Natures like his foster craft in the most pellucid candor.

"How'd ye git away, Rick?" she said instead.

"I won't tell ye," he replied, rudely; "it don't consarn ye ter know." Then suddenly softening, "I take that back, D'rindy. I ain't goin' ter furgit ez ye owned up ye war willin' ter marry me an' live all yer life along with a hunted man in a house that mought be fired over yer head enny time, or a rifle ball whiz in at the winder. I ain't goin' ter furgit that."

Alas! he could not divine how he should remember it!

He fixed his eyes on the fire, as if moodily recalling the scene. She noted that desperate hunted look in his face which it had not worn to-night.

"I war a-settin' thar," he began abruptly, "my feet tied with ropes, and with handcuffs on," — he held his hands together as if manacled; she shuddered a little, — "an' I hearn the hurrahin' an' fuss outside whilst they was all a-rowin' over the gaynder. An' then I hearn a powerful commotion 'mongst the dogs, ez ef they hed started some sorter game or suthin'. An' the fust I knowed thar war a powerful scuttlin' 'round the back o' the blacksmith's shop, an' a rabbit squez in a hole 'twixt the lowes' log an' the groun', — 't warn't bigger 'n a gopher's hole. An' I never thunk nuthin' 'ceptin' them boys outside would be mighty mad ef they knowed thar hounds hed run a rabbit same ez a deer."

Dorinda had sunk into her chair; her hands trembled, her face was pale.

"An' the cur'ous part of it," he continued, now in the full swing of narrative, "war that the hounds would n't gin it up. They jes' kep' a-nosin' an' yappin' roun' that thar little hole. Thar sot the rabbit — she 'minded me o' myself, got in an' could n't git out. Thar war nowhar else fur her ter sneak through. She sot thar ez upright an' trembly ez me; jes' ez skeered, an' jes' about ez little chance. The only dif'fence 'twixt us war I hed a soul, an' that did n't do me enny good, an' the lack o' it did n't do her enny harm; both o' we-uns war more per- tic'lar 'bout keepin' a skin full o' whole bones 'n ennything else. An' then them nosin' hounds began ter scratch an' claw up dirt. Bless yer soul, D'rindy, they hed a hole ez big ez that thar piggin, afore I thunk ennything 'bout'n it. It makes me feel the cold shakes when I 'members ez I mought not hev thunk 'bout'n it till 't war too late. Lord! how slow them hounds seemed! though the rabbit she fund 'em fast enough, I reckon. Ev'y now an' then she 'd hop along this way an' that, an' the hounds would git her scent agin — an' the way they 'd yap! The critter would hop along an' look up at me, — I never will furgit the look in the critter's eyes ez she sot thar an' waited fur the dogs. They war in a hurry an' toler'ble lively, I reckon, but they 'peared ter me ez slow ez ef ev'y one war weighted with a block an' chain. Waal, the hole got bigger an' they yapped louder, an' I got so weak waitin', an' fearin' somebody would hear 'em, an' kem ter see 'bout what they hed got up fur game, an' find that hole, I did n't know how I could bide it. The hole got big enough fur the hounds ter squeeze through, an' hyar they kem bouncin' in. They lept round the shop, an' flopped up agin the door, so that ef thar hed n't been all that fuss outside 'bout takin' the gaynder down, somebody would hev been boun' ter notice it. I hed ter wait fur the dogs ter ketch the rabbit an' shake the life out'n her 'fore I darst move a paig, they kep' up sech a commotion. An' when they hed dragged the critter's little carcass outside an' begun fightin' over it, I got up. I jes' could sheffle along a leetle bit; that eternally cussed scoundrel, Gid Fletcher" — he paused. It was beyond the power of language to express the deep damnation he desired for the blacksmith. His face grew scarlet, the tears started to his angry eyes. How he pitied himself, remembering his hard straits and his cruel indignities! And how she pitied him!

He caught his breath, and went on.

"That black-hearted devil hed tied my feet so close I could sca'cely hobble, an' my hands an' wrists hed all puffed an' swelled up, whar the cords hed been — 't war the sher'ff ez gin me the handcuffs. Waal, I tuk steps 'bout two inches long till I got 'crost the shop ter the hole. Then I jes' flopped down an' croped through. I did n't stan' up outside, though 't war at the back o' the shop an' nobody could see me. Ye know the aidge o' the bluff ain't five feet from the shop; the cliff 's ez sheer ez a wall, but thar's a ledge 'bout twenty feet down. It looked mighty narrer, an' thar war n't no vines ter swing by; but I jes' hed ter think o' them devils on t'other side the shop ter make me willin' ter resk it. Waal, thar war a clump o' sass'fras, — ye know the bark's tough, —

near the aidge. I jes' bruk one o' the shoots ter the root an' turned it down over the aidge o' the bluff an' swung on ter the e-end o' it. Waal, it tore off in my hands, but I did n't fall more 'n a few feet, an' lighted on the ledge. An' I tossed the saplin' away, an' then I walked, — steps 'bout'n two inches long, ef that — ez fur ez the ledge went, cornsider'ble way from the Settlemint, an' 't war two or three hunderd feet ter the bottom, whar I stopped. An' thar war a niche thar whar I could sit an' lay down, sorter. Thar I bided all night. I hearn 'em huntin', an' it made me laff. I knowed they war n't a-goin' ter find me, but I did n't know how I war a-goin' ter git away from thar with them handcuffs on, an' ropes 'roun' my legs; they war knotted so ez I could n't reach 'em fur the irons. I waited all nex' day, though I never hed nuthin' ter eat but some jew-berries ez growed 'mongst the rocks thar. An' the nex' morn'n'," — his eye dilated with triumph, — "the swellin' o' my wrists hed gone down, an' I could draw my hands out'n the handcuffs ez easy ez lyin'."

He held up his hands; they were small for his size, and bore little token of hard work; the wrists were supple.

"An' then," he said, with brisk conclusiveness, "I jes' ontied the ropes 'roun' my feet an' clumb up ter the top o' the mounting by vines an' sech, an' struck inter the laurel, an' never stopped a-travelin' till I got ter Cayce's still."

He drew a long sigh, not unmixed with pleasure. He had a sense of achievement. It gave, perhaps, a certain value to his harsh experience to recount his triumphs to so fair an audience. He was looking at her with a dawning smile in his eyes, and she was silently looking at him. Suddenly she burst into sobs.

"Shucks, D'rindy, it's all over an' done now," he said, appropriating the soft sympathy of her tears.

"An' I'm so glad, Rick; so glad fur that. I'd hev bartered my hope o' heaven fur it," she sobbed. "But I war thinkin' that minit o' the pa'son. They 'rested him in his pulpit, an' they would n't gin him bail, an' they kerried him 'way from the mountings, an' jailed him, an' he'll go ter the pen'tiary, ten year mebbe, fur a crime ez he never done. Ye would n't let him do that ef ye could holp it, would ye, Rick?"

She looked up tearfully at him. His eyes gleamed; his nostrils were quivering; every fibre in him responded to his anger.

"Ef I could, D'rindy Cayce, I'd hev that man chained in the lowest pits o' hell fur all time, so ye mought never see his face agin.

An' ef I could, I'd wipe his mem'ry off'n the face o' the yearth, so ye mought never speak his name."

"Law, Rick, don't!" protested the girl, aghast. "I've seen ye ez jealous o' Amos Jeemes" —

"I don't keer *that* fur Amos Jeemes," he exclaimed, snapping his fingers. "I hev n't seen ye sit an' cry over Amos Jeemes, an' sech cattle, an' say he war like a prophet. I thought ye war thinkin' 'bout *me*, an' — an'" — he paused in mortification.

"D'rindy," he said, suddenly calm, though his eye was excited and quickly glancing, "did ye ax him ef he would do ennything fur me when I war in cust'dy?"

"Naw," said Dorinda, "nobody could do nuthin' fur you-uns, 'kase they'd hev ter resk tharselfs an' run agin the law. But what I want ye ter do fur pa'son air fur jestice. He never done what he war accused of. An' ye *war* along o' Abednego Tynes, though innercent. Law, Rick, ef the murderer would say the word ter set ye free, can't ye do ez much fur the pa'son, ez hev seen so much trouble a'ready?"

"In the name o' Gawd, D'rindy, what air you-uns a-wantin' me ter do?" he asked, in sheer amazement.

She mistook the question for relenting. She caressed his coat sleeve as she stood beside him. All her beauty was overcast; her face was stained with weeping; tears dimmed her eyes, and her pathetic gesture of insistence seemed forlorn. He looked down dubiously at her.

"What I want ye ter do, Rick, fur him, air right, an' law, an' jestice. Nobody could hev done that fur ye, 'cept Abednego Tynes. I want ye ter go ter pa'son's trial fur the rescue, an' gin yer testimony, an' tell the jedge an' jury the tale ye hev tole me — the truth — an' they 'll be obleeged ter acquit."

He flung away in a tumult of rage. It was exhausting to witness how his frequent gusts of passion shook him.

"D'rindy," he thundered, "ye want me ter gin myself up fur the pa'son; ye don't keer nuthin' fur me, so he gits back ter the Big Smoky an' you-uns. I mought be arrested yit on the same indictment; the nolle prosequi don't hender, — it jes' don't set no day fur me ter be tried. An' mebbe Steve Byers hev been foolin' me some. Ye jes' want ter trade me off ter the State fur the pa'son."

"Ye shan't go!" cried the girl. "I did n't know that about the nolle prosequi. Ye shan't go!"

He was mollified for a moment. He noticed

again how pale she was. "Law, D'rindy," he said, "ye fairly wear yerself out with yer tantrums. Why n't ye do like other folks; the pa'son never holped me none, an' I ain't got no call ter holp him."

"Ef ye war ter go afore the squair an' swear 'bout'n the rescue an' sech, an' git him ter write it ter the Court fur the pa'son" —

"The constable o' the deestric' ez hangs 'roun' thar at the jestice's house mought be thar an' arrest me," he said, speciously. "The gov'nor hain't withdrawn that reward yit, ez I knows on."

"Naw," she said, quickly, "I'll make the boys toll the constable down ter the still till ye git through. The jestice air lame, an' ain't able ter arrest ye, an' I'd be thar an' gin ye the wink, ef thar war ennything oncommon ennywhar, or enny men aroun'."

He could hardly refuse. He could not affect fear. He hesitated.

"Ez long ez I thunk he hed rescued ye, I did n't hev no call ter move. But now I know how 't war, I'd fairly die ef he war lef' ter suffer in jail, knowin' he hev done nuthin' agin the law."

Her lip quivered. The tears started to her eyes. The sight of them, shed for another man's sake, excited again the vigilant jealousy in his breast.

"I'll do nuthin' fur Hi Kelsey," he declared. "Ef ye ain't in love with him, ye would be ef he war ter git back ter the Big Smoky. He done nuthin' fur me, an' I hev no call ter do nuthin' fur him."

He looked furiously at her, holding her at arm's length. "Ye hev tole me ye love *me*, an' I expec' ye ter live up ter it. Ye hev promised ter marry me, an' I claim ye fur my wife. Say that man's name another time, an' I'll kill him ef ever he gits in rifle range agin. I'll kill him! I'll kill him!" his right hand was once more mechanically toying with the pistol, while he held her arm with the other, "an' I'll kill ye, too!"

He had gone too far; he had touched the dominant impulse of her nature. Her cheeks were flaring. Her courage blazed in her eyes.

"An' I tell ye, Rick Tyler, that I am not afeard o' ye! An' ef ye let a man suffer fur a word ez ye kin say in safety, an' an act ez ye kin do in ease, ye ain't the Rick Tyler I knowed, — ye air suthin' else. I 'lowed ye war good, but mebbe I hev been cheated in ye, an' ef I hev, I'll gin ye up. I ain't a-goin' ter marry no man ez I can't look up ter, an' say 'he air *good!*' An' ef ye'll meet me a hour 'fore sundown, at the squair's house, ter-morrow evenin', I'll b'lieve in ye, an' I'll marry ye. An' ef ye don't, I won't."

She caught up his hat and gave it to him. Then she opened the door. The white mists stood shivering in the little porch. He turned and looked in angry dismay at her resolute face. But he did not say a word, though he knew her heart yearned for it beneath her inflexible mask. He walked slowly out, and the door closed upon him, and upon the shivering white mists. He paused for a moment, hesitating. He heard nothing within— not even her retreating step. He knew as well as if he had seen her that she was leaning against the door, silently sobbing her heart out.

"D'rindy needs a lesson," he said, sternly. And so he went out into the night.

XIV.

THE rain ceased the next day, but the clouds did not vanish. Their folds, dense, opaque, impalpable, filled the vastness. The landscape was lost in their midst. The horizon had vanished. Distance was annihilated. Only a yard or so of the path was seen by Dorinda, as she plodded along through the white vagueness that had absorbed the familiar world. And yet for all essentials she saw quite enough ; in her ignorant fashion she deduced the moral, that if the few immediate steps before the eye are taken aright, the long lengths of the future will bring you at last where you would wish to be. The reflection sustained her in some sort as she went. She was reluctant to acknowledge it even to herself; but she had a terrible fear that she had imposed a test that Rick would not endure. " Ef he air so powerful jealous ez that, ter not holp another man a leetle bit, when he knows it can't hurt him none, he air jes' selfish, an' nuthin' shorter."

She paused, looking about her mechanically. The few blackberry bushes, almost leafless, stretching out on either hand, were indistinct in the mist, and against the dense vapor they had the meagre effect of a hasty sketch on a white paper. The trees overhung her, she knew, in the invisible heights above; she heard the moisture dripping monotonously from their leaves. It was a dreary sound as it invaded the solemn stillness of the air.

"An' *I* 'm boun' ter try ter holp him, ef I kin. I know too much, sence Rick spoke las' night, ter let me set an' fold my hands in peace. 'Pears like ter me ez that thar air all the diff'ence 'twixt humans an' the beastis, ter holp one another some. An' ef a human won't, 'pears like ter me ez the Lord hev wasted a soul on that critter."

Despite her logic she stood still; her blue eyes were surcharged with shadows as they wistfully turned upward to the sad and sheeted day; her lips were grave and pathetic; her blue dress had gleams of moisture here and there, and a plaid woolen shawl, faded to the faintest hues, was drawn over her dense black hair. She stood and hesitated. She thought of the man she loved, and she thought of the word he denied the man in prison. Poor Dorinda! to hold the scales of Justice unblinded.

"I dunno what ails me ter be 'feard he won't kem!" she said, striving to reassure herself; "an' ennyhow" — she remembered the few immediate steps before her taken aright, and went along down the clouded curtained path that was itself an allegory of the future.

The justice's gate loomed up like fate, — the poor little palings to be the journey's end of hope or despair! A pig, without any appreciation of its subtler significance, had in his frequent wallowings at its base impaired in a measure its stability. He grunted at the sound of a footfall, as if to warn the new-comer that she might step on him. Dorinda took heed of the imperative caution, opened the gate gingerly, and it only grazed his back. He grunted again, whether in meagre surly approval, or reproof that she had come at all, was hardly to be discriminated in his gruff, disaffected tone.

She noticed that the locust leaves, first of all to show the changing season, were yellow on the ground ; a half denuded limb was visible in the haze. There were late red roses, widely a-bloom, by the doorstep of the justice's house, — a large double cabin of hewn logs, with a frame-inclosed passage between the two rooms. There was glass in the windows, for the justice was a man of some means for these parts ; and she saw behind one of the tiny panes his bald polished head and his silver rimmed spectacles gleaming in animated curiosity. He came limping, with the assistance of a heavy cane, to the

"Howdy, D'rindy," he exclaimed, cheerfully, "come in, child. What sort o' weather is this!" In abrupt digression, he looked over her head into the blank vagueness of the world. But for the dim light, it might have suggested the empty inexpressiveness of the periods before the creation, when " the earth was without form and void."

"It air tol'erble airish in the fog," said Dorinda, finding her voice with difficulty.

The room into which she was ushered seemed to her limited experience a handsome apartment. But somehow the passion of covetousness is an untouched spring in the nature of these mountaineers. The idea of ownership did not enter into Dorinda's mind as she gazed at the green plaster parrot that perched in state on the high mantel-piece. She was sensible of its merits as a feature of the domestic landscape at the "jestice's house," precisely as the sight of the distant Chilhowee was company in her lonely errands about the mountain. To be deprived of either would be like a revulsion of nature. She did not grudge the justice his possession, nor did she desire it for herself. She entertained a simple admiration for the image, and always looked to see it on its lofty perch when she first entered the room. There were several books piled beside it, which the justice valued more. There was, too, a little square looking-glass, in which one might behold a distortion of physiognomy. Above all hung a framed picture of General Washington crossing the Delaware. The mantel-piece was to the girl a museum of curiosities. A rag carpet covered the floor; there was a spinning-wheel in the corner; a bed, too, draped with a gay quilt, — a mad disportment of red and yellow patchwork, which was supposed to represent the rising sun, and was considered a triumph of handicraft. The justice's seat was a splint-bottomed chair, which stood near a pine table where ink was always displayed — of a pale green variety — writing-paper, and a pile of books. The table had a drawer which it was difficult to open or shut, and now and then "the squair" engaged in muscular wrestling with it.

He sat down, with a sigh, and drew forth his red bandana handkerchief from the pocket of his brown jeans coat, and polished the top of his head, and stared at Dorinda, much marveling as to her mission. She had not, in her primitive experience, attained to the duplicity of a subterfuge; she declined the invitation to go into the opposite room, where his wife was busy cooking supper, by saying she was waiting for a man whom she expected to meet here to explain something to the justice.

"Is it a weddin', D'rindy?" exclaimed the old fellow, waggishly.

"'T ain't a weddin'," said Dorinda, curtly.

"Ye air foolin' me!" he declared, with a jocose affectation of inspecting his attire. "I hev got another coat I always wears ter marry a couple, an' ye don't want ter gimme a chance ter spruce up, fur fear I'll take the shine off'n the groom. It's a weddin'! Who is the happy man, D'rindy?"

This jesting, as appropriate, according to rural etiquette, to a young and pretty woman as the compliments of the season, seemed a dreary sort of fun to Dorinda, so heavy had her presaging heart become. There was a trifle of sensibility in the old squire, perhaps induced by much meditation in his inactive indoor life, and he recognized something appealing in the girl's face and attitude, as she sat in a low chair before the dull fire that served rather to annul the chilliness of the day than to diffuse a perceptible warmth. The shawl had dropped from her head and loosely encircled her throat; her hand twisted its coarse fringes; she was always turning her face toward the window where only the pallid mists might be seen — the pallid mists and a great glowing crimson rose, that, motionless, touched the pane with its velvet petals. The old justice forbore his jokes, his dignities might serve him better. He entertained Dorinda by telling her how many times he had been elected to office. And he said he would n't count how many times he expected to be, for it was his firm persuasion that " when Gabriel blew that thar old horn o' his'n, he 'd find the squair still a-settin' in jedgment on the Big Smoky." He showed her his books, and told her how the folks at Nashville were constrained by the law of the State to send him one every time they made new laws. And she understood this as a special and personal compliment, and was duly impressed.

Out-doors the still day was dying silently, like the gradual sinking from a comatose state, that is hardly life, to the death it simulates. How did the gathering darkness express itself in that void whiteness of the mists, still visibly white as ever! Night was sifting through them; the room was shadowy; yet still in the glow of the fire she beheld their pallid presence close against the window. And the red rose was shedding its petals! — down dropping, with the richness of summer spent in their fleeting beauty, their fragrance a memory, the place they had embellished, bereft. She did not reflect; she only felt. She saw the rose fade, the sad night steal on apace; the hour had passed, and she knew he would not come. She burst into sudden tears.

The old man, whether it was in curiosity or sympathy, had his questions justified by her self-betrayal, and his craft easily drew the story from her simplicity. He got up suddenly, with an expression of keen interest. She followed his motions dubiously, as he took from the mantel-piece a tallow dip in an old pewter candlestick, and with slow circumspection lighted the sputtering wick. "I want ter look up a p'int o' law, D'rindy," he said, impressively. "Ye jes' set thar an' I'll let ye know d'rec'ly how the law stands."

It seemed to Dorinda a long time that he sat with his book before him on the table, his spectacles gleaming in the light of the tallow dip, close at hand, his lips moving as he slowly read beneath his breath, now and then clutching his big red handkerchief, and polishing off the top of his round head and his wrinkled brow. Twice he was about to close the book. Twice he renewed his search.

And now at last it was small comfort to Dorinda to know that the affidavit would not, in the justice's opinion, have been competent testimony. He called it an *ex parte* statement, and said that unless Rick Tyler's deposition were taken in the regular way, giving due notice to the attorney-general, it could not be admitted, and that in almost all criminal cases witnesses were compelled to testify *viva voce.* Small comfort to Dorinda to know that the effort was worthless from the beginning, and that on it she had staked and lost the dearest values of her life. As he read aloud the prosy, prolix sentences, they were annotated by her sobs.

"Dell-law! D'rindy, 't warn't no good, nohow!" he exclaimed, presently, breaking off with an effort from his reading, for he relished the rotund verbiage, — the large freedom of legal diction impressed him as a privilege, accustomed as he was only to the simple phrasings of his simple neighbors. He could not understand her disappointment. Surely Rick Tyler's defection could not matter, he argued, since the affidavit would have been worthless.

She did not tell him more. All the world was changed to her. Nothing — not her lover himself — could ever make her see it as once it was. She declined the invitation to stay and eat supper, and soon was once more out in the pallid mist and the contending dusk. The scene that she had left was still vivid in her mind, and she looked back once at the lucent yellow square of the lighted window gleaming through the white vapors. The rose-bush showed across the lower panes, and she remembered the melancholy fall of the flower.

Alas, the roses all were dead!

XV.

It was not so dreary in the dark depths of the cavern as in the still white world without; and the constable of the district, one Ephraim Todd, found the flare of the open furnace and the far-reaching lights, red among the glooms, and a perch on an empty barrel, and the warm generosities of the jug, a genial transition. Nevertheless he protested.

" You-uns oughter be plumb 'shamed, Pete," he said, " ter toll me hyar, an' me a off'cer o' the law."

" Ye hev been hyar often afore, the Lord above knows," asseverated Pete, " an' ye needed mighty little tollin'."

" But I warn 't a off'cer o' the law, then," said the constable, wrestling with his official conscience. " An' I hev tuk a oath an' am under bonds. An' hyar I be a-consortin' with law-breakers, an' 't ain't becomin' in a off'cer o' the law."

" Ye ain't tuk no oath, nor entered into no bonds ter keep yer throat ez dry ez a lime-kiln," retorted Pete. " Jes' take a swig at that thar jug an' hand it over hyar, will ye, an' hold yer jaw."

Thus readily the official conscience, never rampant, was pacified. The constable had formerly been, as Pete said, an *habitué* of the place, but since his elevation to office he had made himself scarce, in deference to the promptings of that newly acquired sense of dignity and propriety. Should some chemical process obliterate for a time a leopard's spots, consider the satisfaction of the creature to find himself once more restored to his natural polka-dots; and such was the complacence of the constable, with his artificial conscience evaporated and his heart mottled with its native instincts of good and evil. He was glad to be back in the enjoyment of the affluent hospitalities of the moonshiner's jug.

He was a big, portly fellow, hardly more symmetrical than the barrel upon which he was seated. He had an inexhaustible fund of good humor, and was not even angry when Pete, in sheer contrariety, told him the reason for his enticement to the still. He said he would be glad enough if Rick Tyler could swear out anything that would benefit the parson, and declared that he believed only Micajah Green's malice could have compassed his incarceration.

" 'Cajah inquired o' me whar this place war,

Pete," he said, "a-purtendin' like he hed been hyar wunst. But I jes' tole him 't war ez safe ez a unhatched deedie in a aig — an' I batted my eye, jes' so, an' he shet up purty quick."

The gleam from the furnace door showed Pete's own light gray eyes intently staring at the visitor, but he said nothing and the matter passed.

When the constable's heart was warmed by the brush whiskey he understood the sensation as happiness, and he translated happiness as a religious excitement. He seemed maudlin as he talked about the parson, who, he declared, had led him to grace, and he recited some wonderful stories of religious experience, tending to illustrate his present righteousness and the depths of iniquity from which he had been redeemed. Pete's perversity operated to curtail these. "That's a fac'!" he would heartily assent; "ye useter be one o' the meanes' men on these hyar mountings!" Or "Grace hed a mighty wrastle with Satan in yer soul. I dunno whether he air cast out *yit!*"

The constable — his big owlish head askew — was embarrassed by these manœuvres, and presently the talk drifted to the subject of the parson's spiritual defection. This he considered a mental aberration.

"Hi Kelsey," he said, "war always more or

less teched in the head. I hev noticed — an' ye may sot it down ez a true word — ez ev'y man ez air much smarter 'n other men in some ways, in other ways air foolisher. He mought prophesy one day, an' the nex' ye would n't trest him ter lead a blind goose ter water. He air smarter 'n enny man I ever see — Pa'son Kelsey air. Thar's Brother Jake Tobin ain't got haffen his sense; an' yit nobody can't say ez Brother Jake ain't sensible."

The philosopher upon the barrel, as he made this nice distinction, gazed meditatively into the bed of live coals that flung its red glare on his broad flushed countenance and wide blinking eyes. It revealed the others, too: the old man's hard, lined, wrinkled visage and his stalwart supple frame; Pete, with his long tangled hair, his pipe between his great exposed teeth; Ab, filling the furnace with wood, his ragged beard moved by the hot breath of the fire; the bigboned, callow Sol, with his petulant important face; and Ben, in the dim background tossing the sticks over to Ab from the gigantic woodpile. They fell with a sharp sound, and the cave was full of their multiplied echoes. The men as they talked elevated their voices so as to be heard.

Ab was rising from his kneeling posture. He closed the furnace door, and as it clashed he thought for an instant he was dreaming. In that instant he saw Pete start up suddenly with wild, distended eyes, and with a leveled pistol in his hand. The next moment Ab knew what it meant. A sharp report — and a jet of red light, projected from the muzzle of the weapon, revealed a group of skulking, unfamiliar figures stealthily advancing upon them. The return fire was almost instantaneous, and was followed by multitudinous echoes and a thunderous crash that thrilled every nerve. The darkness was filled with the clamors of pandemonium, for the concussion had dislodged from the roof a huge fragment of rock, weighing doubtless many tons. The revenue raiders lagged for a moment, confused by the overwhelming sound, the clouds of stifling dust, and the eerie aspect of the place. They distinguished a sharp voice presently, crying out some imperative command, and after that there was no more resistance from the moonshiners. They had disappeared as if the earth had swallowed them.

The intruders were at a loss. They could not pursue and capture the men in the dark. If the furnace door were opened they would be targets in the glare for the lurking moonshiners in the glooms beyond. It did not occur to them that the cave had another outlet, until, as the echoes of the fallen fragment grew faint, they heard far away a voice crying out, "Don't leave me!" and the mocking rocks repeating it with their tireless mimicry.

It was the constable. He never forgot that agonized retreat down those unknown black depths. He was hardly able to keep pace with his swifter fellows, falling sometimes, and being clutched to his feet rudely enough, as they pressed on in a close squad; feeling now and then the sudden wing of a bat against his face and interpreting it as the touch of a human pursuer; sometimes despairing, as they scrambled through a long, low, narrow passage, scarcely wide enough for the constable's comfortable fatness. Then it was that fear descended upon him with redoubled force, and he would exclaim in pity of his plight, "An' me a off'cer o' the law!" He impeded their flight incalculably, but to their credit be it said the lighter weights had never a thought of deserting their unfortunate guest despite the danger of capture and the distress of mind induced by the loss of their little "all." The poor constable fitted some of the tube-like passages like the pith in the bark, and as he was at last drawn, pallid, struggling, his garments in shreds, from an aperture of the cave in a dense untrodden jungle of the laurel, he again piteously exclaimed, "An' me a off'cer o' the law!"

There was little leisure, however, to meditate upon his degraded dignity. He followed the example of the moonshiners, and ran off through the laurel as fleetly as a fat man well could.

The raiders showed excellent judgment. They offered no pursuit down those dark and devious underground corridors. Acquiring a sense of security from the echoes growing ever fainter and indicative of lengthening distances, they presently opened the furnace door, and by the aid of the flare cut the tubs and still to pieces, destroyed the worm, demolished the furnace, and captured in triumph sundry kegs and jugs of the illicit whiskey. There was a perfunctory search for the distillers at the log-cabin on the mountain slope. But the officers made haste to be off, for the possibility of rally and recapture is not without parallel facts in the annals of moonshining.

Perhaps the mountain wilds had never sheltered a fiercer spirit than old Groundhog Cayce when he ventured back into his den and stood over the ruins of his scanty fortunes, — the remnants of the still; the furnace, a pile of smoking stones and ashes and embers; the worm in spiral sections; the tubs half burnt, riven in pieces, lying about the ground. The smoke was still dense overhead and the hot stones were sending up clouds of steam. It was as well, perhaps, since the place would never again be free from inspection, that it could not be used as it once was. The great fragment of rock, fallen from the roof, lay in the course of the subterranean stream, and the water, thus dammed, was overflowing its channel and widely spreading a shallow flood all along the familiar ground. It was rising. He made haste to secure the few articles overlooked by the raiders: a rifle, a powder-horn on one of the ledges that served as shelf, a bag of corn, the jovial jug. And for the last time he crept through the narrow portal and left the cavern to the dense darkness, to the floating smoke, to the hissing embers, and the slow rising of the subterranean springs.

For days he nursed his wrath as he sat upon the cabin porch beneath the yellow gourds and the purple blooms of the Jack-bean, and gazed with unseeing eyes at the wide landscape before him. The sky was blue in unparalleled intensity. The great "balds" towered against it in sharp outlines, in definite symmetry, in awful height. The forests were aflame with scarlet boughs. The balsams shed upon the air their perfumes, so pervasive, so tonic, that the lungs breathed health and all the benignities of nature. The horizon seemed to expand, and the exquisite lucidity of the atmosphere revealed vague lines of far away mountains unknown to the limitations of less favored days. In the woods the acorns were dropping, dropping, all the long hours. The yellow sunshine was like a genial enthusiasm, quickening the pulses and firing the blood. The hickory trees seemed dyed in its golden suffusions, and were a lustrous contrast to the sombre pine, or the dappled maple, or the vivid crimson of the black-gum. But the future of the year was a narrowing space; the prospects it had brought were dwarfed in the fulfillment, or were like an empty clutch at the empty air. And winter was afoot; ah, yes, the tenderest things were already dead,— the flowers and the hopes,— and the splendid season cherished in its crimson heart a woeful premonition. And thus the winds, blowing where they listed, sounded with a melancholy cadence; and the burnished yellow sheen was an evanescent light; and the purple haze, vaguely dropping down, had its conclusive intimations in despite that it loitered.

Dorinda, with her hands folded too, sat much of the time in dreary abstraction on the step of the porch, looking down at the yellowed cornfield which she and Rick ploughed on that ecstatic June morning. How long ago it seemed! Sometimes above it, among the brown tassels, there hovered in the air a cluster

of quivering points of light against the blue
mountain opposite, as some colony of gossamer-
winged insects disported themselves in the sunshine. And the crickets were shrilling yet in
the grass. She saw nothing, and it would be
hard to say what she thought. In the brilliancy
of her youthful beauty — a matter of linear
accuracy and delicate chiseling and harmonious
coloring, for nature had been generous to her
— it might seem difficult to descry a likeness
to the wrinkled and weather-beaten features of
her father's lowering face, as he sat in his chair
helplessly brooding upon his destroyed opportunities. But there was a suggestion of inflexi-
bility in both: she had firm lines about her
mouth that were hard in his; the unflinching
clearness of her eyes was a reflection of the unflinching boldness of his. Her expression in
these days was so set, so stern, so hopeless that
one might have said she looked like him. He
beheld his ruined fortunes; she, her bereft heart.

Amos James, one day, as he stood on the
porch, saw this look on her face. She was leaning on her folded arms in the window hard by.
She had spoken to him as absently and with as
mechanical courtesy as the old moonshiner at
the other end of the porch. He came up close
to her. It was a wonderful contrast to the face
she had worn when they talked, that day at the

spring, of Rick Tyler's escape. With the quickened intuition of a lover's heart he divined the connection.

"Ye hain't kep' yer promise, D'rindy," he said, in a low tone.

"What promise?" she demanded, rousing herself and knitting her brows as she looked at him.

"Ye 'lowed ye 'd let me know ef ever ye kem ter think less o' Rick Tyler."

Her eyes, definitely angry, flashed upon him.

"Ye shan't profit by it," she declared.

And so he left her, still leaning in the vine-framed window, the lilac blossoms of the Jackbean drooping until they touched her black hair.

Rick Tyler was dismayed by the result of his jealousy and the strange "lesson" that Dorinda had learned. He found her inflexible. She reminded him sternly of the conditions of her promise and that he had failed. And when he protested that he was jealous because he loved her so, she said she valued no love that for her sake grudged a word, not in generosity, but in simple justice, to liberate an innocent man in the rigors of a terrible doom. And when at this man's very name he was seized with his accustomed impetuous anger, she looked at him with a cool aloof scrutiny that might have expressed a sheer curiosity. It bewildered and tamed him. He had never heard of a Spartan. He only thought of her as immovable, and as infinitely remote from his plane, as the great dome of the mountain. He remembered that she had always softened to his misfortunes, and he talked of how he had suffered. But she said that was all over now, and he had been "mighty lucky." He sought to appeal to her in her own behalf, and reminded her how she had loved him through it all, how she would have married him, despite the fierce pursuit of the law. She had loved him; he would not forget that.

"No," she said, drearily. "I never loved ye. I loved what I thunk ye war. But ye war n't that — nuthin' like it! Ye war suthin' else. I war jes' in love with my own foolishness."

Poor Dorinda! Alas, for the fair ideals! these things are transient.

He went away at last, indignant and amazed. Once he thought of offering to make the affidavit, not cognizant of its fatal defect, and then the conviction took hold upon him that this melancholy was her deep disappointment because she loved the man she sought to aid. And sometimes he could not believe he had lost her heart. And yet when he would go back, her dull indifference to his presence would convince him alike that he was naught to her now and that he had been supplanted.

His contradictions of feeling began to crystallize into a persistent perversity. He took pleasure in denying the story she had told of his escape, and many people hardly knew which version to believe. He congratulated Brother Jake Tobin one evening at the cabin on having turned Hi Kelsey out of the church, and called him a wolf in sheep's clothing. And then for his pains he was obliged to listen to her defense of the absent man; she declared the parson was like one of the prophets, like some man in the Bible. As to that confession he had made in the church, "'t war plain he war out'n his head." Meantime Brother Jake Tobin discreetly bent his attention upon the honey and fried chicken on the supper table, and Rick Tyler fumed in silence.

After the news of the *nolle prosequi* Rick went about the mountain with his former large liberty. His step-brothers were desirous of obliterating his recollection of their avoidance, and made him a present of several head of cattle and some hogs. He lived at home among them, and began to have prospects for the future. He was planning with the younger Cayces to start a new still, for a region is particularly safe for that enterprise immediately after a visit from the revenue officers, their early return being improbable. And he talked about a house-raising while the weather held fine and before snow. " I 'm a-thinkin' 'bout gittin' married, Pete, ter a gal over yander ter the Settlemint," he said, looking for the effect on Dorinda. She was as silent, as stern, as listless as ever. And but for the sheer futility of it he might have fallen to upbraiding her and protesting and complaining as of yore, and repudiated the mythical "gal at the Settlemint."

All the leaves were falling. Crisp and sere, they carpeted the earth and fled before the wind. They seemed in some wise to illumine the slopes as they lay in long yellow vistas under the overhanging black boughs. Many a nest was revealed, — empty, swinging on the bare limb. The mountains near at hand were sad and sombre, the stark denuded forests showing the brown ground among the trees, and great jutting crags, and sterile stretches of outcropping rocks, and fearful abysmal depths of chasms — and streams, too, madly plunging. All the scene was stripped of the garb of foliage, and the illusion of color, and the poetry of the song birds and the flowers. More distant ranges were of a neutral vagueness, and farther still they seemed a nebulous gray under a gray sky. When the sun shone they were blue — a faint, unreal blue, a summer souvenir clinging to the wintry landscape like some youthful trait continued in a joyless age.

For it was November, and the days were drear.

About this time an excited rumor suddenly prevailed that Parson Kelsey had returned to the Great Smoky Mountains. It was widely discredited at first, but proved to be authorized by Gid Fletcher, who was himself just back from Shaftesville, where he had been to testify in the trial for the rescue of Rick Tyler. A story of discomfiture he retailed, and he seemed ill at ease and prone to lay much blame on Rick, whose perverse circulation of diverse accounts of the escape had greatly unnerved him before his journey, and prevented the prosecution from summoning Rick as a witness, if indeed he would have permitted himself to be served with the subpœna. The judge was testy during the trial and charged the jury in favor of the prisoner; after the verdict of acquittal he stated indignantly that there had been practically no evidence against the defendant, and that it was a marked instance of the indifference or ignorance of the committing magistrate and the grand jury that such a case of flagrant malice could get beyond them and into the jurisdiction of the court. Gid Fletcher solaced himself by telling how Green played the fool on the stand when the judge snarled at him, and contradicted himself and cut a " mighty pore figger." " Though ez ter that, the pa'son riz up an' reviled both me an' 'Cajah in open court," said Fletcher. " 'Pears like he hed read the Bible so constant jes' ter l'arn ev'y creepy soundin' curse ez could be called down on the heads o' men. An' somebody said ter the jedge arterward ez he oughter fine pa'son fur contempt o' court. An' the jedge 'lowed he warn 't a statute; he hed some human natur in him, an' he wanted me an' 'Cajah ter hear the truth spoke one time."

The blacksmith declared, too, that he was " fairly afeard o' pa'son " and his fierce threats of revenge, and was glad enough that they were not obliged to make the journey together, for he, having a horse, had ridden, while the parson had been constrained to walk. " I reckon he 's hyar by this time," Fletcher said to Nathan Hoodendin, " but I ain't a-hankerin' ter meet up with him agin. He's more like a wild beastis 'n a man; ter see him cut his blazin' eye aroun' at ye, ye'd 'low ez he'd never hearn o' grace!"

The snow came with Kelsey. One day, when the dull dawn broke, the white flakes were softly falling — silent, mysterious, ghostly invasion of the wild wintry air and the woods. All adown chasms and ravines, unexplored and unknown, the weird palpitating motion animated the wide and desert spaces. The ground was deeply covered; the drifts filled the hollows; they burdened the crests of the jutting crags and found a lodgment in all the fissures of their dark and rugged faces. The white lines on the bare black boughs served to discriminate their sylvan symmetry. Vague solemnities pervaded the silent marshaling of these forces of Nature. The wind held its breath. An austere hush lay upon the chilled world. The perspective had its close limitations and the liberties of vision were annulled. Only the wild things were abroad; but the foot-prints of the rabbit or the deer were freshly filled, and the falling snow seemed to possess the world. When it ceased at last it lay long on the ground, for the cold continued. And the wilderness was sheeted and still.

There were presently visible occasional ruts winding in and out among the trees, marking the course of the road and the progress of some adventurous wagon and ox-team, — sometimes, too, the hoof-prints of a saddle-horse. One might easily judge how few of the mountaineers had ventured out since the beginning of the "cold snap." These marks were most numerous in front of the log-house where Hiram Kelsey and his uncle and the two old men sat around the fire. There was a prevalent curiosity as to how the parson had endured the double humiliation of imprisonment and being cast out of the church. They were hardly prepared for the tempestuous fury which animated him upon the mention of the prosecution and the witnesses' names. But when hesitating inquiries were propounded by those of his visitors disposed to controversy, — seeking to handle his heresies and gauge his infidelity, — he would fall from the ecstasies of rage to a dull despondency.

"I dunno," he would say, looking into the heart of the red fire. "I can't sati'fy my mind. Some things in the Bible air surely set contrariwise. I can't argyfy on 'em. But thar's one thing I kin *feel*— Christ the Lord liveth. An' sometimes that seems doctrine enough. An' mebbe some day I'll find Him."

A thaw came on, checked by a sudden freeze. He thought it as cold as ever one afternoon about sunset as he trudged along the road. He saw a tiny owl, perched in a cedar tree hard by the rail fence. The creature's feathers were ruffled and it looked chill. The atmosphere was of a crystalline clearness. The mountains in the east had dropped the snow from the darkling pines, but above, the towering balds rose in unbroken whiteness, imposed in onyx-like distinctness upon the azure sky. There were vague suggestions of blue and violet and rose on the undulations of the steep snow-covered slopes close at hand. The crags were begirt with icicles, reaching down many feet and brilliant with elusive prismatic glimmers. He heard a sudden crash; a huge scintillating pendant had fallen by its own weight. Chilhowee stood massive and richly purple beyond the snowy valley; above was a long stretch of saffron sky, and in its midst the red sun was going down. He stood to watch its fiery disc slip behind the mountains, and then he turned and pursued his way through the neutral-tinted twilight of the wintry evening.

Old Cayce's log-cabin rose up presently, dark and drear against the high and snowy slopes behind it. The drifts still lay thatch-like on the roof; the eaves were fringed with icicles. The overhanging trees were cased in glittering icy mail. The blackened cornstalks, left standing in the field as is the habit until next spring's ploughing should begin, were writhen and bent, and bore gaunt witness to the devastation of the winter wind. The smoke was curling briskly from the chimney, and as the door opened to his knock, the great fire of hickory and ash, sending up yellow and blue flames all tipped with vivid scarlet, cast a genial flare upon the snowy landscape, slowly darkening without. He experienced a sudden surprise as his eye fell upon old man Cayce, the central figure of the group, having heard stories of the moonshiner's deep depression, consequent upon the disastrous raid, and of the apathy into which he had fallen. They hardly seemed true. He sat erect in his chair, his supple frame alert, his eye intent, every fibre charged with energy, his face deeply flushed. He looked expectant, eager. His stalwart sons sat with him in a semi-circle about the wide warm hearth. All their pipes were freshly alight, for the evening meal was just concluded. They too wore an aspect of repressed excitement.

Kelsey detected it in their abstraction during the formal greetings, and when he was seated among them, ever and anon they shifted uneasily in their chairs, which grated harshly on the puncheon floor. Sometimes there sounded a faint jingling of spurs when they moved their feet on the ill-adjusted stones of the hearth. They had their pistols in their belts and perchance their lives in their hands. His admission was in some sort a confidence, but although he marveled, he said nothing.

The bare and humble furnishing of the room

was very distinct in the rich glow, — the few chairs, the shelves with the cooking utensils, the churn, a chest, the warping-bars, the spinning-wheel; and their simple domestic significance seemed at variance with the stern and silent armed men grouped about the fire.

A vibrant sound — one of the timbers had sprung in the cold. Solomon rose precipitately.

"Nuthin', Sol, nuthin'," said the old man, testily. " 'T ain't nigh time yit."

Nevertheless Sol opened the door. The chill air rushed in. The yellow flames bowed and bent fantastically before it. Outside the gibbous moon hung in the sky, and the light, solemn, ghostly, pervaded with pallid mysteries the snowy vistas of the dense, still woods. The shadow of the black boughs lay in distinct tracery upon the white surface; there was a vague multiplication of effect, and the casual glance could ill distinguish the tree from its semblance. Vacant of illusions was the winding road — silent, and empty, and white, its curve visible from the fire-place through the black rails of the zigzag fence. Hiram Kelsey caught a glimpse, too, of the frosty dilations of a splendid star; then the door closed and Sol came back with jingling spurs to his seat by the fireside.

"Be you-uns sati'fied?" demanded Pete, with a sneer.

Sol, abashed, said nothing, and once more the ominous silence descended, all moodily watching the broad and leaping flames and the pulsating coals beneath.

Somehow the geniality of the fire suggested another bright and dominant presence that was wont in some sort to illumine the room.

"Whar be D'rindy?" asked Kelsey, suddenly.

"Waal — D'rindy," said Ab, the eldest of the sons, evidently withdrawing his mind with an effort, " she hev gone ter Tuckaleechee Cove, ter holp nuss Aunt Jerushy's baby. It's ailin', an' bein' ez it air named arter D'rindy, she sets store by it, an' war powerful tormented ter hear how the critter war tuk in its stummick. She kerried Jacob along, too, 'kase she 'lows she hankers arter him when she's away, an' she makes out ez we-uns cross him in his temper, 'thout she air by ter pertect him. I war willin' 'kase it air peacefuller hyar without Jacob 'n with him — though he air my own son, sech ez he be. An' D'rindy hev pompered him till he air ez prideful ez a tur-r-key gobbler, an' jes' about ez cornsiderate."

"She lef' Mirandy Jane an' me," said Pete, facetiously showing his great teeth.

"Waal," said the old man, speaking with his grave excited eyes still on the fire. " I be toler'ble glad ez D'rindy tuk this time ter leave home fur a few days 'kase she hev been toler'ble ailin' an' droopy. An' t' other day some o' the boys got ter talkin' 'bout'n how sure they be ez 't war 'Cajah Green — dad-burn the critter! — ez gin the revenue hounds the word whar our still war hid. An' D'rindy, she jes' tuk a screamin' fit, an' performed an' kerried on like she war bereft o' reason. An' she got down old Betsy thar " — pointing to a rifle on the rack — " ez Pete hed made her draw a mark on it ter remember 'Cajah Green by, an' his word ez he 'd jail her some day, an' she wanted me an' the boys ter swear on it ez we-uns would never shoot him."

" An' did you-uns swear sech ? " asked Hiram Kelsey, in fierce reprobation. Beneath the broad brim of his hat his eyes were blazing; their large dilated pupils canceled the iris and the idea of color ; they were coals of fire. His shadowed face was set and hard; it bore a presage of disappointment — and yet he was doubtful.

Pete turned and looked keenly at him.

" Waal," said the old man, embarrassed, and in some sort mortified, " D'rindy, ye see, war ailin', an', an' — I never hed but that one darter an' sech a pack o' sons, an it 'pears like she *oughter* be humored — an' " —

" Ye w-wants him shot, hey, pa'son ? " Pete

interrupted his critical study of the unconscious subject.

Kelsey's eyes flashed.

"I pray that the Lord may cut him off," he said.

"Waal, the Lord ain't obleeged ter use a rifle," said Pete, pertinently. "Even we-uns kin find more ways than that."

"The pa'son mought ez well go along an' holp," said Groundhog Cayce.

Kelsey turned his eyes in blank inquiry from the old man to Pete by his side.

"We air a-layin' fur him now," Pete explained.

"He hain't been so delivered over by the Lord ez ter kem agin, arter informin' the raiders, inter the Big Smoky?" Kelsey asked, forgetting himself for the moment, and aghast at the doomed man's peril.

Pete tapped his head triumphantly.

"'T ain't stuffed with cotton wool," he declared. "We let on ter the mounting ez we never knowed who done it. An' we jes' laid low, an' held our tongues betwixt our teeth, when we hearn 'bout'n his 'quirin' round 'bout'n the still, from this'n an' that'n, d'rectly arter the 'lection. We got him beat fur that, jes' 'count o' what he said ter D'rindy, 'kase she would n't g-g-gin her cornsent ter shootin' him, an' got dad set so catawampus, he obeyed her like Jacob would n't fur nuthin'. An' " — with rising emphasis, " th-th-the blamed critter 'lows he lef' no tracks an' ain't been fund out yit! An' hyar he be on the Big Smoky agin, a-finishin' up some onsettled business with his old office. I seen him yander ter the Settlemint, an' talked with him frien'ly an' familiar, along o' Gid Fletcher, an' fund out when he war ter start down ter Eskaqua Cove, ter bide all night at Tobe Grimes's house."

"But — but — ef they never tole him, — surely none o' 'em told him " — argued Kelsey, breathlessly.

Pete showed his long teeth. "Somebody tole him," he said, with a fierce smile. "H-h-he could n't git the mounting ter t-t-turn agin we-uns; they war *afeard!*" cynically discriminating the motive. "So he kem nosin' roun' 'mongst our c-c-chillen — the little chillen, ez did n't know what they war a-tellin', an' Jacob tole him whar the cave war, an' 'bout haulin' the apples fur pomace. Jacob war the man, fur Mirandy Jane hearn him say it. She hed seen 'Cajah Green afore, when he war sher'ff."

It was a palpable instance of bad faith and imposition, and it tallied well with Hiram Kelsey's own wrongs. He sat brooding upon them, and looking at the fire with dulled meditative eyes. One of the logs, burnt in twain, broke with a crash under the burden of the others, and the fire, quickening about them, sent up myriads of sparks attendant upon the freshening flames; among the pulsating red coals there were dazzling straw-tinted gleams, and a vista of white heat that repelled the eye. Outside the wind was rising — its voice hollow, keen, and shrill as it swept over the icy chasms; the trees were crashing their bare boughs together. It was a dreary sound. From far away came the piercing howl of some prowling hungry wolf, familiar enough to the ears that heard it, but its ravening intimations curdled the blood. A cock's crow presently smote the air, clear and resonant as a bugle, and with a curse on tardiness the impatient Sol once more rose and opened the door to look out.

A change was impending. Clouds had come with the wind, from the west to meet the moon. Though tipped with the glint of silver, the black portent was not disguised. Rain or snow, it mattered not which. The young mountaineer held the door open to show the darkening sky and the glittering earth, and looked over his shoulder with a triumphant glance.

"That will settle the footprints," he said.

There was something so cruel in his face, so

deadly in his eye, a ferocious satisfaction in the promised security so like the savage joy of a skulking beast, that it roused a normal impulse in the breast of the man who read the thoughts of his fellow-men like an open book. Kelsey was himself again.

He raised his hand suddenly, with an imperative gesture.

"Listen ter me!" he said, with that enthusiasm kindling in his eyes which they honored sometimes as the light of religion, and sometimes reviled as frenzy. "Ye'll repent o' yer deeds this night! An' the jedgmint o' the Lord will foller ye! Yer father's gray hairs will go down in sorrow ter the grave, but his mind will die before his body. An' some o' you-uns will languish in jail, an' know the despair o' the bars. An' he that is bravest 'mongst ye will mark how his shadder dogs him. An' ye will strike yer hands tergether, an' say, 'That the day hed never dawned, that the night hed never kem fur we-uns!' An' ye'll wisht ye hed died afore! An' but for the coward in the blood, ye would take yer own life then! An' ye'll look at the grave before ye, an' hope ez it all ends thar!"

His eye blazed. He had risen to his feet in the intensity of his fervor. And whether it was religion or whether it was lunacy, it transfigured him.

They had all quailed before him, half overborne by the strength of his emotion, and half in deprecation, because of their faith in his mysterious foreknowledge. But as he turned, pushed back his chair, and hastily started toward the door, they lost the impression. Pete first recovered himself.

"Wh-wh-whar be you-uns a-goin'?" he demanded, roughly.

The parson turned fiercely. He thrust out his hand with a gesture of repudiation, and once more he lifted the latch.

"Naw, ye ain't g-g-goin'," said Pete, with cool decision, throwing himself against the door. "Ye hev sot 'mongst we-uns an' h-hearn our plans. Ye 'peared ter gin yer cornsent w-when dad said ye could go 'long. Dad thought ye'd like ter hev a s-sheer in payin' yer own grudge. We hev tole ye what we hev tole no other livin' man. An' now ye hev got ter hev our reason ter h-h-hold yer jaw. I don't like ter s-shoot a man down under our own roof ez kem hyar frien'ly, but ef ye fools with that thar latch agin, I reckon I'll be obleeged ter do it."

If Pete Cayce had possessed an acute discrimination in the reading of faces, he might have interpreted Kelsey's look as a pondering dismay; the choice offered him was to do murder or to die! As it was, Pete only noted the relinquishment of the parson's design when he sat down silent and abstracted before the fire.

But for his deep grudge, it might have seemed that Kelsey had intended to forewarn Micajah Green of the danger in the path, and to turn him back. Pete did not feel entirely reassured until after he had said, —

"I 'lowed ez ye s-s-swore ye fairly *de*-spise 'Cajah G-G-Green, an' r-raged ter git even with him."

"I furgits it sometimes," rejoined Kelsey.

And Pete did not apprehend the full meaning of the words.

"An' don't do no more o' yer prophesyin' ternight, Hiram," said the old man, irritably. "It fairly gins me the ager ter hear sech talk."

The night wore on. The fire roared; the men, intently listening sat around the hearth. Now and then a furtive glance was cast at Hiram Kelsey. He seemed lost in thought, but his eye glittered with that uninterpreted, inscrutable light, and they were vaguely sorry that he had come among them. They took scant heed of his reproach. It has been so long the unwritten law of moonshiners that the informer shall perish as the consequence of his malice and his rashness, that whatever normal moral sense they possess is in subjection to their arbitrary code of justice and the savage custom of the region. The mysterious disappearance of a horse-thief or a revenue spy, dramatically chronicled, with a wink and a significant grin, as "never hearn on no more," or, " fund dead in the road one mornin'," affects the mountaineers much as the hangman's summary in the Friday evening papers impresses more law-abiding communities — shocking, but necessary.

The great fire was burnt to a mass of coals. The wind filled the ravines with a tumult of sound. The bare woods were in wild commotion. The gusts dashed upon the roof snow perhaps, or sleet, or vague drizzling rain ; now discontinued, now coming again with redoubled force. Suddenly, a growl from the dogs under the house ; then the sound of a crunching hoof in the snow.

The men sallied forth, swift and silent as shadows. There was a frantic struggle in the road ; a wild cry for help ; a pistol fired wide of the mark, the report echoing in the silence from crag to crag, from chasm to chasm with clamorous iteration, as if it would alarm the world. The horses were ready. The men hastily threw themselves into the saddle.

It had been arranged that Kelsey, who had no horse, should ride before the prisoner. He mounted, drew about his own waist the girth which bound the doomed man, buckling it securely, and the great gray horse was in the centre of the squad.

Micajah Green begged as they went — begged as only a man can for his life. He denied, he explained, he promised.

"Ye cotton ter puttin' folks in jail, 'Cajah! Yer turn now! We'll put ye whar the dogs won't bite ye," said the old man, savagely. And the rest said never a word.

The skies were dark, the mountain wilds awful in their immensity, in their deep obscurities, in the multitudinous sounds of creaking boughs and shrilling winds.

They were in the dense laurel at last. The branches, barbed with ice, and the evergreen leaves, burdened with snow, struck sharply in their faces as they forced their way through. The swift motion had chilled them; icicles clung to their hair and beard; each could hardly see the dark figures of the others in the dense umbrageous undergrowth as they recognized the spot they sought and called a halt. It was the mouth of the cave; they could hear the sound of the dark cold water as it rippled in the vaulted place where the dammed current rose now half-way to the roof. Their wretched prisoner, understanding this fact and the savage substitute for the rifle, made a despairing struggle.

"Lemme git a holt of him, Hi," said Pete, his teeth chattering, his numbed arms stretched up in the darkness to lay hold on his victim.

"Hyar he be," gasped the parson.

There was another frantic struggle as they tore the doomed man from the horse; a splash, a muffled cry — he was cast headlong into the black water. A push upon a great bowlder hard by — it fell upon the cavity with a crash, and all hope of egress was barred. Then, terrorized themselves, the men mounted their horses; each, fleeing as if from pursuit, found his way as best he might out of the dark wilderness.

One might not know what they felt that night when the rain came down on the roof. One might not dare to think what they dreamed.

The morning broke, drear, and clouded, and full of rain, and hardly less gloomy than the night. The snow, tarnished, and honeycombed with dark cellular perforations, was melting and slipping down and down the ravines. The gigantic icicles encircling the crags fell now and then with a resounding crash. The drops from the eaves dripped monotonously into the puddles below. The roof leaked. Sol's bridle-hand had been frozen the night before in the long swift ride.

But the sun came out again; the far mountains smiled in a blue vagueness that was almost a summer garb. The relics of the snow exhaled a silvery haze that hung airily about the landscape. Only the immaculate whiteness of those lofty regions of the balds withstood the thaw, and coldly glittered in wintry guise.

A strange sensation thrilled through the fireside group one of these mornings when Amos James came up from the mill, and as he smoked with them asked suddenly, all unaware of the tragedy, " What ailed 'Cajah Green ter leave the Big Smoky in sech a hurry ? "

" Wh-wh-at d'ye mean ? " growled Pete, in startled amaze.

And then Amos James, still unconscious of the significance of the recital, proceeded to tell that shortly after daybreak on last Wednesday morning he heard a " powerful jouncin' of huffs," and looking out of the window he saw Micajah Green on his big gray horse, flying along the valley road at a tremendous rate of speed. Before he could open the window to hail him, man and horse were out of sight.

It was a silent group that Amos left, all meditating upon that swift equestrian figure, pictured against the dreariness of the rainy dawn, and the gray mist, and the shadowing mountains.

"Amos seen a ghost," said Pete, presently. He looked dubiously over his shoulder, though the morning sunshine came flickering through the door, widely ajar.

"That ain't nuthin' oncommon," said the old man, sturdily. Then he told a ghastly story of a legal execution, — that the criminal was seen afterward sitting in the moonlight under the gallows on his coffin-lid; and other fearful fantasies of the rural mind, which, morbidly excited, will not accept the end of the rope as a finality.

It was only when Obediah Scruggs came to their house searching for his nephew, saying that Hiram had not been seen nor heard of since he had set out one evening to visit them, that a terrible premonition fell upon Groundhog Cayce. His iron will guarded it for a time, till some one journeying from Shaftesville reported having seen there Micajah Green, who was full of a terrible story of a midnight attack upon him by the Cayce tribe, from whom he had miraculously escaped in the midst of the struggle and darkness, he declared, and more dead than alive. Then mysteriously and with heavy presage Pete and his father made a pilgrimage to the cave. They pried up the bowlder over the cavity. They heard the deep water held in the subterranean reservoir still sighing and echoing with the bubbling of the mountain spring. On the surface there floated a hat — Hi Kelsey's limp and worn old hat.

They never told their secret. They replaced the bowlder, and sealed their lips. The old man began to age rapidly. His conscience was heavier than his years. But it was a backwoods conscience, and had the distortions of his primitive philosophy. One day he said piteously, "It air a dreadful thing, Pete, ter kill a man by accident."

And Pete replied meditatively, "I dunno but what it air."

By degrees, as they reflected upon the incredible idea that a mistake could have been made between the two men, the truth percolated through their minds. It was a voluntary sacrifice. "He war always preachin' agin killin'," said the old man, "an' callin' folks," his voice fell to a whisper — "Cain!"

It was well for him, perhaps, when he presently fell into mental decrepitude, and in vacancy was spared the anguish of remorse.

And Pete fearfully noted the fulfillment of the prophecy.

No one could account for the change in Pete Cayce. He patched up old feuds, and forgave old debts, and forgot his contentious moods, and was meek and very melancholy. And although the parson preached no more, who shall say his sermons were ended? As to him, surely his doubts were solved in knowing all, and perhaps in the exaltations of that sacrificial moment he found Christ.

The mystery of his fate remained unexplained. The search for him flagged after a time, and failed. There were many conjectures, all wide of the truth. Dorinda believed that, like the prophet of old, he had not been suffered to taste death, but was caught up into the clouds. And with a chastened solemnity she cherishes the last of her illusions.

Works of Fiction

PUBLISHED BY

HOUGHTON, MIFFLIN AND COMPANY,

4 PARK ST., BOSTON; 11 E. 17TH ST., NEW YORK.

Thomas Bailey Aldrich.

Story of a Bad Boy. Illustrated. 12mo $1.50
Marjorie Daw and Other People. 12mo 1.50
The Same. Riverside Aldine Series. 16mo . . . 1.00
Prudence Palfrey. 12mo 1.50
The Queen of Sheba. 12mo 1.50
The Stillwater Tragedy. 12mo 1.50

Hans Christian Andersen.

Complete Works. In ten uniform volumes, crown 8vo.
The Improvisatore; or, Life in Italy 1.50
The Two Baronesses 1.50
O. T.; or, Life in Denmark 1.50
Only a Fiddler 1.50
In Spain and Portugal 1.50
A Poet's Bazaar 1.50
Pictures of Travel 1.50
The Story of my Life. With portrait 1.50
Wonder Stories told for Children. Illustrated . . 1.50
Stories and Tales. Illustrated 1.50
    The set 15.00
A new and cheap Edition, in attractive binding. Sold
    only in sets 10.00

William Henry Bishop.

Detmold: A Romance. "Little Classic" style. 18mo 1.25
The House of a Merchant Prince. 12mo 1.50
Choy Susan, and other Stories. 16mo 1.25

Works of Fiction Published by

Björnstjerne Björnson.
Works. *American Edition*, sanctioned by the author, and translated by Professor R. B. Anderson, of the University of Wisconsin. In seven volumes, 16mo.

Synnöve Solbakken.
Arne.
A Happy Boy.
The Fisher Maiden.
The Bridal March, and Other Stories.
Captain Mansana, and Other Stories.
Magnhild.

Each volume $1.00
The Same. In three volumes, 12mo 4.50

Alice Cary.
Pictures of Country Life. 12mo 1.50

John Esten Cooke.
My Lady Pokahontas. 16mo 1.25

James Fenimore Cooper.
Complete Works. New *Household Edition*, in attractive binding. With Introductions to many of the volumes by Susan Fenimore Cooper, and Illustrations. In thirty-two volumes, 16mo.

Precaution.	The Prairie.
The Spy.	Wept of Wish-ton-Wish.
The Pioneers.	The Water Witch.
The Pilot.	The Bravo.
Lionel Lincoln.	The Heidenmauer.
Last of the Mohicans.	The Headsman.
Red Rover.	The Monikins.
Homeward Bound.	Miles Wallingford.
Home as Found.	The Red Skins.
The Pathfinder.	The Chainbearer.
Mercedes of Castile.	Satanstoe.
The Deerslayer.	The Crater.
The Two Admirals.	Jack Tier.
Wing and Wing.	The Sea Lions.
Wyandotté.	Oak Openings.
Afloat and Ashore.	The Ways of the Hour.

(*Each volume sold separately.*)

Each volume 1.00
The set 32.00
Half calf 80.00

New Fireside Edition. With forty-five original Illustrations by Darley, Dielman, Fredericks, Sheppard, and Waud. In sixteen volumes, 12mo.
 The set $20.00
 Half calf 45.00
   (*Sold only in sets.*)

Sea Tales. New *Household Edition*, in attractive binding, the volumes containing Introductions by Susan Fenimore Cooper. Illustrated.
First Series. Including —
The Pilot.	The Red Rover.
The Water Witch.	The Two Admirals.
Wing and Wing.	

Second Series. Including —
The Sea Lions.	Afloat and Ashore.
Jack Tier.	Miles Wallingford.
The Crater.	

 Each set, 5 vols. 16mo 5.00
 Half calf 12.50
Leather-Stocking Tales. New *Household Edition*, in attractive binding, the volumes containing Introductions by Susan Fenimore Cooper. Illustrated. In five volumes, 16mo.
The Deerslayer.	The Pioneers.
The Pathfinder.	The Prairie.
Last of the Mohicans.	

 The set 5.00
 Half calf 12.50
Cooper Stories; being Narratives of Adventure selected from his Works. With Illustrations by F. O. C. Darley. In three volumes, 16mo, each 1.00

Charles Egbert Craddock.

In the Tennessee Mountains. 16mo 1.25
The Prophet of the Great Smoky Mountains. 16mo . 1.25
Down the Ravine. A Story for Young People. Illustrated. 16mo 1.00

F. Marion Crawford.

To Leeward. 16mo 1.25
A Roman Singer. 16mo 1.25
An American Politician. 16mo 1.25

Maria S. Cummins.

The Lamplighter. 12mo 1.50
El Fureidîs. 12mo 1.50
Mabel Vaughan. 12mo 1.50

Works of Fiction Published by

Daniel De Foe.
Robinson Crusoe. Illustrations by Thomas Nast and
E. Bayard. 16mo $1.00

P. Deming.
Adirondack Stories. "Little Classic" style. 18mo . .75
Tompkins and other Folks 1.00

Thomas De Quincey.
Romances and Extravaganzas. *Riverside Edition.*
12mo 1.50
Narrative and Miscellaneous Papers. *Riverside Edition.* 12mo 1.50

Charles Dickens.
Complete Works. *Illustrated Library Edition.* With Introductions, biographical and historical, by E. P. Whipple. Containing all the Illustrations that have appeared in the English edition by Cruikshank, Phiz, Seymour, John Leech, Maclise, Marcus Stone, and others, engraved on steel, to which are added the designs of F. O. C. Darley and John Gilbert, in all numbering over 550. Handsomely bound, and complete in twenty-nine volumes, 12mo.

The Pickwick Papers, 2 vols. Dombey and Son, 2 vols.
Nicholas Nickleby, 2 vols. Pictures from Italy, and
Oliver Twist. American Notes.
Old Curiosity Shop, and Reprinted Pieces, 2 vols. Bleak House, 2 vols.
  Little Dorrit, 2 vols.
Barnaby Rudge, and Hard Times, 2 vols. David Copperfield, 2 vols.
  A Tale of Two Cities.
Martin Chuzzlewit, 2 vols. Great Expectations.
Our Mutual Friend, 2 vols. Edwin Drood, Master
Uncommercial Traveller. Humphrey's Clock, and
A Child's History of England, and Other Pieces. Other Pieces.
  Sketches by Boz.
Christmas Books.

Each volume 1.50
The set. With Dickens Dictionary. 30 vols . . 45.00
Half calf 100.00

Globe Edition. Printed in large type (long primer) on good paper, and containing all the Illustrations of Darley and Gilbert (55 in number) on steel, and the Index of Characters. In fifteen volumes, 12mo.
Each volume 1.25
The set 18.75
Half calf, or half morocco 40.00

Christmas Carol. Illustrated. 8vo, full gilt $3.00
 Morocco 7.00
The Same. 32mo 75
Christmas Books. Illustrated. 12mo 2.00
 Morocco 5.00

Edgar Fawcett.
A Hopeless Case. "Little Classic" style. 18mo . 1.25
A Gentleman of Leisure. "Little Classic" style. 18mo 1.00
An Ambitious Woman. 12mo 1.50

Fénelon.
Adventures of Telemachus. 12mo 2.25

Harford Flemming.
A Carpet Knight. 16mo 1.25

Baron de la Motte Fouqué.
Undine, Sintram and his Companions, with St. Pierre's
"Paul and Virginia," 32mo 75
Undine and other Tales. Illustrated. "Riverside
Classics." 16mo 1.00

Johann Wolfgang von Goethe.
Wilhelm Meister. Translated by Thomas Carlyle.
Portrait of Goethe. In two volumes. 12mo . . 3.00
The Tale and Favorite Poems. 32mo 75

Oliver Goldsmith.
Vicar of Wakefield. *Handy-Volume Edition.* 32mo,
 gilt top 1.25
The Same. "Riverside Classics." Illustrated. 16mo 1.00

Jeanie T. Gould (Mrs. Lincoln).
Marjorie's Quest. Illustrated. 12mo 1.50

Thomas Chandler Haliburton.
The Clockmaker; or, The Sayings and Doings of
Samuel Slick of Slickville. "Riverside Classics."
Illustrated by Darley. 16mo 1.00

A. S. Hardy.
But Yet a Woman. 16mo 1.25

Miriam Coles Harris.
Rutledge.   A Perfect Adonis.
The Sutherlands.   Missy.
Frank Warrington.   Happy-Go-Lucky.
St. Philips.   Phœbe.
Richard Vandermarck.
Each volume, 12mo 1.25

Works of Fiction Published by

Bret Harte.

The Luck of Roaring Camp, and Other Sketches. 16mo $1.50
The Same. Riverside Aldine Series. 16mo . . . 1.00
Condensed Novels. Illustrated. 16mo 1.50
Mrs. Skaggs's Husbands, and Other Sketches. 16mo. 1.50
Tales of the Argonauts, and Other Stories. 16mo . 1.50
Thankful Blossom. "Little Classic" style. 18mo . 1.25
Two Men of Sandy Bar. A Play. "Little Classic" style. 18mo 1.00
The Story of a Mine. "Little Classic" style. 18mo 1.00
Drift from Two Shores. "Little Classic" style. 18mo 1.25
The Twins of Table Mountain, and Other Sketches. "Little Classic" style. 18mo. 1.25
Works. Rearranged, with an Introduction and a Portrait. In five volumes, crown 8vo.
Poetical Works, and the drama, "Two Men of Sandy Bar," with an Introduction and Portrait.
The Luck of Roaring Camp, and Other Stories.
Tales of the Argonauts and Eastern Sketches.
Gabriel Conroy.
Stories and Condensed Novels.

    Each volume 2.00
    The set 10.00
    Half calf 20.00

Flip, and Found at Blazing Star. "Little Classic" style. 18mo 1.00
In the Carquinez Woods. "Little Classic" style. 18mo 1.00
On the Frontier. "Little Classic" style. 18mo . . 1.00
By Shore and Sedge. "Little Classic style." 18mo. 1.00
Maruja. A Novel. "Little Classic" Style. 18mo. 1.00

Nathaniel Hawthorne.

Works. *New Riverside Edition*. With an original etching in each volume, and a new Portrait. With bibliographical notes by George P. Lathrop. Complete in twelve volumes, crown 8vo.
Twice-Told Tales.
Mosses from an Old Manse.
The House of the Seven Gables, and the Snow-Image.
The Wonder-Book, Tanglewood Tales, and Grandfather's Chair.
The Scarlet Letter, and The Blithedale Romance.
The Marble Faun.
Our Old Home, and English Note-Books. 2 vols.
American Note-Books.
French and Italian Note-Books.

Houghton, Mifflin and Company. 7

The Dolliver Romance, Fanshawe, Septimius Felton, and, in an Appendix, the Ancestral Footstep. Tales, Sketches, and Other Papers. With Biographical Sketch by G. P. Lathrop, and Indexes.
- Each volume $2.00
- The set 24.00
- Half calf 48.00
- Half crushed levant 60.00

"*Little Classic*" *Edition.* Each volume contains a new Vignette Illustration. In twenty-five volumes, 18mo.
- Each volume 1.00
- The set 25.00
- Half calf, or half morocco 62.50
- Tree calf 81.00

A Wonder-Book for Girls and Boys. *Holiday Edition.* With Illustrations by F. S. Church. 4to . . 2.50

Twice-Told Tales. *School Edition.* 18mo 1.00

The Scarlet Letter. *Holiday Edition.* Illustrated by Mary Hallock Foote. Red-line border. 8vo, full gilt 4.00
- Half calf 6.00
- Morocco, or tree calf 9.00

Popular Edition. 12mo 1.00
True Stories from History and Biography. 12mo . 1.50
The Wonder-Book. 12mo 1.50
Tanglewood Tales. 12mo 1.50
Tales of the White Hills, and Legends of New England. 32mo 75
Legends of Province House, and A Virtuoso's Collection. 32mo 75

Oliver Wendell Holmes.

- Elsie Venner. A Romance of Destiny. Crown 8vo . 2.00
- The Guardian Angel. Crown 8vo 2.00
- The Story of Iris. 32mo 75
- My Hunt after the Captain. 32mo 40

Blanche Willis Howard.

- One Summer. A Novel. "Little Classic" style. 18mo 1.25
- *Holiday Edition.* Illustrated by Hoppin. Square 12mo 2.50

Augustus Hoppin.

- Recollections of Auton House. Illustrated. Small 4to 1.25
- A Fashionable Sufferer. Illustrated. 12mo . . . 1.50
- Two Compton Boys. Illustrated. Square 16mo . . 1.50

8 *Works of Fiction Published by*

William Dean Howells.
Their Wedding Journey. Illustrated. 12mo . . . $1.50
The Same. Illustrated. Paper covers. 16mo 50
The Same. "Little Classic" style. 18mo 1.25
A Chance Acquaintance. Illustrated. 12mo . . . 1.50
The Same. Illustrated. Paper covers. 16mo 50
The Same. "Little Classic" style. 18mo 1.25
A Foregone Conclusion. 12mo 1.50
The Lady of the Aroostook. 12mo 1.50
The Undiscovered Country. 12mo 1.50
A Day's Pleasure, etc. 32mo 75

Thomas Hughes.
Tom Brown's School-Days at Rugby. *Illustrated Edition.* 16mo 1.00
Tom Brown at Oxford. 16mo 1.25

Henry James, Jr.
A Passionate Pilgrim, and Other Tales. 12mo . . . 2.00
Roderick Hudson. 12mo 2.00
The American. 12mo 2.00
Watch and Ward. "Little Classic" style. 18mo . 1.25
The Europeans. 12mo 1.50
Confidence. 12mo 1.50
The Portrait of a Lady. 12mo 2.00

Anna Jameson.
Studies and Stories. "Little Classic" style. 18mo . 1.50
Diary of an Ennuyée. "Little Classic" style. 18mo . 1.50

Douglas Jerrold.
Mrs. Caudle's Curtain Lectures. Illustrated. "Riverside Classics." 16mo 1.00

Sarah Orne Jewett.
Deephaven. 16mo 1.25
Old Friends and New. 18mo 1.25
Country By-Ways. 18mo 1.25
The Mate of the Daylight. 18mo 1.25
A Country Doctor. 16mo 1.25
A Marsh Island. 16mo 1.25

Rossiter Johnson.
"Little Classics." Each in one volume. 18mo.
   I. Exile.   IV. Life.
   II. Intellect.   V. Laughter.
   III. Tragedy.   VI. Love.

VII. Romance.
VIII. Mystery.
IX. Comedy.
X. Childhood.
XI. Heroism.
XII. Fortune.
XIII. Narrative Poems.
XIV. Lyrical Poems.
XV. Minor Poems.
XVI. Nature.
XVII. Humanity.
XVIII. Authors.

Each volume $1.00
The set 18.00
Half calf, or half morocco 45.00
The Same. In nine volumes, square 16mo.
The set 13.50
Half calf 27.00
Tree calf 40.50
(*Sold only in sets.*)

Charles and Mary Lamb.
Tales from Shakespeare. 18mo 1.00
The Same. Illustrated. 16mo 1.00
The Same. *Handy-Volume Edition.* 32mo, gilt top . 1.25

Henry Wadsworth Longfellow.
Hyperion. A Romance. 16mo 1.50
Popular Edition. 16mo 40
Popular Edition. Paper covers, 16mo 15
Outre-Mer. 16mo 1.50
Popular Edition. 16mo 40
Popular Edition. Paper covers, 16mo 15
Kavanagh. 16mo 1.50

S. Weir Mitchell.
In War Time. 16mo 1.25

Nora Perry.
The Tragedy of the Unexpected, and Other Stories.
"Little Classic" style. 18mo 1.25

Elizabeth Stuart Phelps.
The Gates Ajar. 16mo 1.50
Beyond the Gates. 16mo 1.25
Men, Women, and Ghosts. 16mo 1.50
Hedged In. 16mo 1.50
The Silent Partner. 16mo 1.50
The Story of Avis. 16mo 1.50
Sealed Orders, and Other Stories. 16mo . . 1.50
Friends: A Duet. 16mo 1.25
Doctor Zay. 16mo 1.25
An Old Maid's Paradise. 16mo 50

Marian C. L. Reeves and Emily Read.
Pilot Fortune. 16mo 1.25

Riverside Paper Series.

A Series of Novels by the best American Authors.
1. But Yet a Woman. By A. S. Hardy.
2. Missy. By the author of "Rutledge."
3. The Stillwater Tragedy. By T. B. Aldrich.
4. Elsie Venner. By O. W. Holmes.
5. An Earnest Trifler. By Mary A. Sprague.
6. The Lamplighter. By Maria S. Cummins.
7. Their Wedding Journey. By W. D. Howells.
8. Married for Fun. Anonymous.
9. An Old Maid's Paradise. By Elizabeth Stuart Phelps.
10. The House of a Merchant Prince. By W. H. Bishop.
11. An Ambitious Woman. By Edgar Fawcett.
12. Marjorie's Quest. By Jeanie T. Gould (Mrs. Lincoln).
13. Hammersmith. By Mark Sibley Severance.

Each volume, 16mo, paper covers . . . . $ .50

Joseph Xavier Boniface Saintine.

Picciola. "Riverside Classics." Illustrated. 16mo . 1.00

Jacques Henri Bernardin de Saint-Pierre.

Paul and Virginia. "Riverside Classics." Illustrated. 16mo 1.00
The Same, together with Undine, and Sintram. 32mo .75

Sir Walter Scott.

The Waverley Novels. *Illustrated Library Edition.* This edition has been carefully edited, and is illustrated with 100 engravings by Darley, Dielman, Fredericks, Low, Share, Sheppard, and has also a glossary and a very full index of characters. In 25 volumes, 12mo.

Waverley.
Guy Mannering.
The Antiquary.
Rob Roy.
Old Mortality.
Black Dwarf, and Legend of Montrose.
Heart of Mid-Lothian.
Bride of Lammermoor.
Ivanhoe
The Monastery.
The Abbot.
Kenilworth.

The Pirate.
The Fortunes of Nigel.
Peveril of the Peak.
Quentin Durward.
St. Ronan's Well.
Redgauntlet.
The Betrothed, and the Highland Widow.
The Talisman, and Other Tales.
Woodstock.
The Fair Maid of Perth.
Anne of Geierstein.

Houghton, Mifflin and Company.

Count Robert of Paris. The Surgeon's Daughter, and Castle Dangerous.
    Each volume $1.00
    The set 25.00
    Half calf 62.50
    Half seal 75.00
Globe Edition. Complete in 13 volumes. With 100 Illustrations. 16mo.
    The set 16.25
    Half calf, or half morocco 35.00
    (*Sold only in sets.*)
Tales of a Grandfather. *Illustrated Library Edition.* With six steel plates. In three volumes, 12mo . . 4.50
    Half calf 9.00
Ivanhoe. Fancy binding. 8vo 1.00
    Half calf 2.50

Horace E. Scudder.
The Dwellers in Five-Sisters' Court. 16mo 1.25
Stories and Romances. 16mo 1.25

Mark Sibley Severance.
Hammersmith: His Harvard Days. 12mo 1.50

T. D. Sherwood.
Comic History of the United States. Illustrated. 12mo 2.50

J. E. Smith.
Oakridge: An Old-Time Story of Maine. 12mo . . 2.00

Mary A. Sprague.
An Earnest Trifler. 16mo 1.25

Harriet Beecher Stowe.
Agnes of Sorrento. 12mo 1.50
The Pearl of Orr's Island. 12mo 1.50
Uncle Tom's Cabin. *Popular Illustrated Edition.*
  12mo 2.00
The Same. *Popular Edition.* 12mo 1.00
The Minister's Wooing. 12mo 1.50
The Mayflower, and Other Sketches. 12mo . . . 1.50
Dred. 12mo 1.50
Oldtown Folks. 12mo 1.50
Sam Lawson's Fireside Stories. Illustrated. *New Edition*, enlarged 1.50
My Wife and I. Illustrated. 12mo 1.50
We and Our Neighbors. Illustrated. 12mo . . . 1.50
Poganuc People. Illustrated. 12mo 1.50
  The above eleven volumes, in box 16.50

Works of Fiction.

Uncle Tom's Cabin. *Holiday Edition.* With red line border, Introduction, and a Bibliography by George Bullen, of the British Museum. Over 100 Illustrations. 12mo $3.50
 Half calf 6.00
 Morocco, or tree calf 7.50
Popular Edition. 12mo 1.00
A Dog's Mission, etc. Illustrated. Small 4to . . . 1.25
Queer Little People. Illustrated. Small 4to . . . 1.25
Little Pussy Willow. Illustrated. Small 4to . . . 1.25

Gen. Lew Wallace.
The Fair God; or, The Last of the 'Tzins. 12mo . 1.50

Henry Watterson.
Oddities in Southern Life and Character. Illustrated. 16mo 1.50

Richard Grant White.
The Fate of Mansfield Humphreys, together with the Episode of Mr. Washington Adams in England. 16mo 1.25

Adeline D. T. Whitney.
Faith Gartney's Girlhood. Illustrated. 12mo . . . 1.50
Hitherto: A Story of Yesterdays. 12mo 1.50
Patience Strong's Outings. 12mo 1.50
The Gayworthys. 12mo 1.50
Leslie Goldthwaite. Illustrated. 12mo 1.50
We Girls: A Home Story. Illustrated. 12mo . . 1.50
Real Folks. Illustrated. 12mo 1.50
The Other Girls. Illustrated. 12mo 1.50
Sights and Insights. 2 vols. 12mo 3.00
Odd, or Even? 12mo 1.50
Boys at Chequasset. Illustrated. 12mo 1.50
Bonnyborough. (*In press.*)
The above twelve volumes in box 18.00

*** *For sale by all Booksellers. Sent, post-paid, on receipt of price (in check on Boston or New York, money-order, or registered letter) by the Publishers,*

HOUGHTON, MIFFLIN AND COMPANY,

4 PARK ST., BOSTON, MASS.; 11 EAST SEVENTEENTH ST., NEW YORK.

A Catalogue containing portraits of many of the above authors, with a description of their works, will be sent free, on application, to any address.

www.ingramcontent.com/pod-product-compliance
Lightning Source LLC
Chambersburg PA
CBHW030743230426
43667CB00007B/816